D1370024

Negotiating the Net
in Africa

iPOLITICS: Global Challenges in the Information Age

RENÉE MARLIN-BENNETT, SERIES EDITOR

Negotiating

the Net in Africa

The Politics of Internet Diffusion

edited by
Ernest J. Wilson III
Kelvin R. Wong

LYNNE
RIENNER
PUBLISHERS

BOULDER
LONDON

Published in the United States of America in 2007 by
Lynne Rienner Publishers, Inc.
1800 30th Street, Boulder, Colorado 80301
www.rienner.com

and in the United Kingdom by
Lynne Rienner Publishers, Inc.
3 Henrietta Street, Covent Garden, London WC2E 8LU

Library of Congress Cataloging-in-Publication Data
Negotiating the net in Africa : the politics of internet diffusion / edited by Ernest J. Wilson III
and Kelvin R. Wong.
    p.   cm. — (iPolitics: global challenges in the information age)
  Includes bibliographical references and index.
  ISBN-13: 978-1-58826-421-3 (alk. paper)
  ISBN-10: 1-58826-421-1 (alk. paper) O5-O7-O7
    1. Internet—Africa.   2. Information technology—Economic aspects—Africa.
3. Information technology—Social aspects—Africa. I. Wilson, Ernest J. II. Wong, Kelvin R.
III. Series: iPolitics.
ZA4201.N44 2006
025.04096—dc22

                                         2006011926

British Cataloguing in Publication Data
A Cataloguing in Publication record for this book
is available from the British Library.

Printed and bound in the United States of America

The paper used in this publication meets the requirements
of the American National Standard for Permanence of
Paper for Printed Library Materials Z39.48-1992.

5 4 3 2 1

To the youth of today—

to Lilia Blumel Wong (who arrived during the project!),
Malik Ernest Wilson, and Rodney Rusan Gregory Wilson—

and to all youth struggling to build a better tomorrow in Africa

Contents

Preface

THIS BOOK BEGAN WITH an incorrect assumption about what practitioners in the Internet sector wanted to know. After researching and writing on information communication technologies (ICTs) in Africa for several years, we had a particular view of what would constitute useful knowledge for Internet professionals. In 2001 we put this view to a gathering of African experts in Washington, D.C.—people whose jobs were to promote Internet supply and demand in Africa. Alas, the guidance they gave us was at variance with our expectations. They told us that they wanted to know what things had worked for people like them in other African countries when trying to negotiate greater access to the Internet. They said they didn't need copies of formal laws and regulations; they didn't need restatements of highblown rhetoric from ministers and presidents boasting about what they *would* do, someday. They wanted the real stories behind the official stories. They wanted to know how others in similar positions in other countries had been able to negotiate good outcomes successfully, even when confronted by very conservative and sometimes hostile officials. Which tactics worked politically, which didn't, and for what reasons? Developing better listening skills proved invaluable in our research, and in putting together this book.

The idea for the volume had its roots back in 1998–1999, when the Center for International Development and Conflict Management (CIDCM) at the University of Maryland in College Park, partnered with K. Y. Amoako, then executive secretary of the UN's Economic Commission for Africa (ECA), to organize jointly an international colloquium titled "New IT and Inequality: Resetting the Research and Policy Agendas" (Wilson and Wong, 2000). That conference in College Park brought together top experts from across Africa and all over the world, and served as the trial run for the ECA's inaugural

African Development Forum in October 1999 in Addis Ababa: "The Challenge to Africa of Globalisation and the Information Age."

The important lesson that we took away from the conferences and our subsequent meetings with African experts in Washington was that outside observers, scholars, and international practitioners need to listen attentively to the multiple voices and the multiple messages of local people doing local work. This also means being attentive to local conditions and local histories. We found that the risk of arrogance was quite high, even among the most sympathetic outsiders. There was much external advice and eager instruction given by nonlocal experts and global techno-gurus that dominated academic writing and policy prescriptions, much of it quite dismissive of local concerns and preferences.

Over the course of this project we also learned two other lessons. First, there is no such thing as *the* local "African" voice; rather, there are many local voices competing to tell their own versions of African Internet reality, from government officials to academics to local nonprofit community groups to local businesspeople. All these groups reported on the history of "Internet diffusion" as they themselves experienced it. Second, there were far too few efforts under way to capture this rich, complex history of Internet diffusion into the least-developed parts of the globe. Most of the knowledgeable people were too busy making history to take time out to record it.

With these normative and intellectual priorities, we elaborated an initial theoretical and analytic framework for this volume, and then selected and began to collaborate closely with a talented group of well-traveled local experts to design an approach that would be faithful to local knowledge, but that would also result in country chapters that could yield comparability and help aggregate knowledge. In 2002, under a generous Hewlett Foundation grant and with support from the US Agency for International Development (USAID), we invited a group of experts to come to College Park for an initial colloquium on methods and cases, which included outside experts from USAID, the World Bank, private companies, and other sources of expertise. The chapter contributors returned to Africa to conduct and write up their initial research. This was followed by a second full meeting of the group in South Africa in October 2002, where the papers were presented at the Tel.Com Africa Conference and then the drafts were critiqued and the framework for the book was strengthened. Still more rewriting and critiques preceded an authors' conference in College Park in 2004 and presentation of the results to a seminar at the Information for Development (InfoDEV) group at the World Bank. Then more editing and rewriting.

Our approach, which we term "negotiating the Net," is built around a core concept of universal critical negotiation issues (CNIs) and allows us to extract both analytic and theoretical insights and practical lessons from the material while sticking close to the storyline of local history as it was actually lived in six African countries. Each chapter follows the same jointly developed format: after a brief introduction the author moves quickly to identify and analyze three or four of the most critical and controversial negotiation issues in the country's Internet sector. Each author asks and answers the same questions about these critical issues. Each author extracts lessons and insights about Internet diffusion in that country.

We believe we have succeeded in reaching our twin goals: this volume reflects practical lessons, as well as better conceptualization and theory. The results of our collaboration are before you; you must now judge whether we have indeed succeeded in listening well enough.

*   *   *

This volume has been a collective and cooperative venture from beginning to end. Funders, friendly collaborators, publishers, and attendees at various conferences and seminars where we presented our ideas all helped make it a better book.

In addition to the authors listed in the table of contents, we wish to acknowledge the participation of Reine Boni, whose early contributions on Internet expansion in Côte d'Ivoire were very valuable and whose further work on this project was made impossible by the regrettable turmoil in her country. We also acknowledge the contributions of Simbo Ntiro to the Tanzania chapter. Lane Smith, the heart and soul behind the Leland Initiative of USAID, has been a constant friend and companion over the life of this project and well before it began officially. John Daly, too, has been unstinting in his suggestions about the text and in providing helpful references to other material we should read and take into account.

Good feelings and fraternal sympathies are never adequate for a major multiyear project like this one—we also needed material support. Happily the Hewlett Foundation provided fellowship support to our chapter contributors through a generous grant that made this project possible. The Leland Initiative was also willing to step in and help us with financial support. CIDCM provided the infrastructure we needed to make this project a success; we heartily acknowledge the continuing encouragement of its director, Jonathan Wilkenfeld, who participated in some of our sessions, and of Jarrod Bailey, Betsy Kielman, Poupak Moallem, and Tanja Owe. We acknowledge, too, the professional editing provided by Anne Santiago and Michael Dravis.

We also wish to thank Mustapha Terrab and Kerry McNamara, colleagues at the InfoDEV project, housed at the World Bank, for sponsoring a research seminar at which we presented our findings. We thank Jonathan Miller and

Charley Lewis for organizing our participation in a seminar at the 2002 Tel.Com Africa Conference, as well as our contributor conference in South Africa.

We wish especially to thank our wives, Christina Blumel and Francille Rusan Wilson, for putting up with our overseas travel and our local absences as we put together this book.

—Ernest J. Wilson III and Kelvin R. Wong

Negotiating the Net
in Africa

1

Introduction: Negotiating the Net in Africa

*Ernest J. Wilson III
and Kelvin R. Wong*

THE DIFFUSION OF MODERN information and communications technologies in developing countries is a subject of growing importance for entrepreneurs, government officials, and leaders of civil society. They are beginning to recognize that their own future—and the future of the institutions, nations, and cultures they lead—will hinge substantially on their capacity to harness the beneficial effects of powerful new communications and information resources, while minimizing the disruptive influences of those resources. Scholars, too, are trying to understand and explain the diffusion of these new information and communication technologies (ICTs). Yet many of the available explanations are either highly aggregated descriptions of global ICT diffusion measured against indicators like gross domestic product (GDP) per capita, or descriptive accounts of specific local projects in Africa, Asia, or Latin America, such as telecenters or cybercafes, for which each description is unique and fails to contribute to an aggregate understanding of the reasons for the spread of ICTs.

Thus, analysts of ICT diffusion are confronted with 200 countries with 200 seemingly distinct experiences. We lack an approach that can incorporate distinct experiences and different cases into a single analysis, one that can provide a coherent narrative and comparative analysis of how the Internet, for example, spreads through society. Absent this kind of a framework, we have a jumble of stories of false starts, half initiatives, some successes, and many failures. Confronted with these contradictory accounts, many questions remain about the spread of these technologies: What drives their diffusion—the technology itself, policy, or money? What explains national and regional differences in their spread? How are the "rules of the game" rewritten to create new ICT markets and sectors, and whom do they benefit? And especially important, why does the Internet spread faster and farther in some countries and

1

communities than in others? These questions and this kind of analysis are central to a whole range of policy questions.

Ultimately, these and other central questions can be answered by means of careful empirical research. Yet careful research alone is not enough; advancing knowledge also requires clear conceptual frameworks and compelling theoretical claims. Such is the ambition of this volume.

Project Framework

Our framework, termed "Negotiating the Net" (NTN), was designed to answer policy-relevant and theoretically important questions—principally, how to best explain the patterns of Internet expansion we observe in Africa and what kinds of purposeful interventions shape their performance. We found most explanations to be apolitical, naive, and technodeterminist. Thus we developed an alternative negotiation model based on our initial observations in Africa and drawing on previous research conducted in China, Brazil, and India. Our new model is built around a theory of "strategic restructuring" (Wilson, 2004). The initial NTN model was then further refined by the contributors to this volume over the three-year life of the project to capture several societal elements that other models seemed to ignore: politics; winners and losers; the nonautomatic, negotiated nature of technological diffusion; and indigenous innovation. The NTN framework is unambiguously built on the premise that politics and policy are primary to understanding the diffusion of the Internet.

Certainly, like other scholars, we recognize that the level of economic development, capacity for wealth creation, and technological advances are key determinants of the pace and extent of diffusion. A high level of GDP per capita in a country means more people can afford to pay for a "luxury" like the Internet. Widespread telephone infrastructure contributes positively to the availability of Internet services. Lower levels of education mean fewer people can fruitfully access the Internet. And a repressive military government will tend to thwart widespread Internet use. We appreciate the role played by these broad contextual factors. However, our singular contribution is to concentrate on precisely those important features of information technology (IT) diffusion that other analysts omit—the details of politics, processes, and policy.

Other analysts have recognized the centrality of policy and politics, of course, from the architects of the World Bank's structural adjustment policies to the implementers of the Leland Initiative of the US Agency for International Development (USAID). Recognition of policy and politics as a key factor in diffusion is not entirely new. What is new is that the NTN framework insists on locating politics and policy at the center of our model, not as an adjunct or add-on. We also provide a unique set of analytic building blocks, which we call critical negotiation issues (CNIs), that give more focus and structure to the political and policy analysis, and facilitate greater comparative examination. There are, of course, many anecdotes about why an Internet or radio license application was first rejected and then accepted, why a contender failed at one point and succeeded at another, and why a minister, regulator, or telecommunications boss was sacked. Such stories abound. What has been missing and what we provide is a systematic way to process these anecdotes and other information.

Project Essentials

The NTN project explains the diffusion of the Internet in terms of negotiations that take place among variously competing and cooperating parties in society, focusing on a dozen critical policy issues negotiated among different groups (see Figure 1.1 on p. 7). The means by which these dozen issues are negotiated and resolved (or not) in turn affect Internet diffusion in a society, including its pace and extent. This process of negotiation and diffusion differs in its details from country to country, but there are important underlying elements common to all countries. Before we straightforwardly describe the why, what, who, when, and where of the NTN model, a brief definition: we use the term "negotiation" to indicate a multiparty interaction in which actors come together to seek accommodation and accord from other actors in order to advance their own interests (Boyer, Starkey, and Wilkenfeld, 2005).

These interactions may occur in formal settings like open regulatory hearings or legislative sessions. They also may occur in informal settings like hotel bars; they occur during commercial transactions among buyers and sellers. Negotiations involve all manner of actors—private-company executives, government officials, university professors, representatives of multilateral or bilateral institutions, and representatives of nongovernmental organizations (NGOs). Readers will find examples of all of them. We do not claim that negotiations are good or bad, or lead always to positive outcomes. Nor do we believe that all negotiations are fully "rational" in the sense that neoclassical economists use the term. As often as not, stakeholders possess partial information, hold narrow perspectives on their own and others' positions, and can be incompetent or competent negotiators.

Why Do the Negotiations Occur?

Why do people compete and negotiate over the Internet? For the same reasons they negotiate over land, education, or freedom of speech. Negotiations occur because different stakeholders have conflicting views on how Internet services should be owned, controlled, regulated, used, and distributed. These stakeholders, moreover, are willing to fight to obtain their favored solutions. This reality drives the "why" of the CNIs. Suppliers negotiate with customers and vice versa. Large monopoly suppliers negotiate with small startup suppliers.

Foreign interests negotiate with local interests. They seek not only onetime benefits from onetime transactions; they also seek to benefit repeatedly over many transactions. Therefore, they enter into negotiations to change the rules and regulations that structure all the relevant transactions to their benefit, which are described more fully below.

What Is Being Negotiated?

All countries in the world confront a set of common issues that must be resolved if the Internet, and other telecommunications services, are to be diffused effectively. Taken together, these issues constitute some of the most basic "rules of the game" that guide the behavior of all the players in the Internet arena. Depending on how they are resolved, issues of Internet governance provide positive incentives for some activities and negative sanctions for others. Our NTN team identified twelve basic issues of Internet diffusion, ranging from market structure to issuance of a specific license. These constitute our critical negotiation issues, and they fall into four main categories: policy reform, access, national ICT policy, and technical issues.

Who Is Doing the Negotiation?

A number of different groups and their representatives are involved in Internet negotiations. In general, they are drawn from five distinct institutional areas: government, the private sector, the research and development community, nongovernmental organizations, and international organizations. More specifically, negotiations are conducted by a small handful of individuals located in institutions such as the country's telecommunications ministry or its equivalent, the office of the president or prime minister, the state-owned telephone monopoly, and the state regulator. In the private sector, interested parties include small startup companies that create the first commercial Internet service providers (ISPs), and representatives of large, private companies (mostly foreign but also sometimes domestic). University professors and researchers often play important roles early in the game, as do selected officials from multilateral and bilateral aid agencies.

In the early years of Internet diffusion, the number of people involved is relatively small, and most are from the university and research communities. The number of players grows as interest in the Internet increases. These innovators and early adopters can be thought of as "information champions," because of their fierce commitments to promoting the Internet. The champions clash with the "information conservatives," who seek to preserve the prevailing monopoly and statist system. The conservatives seek to block the Internet completely or to control it so that the new technology will not compromise their professional and personal interests. Typically, Internet opponents are the executives of the country's state-run telephone monopoly or senior government ministers. In this study we pay especially close attention to the Internet champions who launch ISPs, and examine how they negotiate with their suppliers, their regulators, their clients, and so forth.

From country to country, the early Internet leaders often share a common background. They are well educated, often have studied overseas, and are typically based in universities and motivated by civic-mindedness. As such individuals make contact with others like themselves, in different sectors, who are equally interested in Internet diffusion, they eventually come to constitute an evolving "mode of cooperation" across the four key sectors: public, private, nonprofit, and research and education. It seems that the more robust these cross-sector partnerships, the more successful the diffusion.

Over time, relationships based on negotiation and cooperation thicken and become institutionalized, and new groups form to protect their interests and perspective (Wilson, 2003).

When Do the Negotiations Occur?

This study examines the negotiations that transpired between the time just before the invention of the basic Internet-protocol technology and the present— that is, the 1990–2005 period. Within this fifteen-year period, distinct phases have appeared in all countries and the character of the negotiations within each phase has been similar. The first phase is an experimental, precommercial period based in universities and carried out by "geeks." The second phase begins when an ambitious entrepreneur launches the first open, commercial ISP in the country (this typically happened in the mid-1990s). The third phase, qualitatively different from the others, occurs when several new ISPs are launched, creating competition, which typically drives prices down and improves services for consumers. In the fourth phase (following the burst of the Internet bubble in 2000), there is simultaneously competition and some consolidation.

Where Do the Negotiations Occur?

The twelve important issues are negotiated among all interested parties. Some negotiations take place between the startup ISP owner and representatives of the incumbent telecommunications company over issues like interconnection fees; such issues may be thrashed out in meetings held at the country's communications ministry or in the office of the post, telephone, and telegraph (PTT) entity. Other negotiations occur between local champions and foreign suppliers of technology or finance. When ISP business associations appear, negotiations take place among the ISP owners themselves, and their associations become key sites of negotiations. Increasingly, negotiations are migrating beyond the closed "iron triangle" (state monopoly, ministry, and political authorities) within which ICT policies were invariably determined in the past, toward more open, transparent, and democratic sites where more stakeholders can participate effectively. By 2000, many governments of least-developed countries (LDCs) had appointed various national consultative groups to address themes like "information society," often bringing together four key interests—public, private, nonprofit, and research and education. The shift from closed iron triangle to a more genuinely open, inclusive, four-actor quad remains important, but differs from country to country.

Critical Negotiation Issues

Formally, we define a critical negotiation issue in the area of Internet diffusion as an issue having three components: it has high relevance to Internet diffusion, parties contend over it, and if left unresolved diffusion is seriously impeded. To identify, analyze, and explain a country's CNIs, each chapter contributor agreed to address the following set of questions:

- Who were the main actors and what were their positions?
- What was the key issue of contention, what was its extent, and what was the nature of the conflict?
- How did the negotiations evolve over time? Did positions, strategies, and forums change?
- What alliances and coalitions emerged, and on what basis?
- How did the issue come to a head, and how was it resolved?
- What was the outcome? Was there any impact on Internet diffusion?

Focusing their analyses on these questions, the contributors initially identified more than twenty CNIs based on their observations across multiple countries. We pared the number down to the most significant twelve. Of course, any classification scheme is imperfect. Some of our CNIs overlap with others, and the dividing line between any two may be fuzzy. Some CNIs are almost always more important than others, while several CNIs prove more significant in some countries than in others (see Chapter 9). Still, in giving multiple presentations to scholars, policymakers, and activists in many countries over several years, our team observed again and again that audiences found these categories intuitively and experientially accurate and useful for framing complex processes using consistent terms.

Among the CNIs, some are quite obvious, such as policy decisions about privatization (private sector ownership) and liberalization (more than one actor in the market). Others, such as policymaking capacity, are not so obvious, and of course the dividing line between them is fluid. To preserve comparability and prevent unwieldy analysis, we decided that each contributor would focus on the four CNIs most important to his or her country case. As mentioned above, the twelve CNIs cluster into four broader categories: policy reform, access, national ICT policy, and technical issues (see Figure 1.1).

Policy issues reflect the ongoing rules of the game, who can play and how basic rules are interpreted: Are private sector actors allowed to play, and if so, under what conditions and in which service sector? Is voice over Internet protocol (VOIP) an information or telecommunications service? What level of cross-subsidy will be allocated to underserved users? Here the dominant questions for us pertain to privatization, liberalization, and regulation.

These CNIs are almost always politically very sensitive, as they have important and direct implications for ownership, competition, and control. "Privatization" means transferring part (rarely all) of the ownership from public to private groups, "liberalization" means introducing more competition into a market, and "regulation" brings into the market a body designed to ensure fair-

Figure 1.1   Critical Negotiation Issues

Policy reform issues

1. Privatization
2. Liberalization
3. Regulation

Access issues

4. Access to facilities
5. Monopoly pricing
6. Access legality

National ICT policy issues

7. Information society
8. Universal access and services
9. Policymaking capacity
10. Implementation capacity

Technical issues

11. Internet exchange point (IXP)
12. Voice over Internet protocol (VOIP)

ness, transparency, and competitive conditions while promoting consumer welfare.

Since in most African countries (as elsewhere) the traditional telephone company monopoly was, or is, owned by the state, an early and contentious step to reform is privatization of state ownership, often accompanied by more competition (i.e., sector liberalization). Regulation then shapes the form of the sector according to government policy and maintains public goods, such as stability, order, and harmony, among competing interests. Policy reform issues are particularly contentious because they define and change permissible ranges of behavior, and winners and losers.

Access issues, the second category, groups together three CNIs that reflect conditions and terms prevailing upon users' and service providers' ability to plug into networks: monopoly pricing, access to facilities, and legality of access. Access itself is the ability of users and service providers to effectively connect to the Internet.

Monopoly pricing issues center on negotiations over prices charged by the monopoly, and hence touch on cost as well as cross-subsidies (when one service subsidizes another). Monopoly pricing is an access issue (especially in poor countries) because the monopolies usually set very high prices, resulting in very limited actual demand and access despite high potential demand (Wilson and Wong, 2003). The very high cost of Internet service results in decreased access (Daly, 1999).

With the end of the "monopoly" and the introduction of some competition, dominant providers (former monopolies) often sought to disadvantage others by restricting access to "their" networks facilities. They did this by limiting telephone-line availability (needed for dial-up customers at an ISP) and generally providing less reliable and inferior service, and as a result, access to their facilities becomes an issue. Thus, access to facilities centers on negotiations over access to equipment and the physical connections that users and service providers have to telephone and data networks. Not surprisingly access to facilities is particularly contentious when monopolies from the ancien régime first connect with other service providers. Here, negotiations are essentially about terms and conditions for new entrant access to the dominant provider's network facilities.

Legality of access refers to the authoritative setting and enforcing of the terms for access to facilities by different service providers—how, when, and by whom. Here, points of contention center on interpretations and enforcement of laws, regulations, and other authoritative terms governing connections and plug-ins.

These two CNIs, access to facilities and legality of access, have been identified as different CNIs. The issues in contention, and stakeholder strategies associated with getting initial connection and maintaining it, are quite distinct.

The third category of CNIs, national ICT policy issues, centers on how countries define and integrate ICT into their strategy of national development. These are essentially issues about national objectives for ICT. This category includes information society policy as well as universal access. In addition, technical capacity to make and implement policy is a critical issue, because in many African contexts expertise required for informed decisionmaking and policy implementation is a significant burden and is critical to success of national objectives.

The final category of CNIs involves very technical issues and includes establishing an Internet exchange point (IXP) and use of VOIP. An IXP connects the local Internet facilities to one another and increases efficiency and reduces cost, but requires some trust among those cooperating. VOIP is among the newer technologies for voice traffic and, as with an IXP, can significantly reduce calling costs. VOIP is also at the leading edge of data convergence.

Table 1.1 demonstrates the most important CNIs in each of the six country cases as well as continentwide. Of the CNIs examined in each of the case studies, the most prevalent involved issues of policy reform. This should not be surprising to anyone familiar with the disposition of a monopoly, in Africa or elsewhere, to resist liberalization. The least prevalent involved issues of national policy.

Table 1.1   Critical Negotiation Issues by Country

	CNI 1	CNI 2	CNI 3	CNI 4
Ghana	Access: international gateways	VOIP	Universal service	IXP
Guinea-Bissau	Privatization	Liberalization	Licensing, regulation	VOIP
Kenya	Access: ISP licensing	Access: national backbone	Regulation	IXP
Rwanda	Access: facilities	Pricing	Licensing	IXP
South Africa	Access: anti-competitive behavior	Access: facilities	Liberalization, privatization, regulation	E-commerce policy
Tanzania	Access: initial licensing	Sectorwide reform	ISP licensing	—
Continental	Access	Privatization	Cost-based pricing	

The Diffusion Outcomes

One of our primary goals was to explain the particular national stairstep diffusion pattern illustrated in Figure 1.2. We reasoned that there should be something about Internet politics and negotiations at the local level that affected the curves of Internet diffusion at the national level. That is, we should be able to link changes in indicators like numbers of Internet users and bandwidth availability to political bargaining and decisions surrounding critical Internet issues. We assumed we would be able to explain these patterns through the kinds of policy innovations that African governments pursued (Wilson and Wong, 2003).

At the broadest level, these patterns are not unique to Africa. The ultimate structural causes most likely to shape the baseline pattern (including the level of penetration) would be a mix of factors like level of economic development or education. But why do specific African countries exhibit certain outcomes? The most immediate determinants of the stairstep pattern, we reasoned, should be the nature and results of negotiations.

Figure 1.2 shows that all the national figures in Africa trend upward, and that many exhibit a visible uptick in 2000–2001. Yet beyond these similarities, there are also important differences cross-nationally: the country with the highest GDP—South Africa—exhibits curves that are more moderate and less sharp, while Rwanda and Tanzania, starting from a lower base, have steeper penetration curves. The question we seek to understand is why an uptick occurs when it does; our hypothesis is that changes in politics and policy are at least as important as other factors.

Field Methods

The methodologies employed to answer our research questions involved prodigious amounts of field interviews in each country with dozens of key actors, and an extensive review of local records. Over a period of almost two years, the chapter contributors analyzed the CNIs in painstaking detail by carefully interviewing and reinterviewing dozens of people from the public, private, research, and civil society sectors. Our project research team met with officials of international organizations like the World Bank. They poured over public and private records. All of the contributors already had substantial professional engagement with Internet issues and thus were "participant-observers." They asked Internet stakeholders a uniform set of questions developed by the research team (see p. 6).

In almost every instance, the project's researchers were the very first, or among the first, in their country to craft rigorous histories of the diffusion process and certainly among the first to create Internet biographies. Early on,

Figure1.2 Total Outbound Bandwidth by Country, 1998–2002

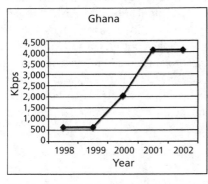

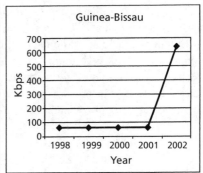

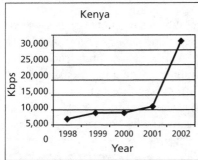

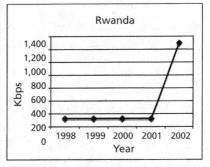

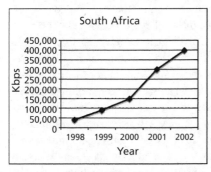

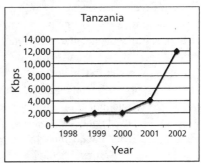

Source: Jensen, 2002.

we did not appreciate how important it would be to document the history of the participants themselves, from their own unique perspectives. As researchers, we found ourselves listening to new narratives, and even to counternarratives to the "official" or conventional understandings of Internet diffusion contained in other accounts produced by international organizations and national governments. These unique grassroots histories and biographies greatly enriched each of the national case studies, but they also fed into the common NTN research framework (Project for Information Access and Connectivity, 2002). Interesting commonalities existed across the cases, even at the micro level. Sustained interaction between our chapter contributors and their subjects led our researchers to refine the meanings of the CNIs and their implications for Internet diffusion.

Selecting the Cases

Why did this project focus on the Internet? Why were national cases selected? The Internet was a natural focus of our research because it is becoming the essential communications medium through which contemporary societies are linked together in a globalizing world. The Internet is allowing local people to communicate with one another in new ways. It is increasingly linked to other media like broadcasting and print, and advances freedom of expression. This new technology is also a critical core infrastructure for businesses. Yet despite its growing visibility and importance, the Internet in Africa is vastly underanalyzed and poorly understood.

We selected national cases in Africa that illustrate the wide range of country circumstances across the continent: countries that are richer and poorer; anglophone, francophone, and lusophone; capitalist and socialist; eastern, western, and southern; and more and less democratic. We decided to use these dimensions for selection because they are proxies for independent variables that experts believe will shape diffusion outcomes. Just as wealth, education, political regime, and access to telephone lines might create differences in Internet diffusion patterns across African nations, so too might colonial heritage make a difference— contrast the British with the Portuguese in their colonial telecommunication policies and their current behaviors. Our six cases are Ghana, Guinea-Bissau, Kenya, Rwanda, South Africa, and Tanzania. While we have included two West African cases, we were not able to include Nigeria, resulting from complexity on the ground and a shortage of experts available at the time to do original research and write a chapter. This volume features an overarching examination of CNIs across Africa. and a survey of negotiations between local stakeholders and international actors.

What the Model Excludes

By definition, a model excludes a great deal in order to concentrate on a narrow range of factors. The NTN model excludes several factors, most notably demand-side issues such as individual user profiles of education or income. Nor does the NTN model capture the details of the downstream social or economic effects of Internet expansion—for example, the Internet's impact on the digital divide (see Wilson 2004, chap. 6) or export competitiveness. The NTN model is explicitly concerned with the politics of the "supply side" of the story and concentrates on the individuals and groups seeking to introduce new ICT resources into communities otherwise underserved.

Case Summaries

Using our NTN framework, the chapter contributors analyzed in great detail the CNIs that emerged in our six case selections, individually as well as continentwide.

The continental case study has two focal points. One is the role of donors and international cooperation in ICT diffusion. Lishan Adem addresses important differences among donors and provides a concise chronology and analysis of ICT diffusion from the early 1990s to 2004. The other focal point is his analysis of the CNI process of two donor ICT programs. Adem undertakes this from a continental programmatic perspective as well as from a national programmatic view. The discussion of SatelLife and its negotiations for a license to access satellite-based Internet in the early 1990s in Ethiopia, and the Leland Initiative's negotiations on cost-based pricing in Mali, illustrate how politics and the policy process are captured within the NTN framework and the use of CNIs as analytical building blocks.

The six individual country cases range from South Africa, with a well-developed and sophisticated political system and robust economy; to Kenya and Ghana, with stable and promising economies; to Rwanda, which emerged from its 1994 genocide with less than a handful of telephone lines; to Guinea-Bissau, which experienced a coup and strong intervention from multinational corporations.

The South Africa case focuses on the long contest between the South African telecommunications monopoly and local, privately owned competitor ISPs. South Africa had a liberalized and privatized ISP sector that predated Telkom South Africa's entry into the Internet business. Telkom, with some myopia, had ignored the Internet until, like Gulliver, it found the local Internet market captured by a myriad of smaller ISPs. Then, as a giant awaking to a new predicament, Telkom South Africa turned to anticompetitive tactics and attempted to quash the ISPs, which resulted in serious litigiousness. In the background of course, though not at the core of these contests, was the country's remarkable transition toward political and racial equality.

Ghana, like South Africa, entered the Internet era led by a private sector Internet company, National Computer Systems (NCS), which dominated the market well beyond its infancy. The Ghana case demonstrates the important role of international financial institutions, broad-based national policy reform, and the economic pressures and incentives of VOIP and universal access. The case also highlights how a fragmented regulatory approach to modern ICTs, with ambiguous roles and responsibilities among government agencies, and among powerful individuals, can hamper diffusion and complicate negotiations.

The Kenya case analyzes push-pull dynamics and linkages between the diffusion of the Internet and the democratization process, which culminated in the defeat of longtime president Daniel arap Moi. At the same time, the country reflects the continuing monopolistic tendencies held by most telecommunications companies. In Kenya the Internet had, until recently, found a cold host in government agencies. At one point government employees were forbidden to have e-mail accounts. In a telling statement, the telecommunications regulator remarked, "We were shocked to learn Telecommunications Service Providers of Kenya launched the new [IXP] service without applying for a license."[1] Despite this kind of governmental reticence, the ISP association and the Kenya Education Network, working separately, were able to make government policy more progressive. The Kenya and Ghana cases reflect interesting similarities, especially with respect to relatively well-developed de jure regulatory structures, yet in practice the Communications Commission of Kenya has been more successful than Ghana's National Communication Authority in its quest to introduce policy reform.

The Rwanda case illustrates how a small, war-torn country, having emerged from genocide in 1994, coped with a highly monopolistic telecommunications company and eventually made giant steps forward in bringing the benefits of the Internet to the country through a partnership between a domestic education coalition and international donors. With significant human resource shortfalls on all fronts, this small poor country, which experienced a genocide, a civil war, two significant militarized cross-border disputes, and continuing high-level insecurity in the past decade, was among the first in Africa to liberalize the Internet access providers (IAPs), even though their interconnection was only fully realized in 2004.

Like Rwanda, Guinea-Bissau is small and poor, and has experienced more than its share of instability. A coup was followed by a civil war. The Guinea-Bissau case, unlike the others, highlights how an international corporation hampered progress for a number of years.

Tanzania reflects the importance of telecommunications reform writ large, and the case study provides in-depth analysis of the country's experience with SatelLife. While Tanzania's policy posture with respect to privatization and liberalization was seemingly quite advanced in the early days, soon thereafter the telecommunications regulator was sacked and the telecommunications board became ineffective for nearly three years.

Democracy and Markets, David and Goliath, and the Second Speech in the Hotel Bar

Five of the six countries covered in this volume experienced a massive tectonic shift in their political economy during the 1990s. These remarkable, far-reaching changes were part of a larger wave of change that rolled across the entire African continent and other areas of Asia, Latin America, and Europe. One historic trend was the transition from socialist and command economies to more market-driven arrangements. A key aspect of this economic reform process was privatization and commercialization. Simultaneously, Africa was rocked by an unanticipated upsurge in political liberalization and democracy (Bratton and van de Walle, 1997). These two intertwined trends—more capitalism and more democracy—provided the sustaining environment within which the Internet diffused in Africa and, as we will see in some of the case studies (e.g., Kenya and Guinea-Bissau), the relationships among the Internet and political and economic liberalization could sometimes flow in both directions. Our evidence, however, suggests that prior economic and political liberalizations facilitated Internet diffusion more than technological diffusion generated political liberalization. This may change in the future, but it is the reality on the ground today.

One of the main themes to emerge from the studies contained in this volume is that whatever the specific details in each national case, and despite nuances across the CNIs, the story of Internet diffusion in Africa is very much a "David and Goliath" scenario. In each country, the incumbent national telecommunications company and its political allies elsewhere in government aggressively pursued multiple strategies against the small, private, and locally owned "impudent" startups. Entrenched interests, the Goliaths, used every means to protect their privileged position in the market and in powerful domestic political circles: discriminatory technological standards, discriminatory pricing, predatory regulatory controls, and even police raids. Unlike in the biblical tale, however, the little Davids did not slay the giant Goliaths. Instead, the Goliaths survived, but had to live in an increasingly competitive commercial environment surrounded by a growing number of Davids.

All matters of importance involve a compelling story or two. The dominant story—the conventional wisdom, the "way it is," the public truth—is widely accepted and widely repeated, and usually has some significant elements of veracity and accuracy. From the point of view of the "geek" community of ICT experts, the dominant story and conventional wisdom of Internet diffusion in Africa and elsewhere is that if you build it, users will come. As one world-class ICT intellectual, Nicholas Negroponte, boldly said at a meeting in Rome recently, "Yes, indeed, if you drop a laptop in a poor rural school it really will transform the children."[2] The other story, told by Africa experts, is more likely to convey the deeply embedded institutional, cultural, and economic challenges that will shape—and often sink—Internet diffusion efforts: African society captures everything including a laptop's effectiveness in rural areas. The "geek" ICT expert's story is often overly optimistic about diffusion outcomes; by contrast, the Africa expert's story can be overly pessimistic.

Our third theme is that a new narrative is needed, one that tells a more nuanced and critical story of Internet diffusion in Africa. Whether novice or seasoned expert, many have probably heard the polite version of the "Africa Internet story" in countless conferences and seminars from South Africa to Senegal, from Cambridge, England, to Cambridge, Massachusetts. In this narrative, the African Internet expert offers up a story of great individual and social needs that will soon be met with adequate bandwidth, shining new hand-held devices like mobile phones or personal digital assistants (PDAs), steadily falling prices, and proper policies that allow for an adequate "enabling environment" for ICT. To achieve this, three "next steps" are called for, and the audience applauds politely. Then the speaker and a few senior audience members head to the hotel bar, where someone quickly asks, "Now tell me what is really going on," and why the Ethiopians (or the Thais or the French) are not pursuing what the conventional wisdom and technological logic suggest. At this prompt, there in the hotel bar, the speaker gives his "after-the-speech speech." This second narrative points to entrenched political and institutional interests, failures to reach political consensus, and frustrations among the incumbents and the new ISPs—the roadblocks and the blockbusters. This second narrative engages with the difficult realities of the critical negotiation issues—their coalitions, leaders, and followers—and is really more helpful for understanding Africa's advancement toward a more knowledge-intensive society at a time when many African countries are moving backward and away from such a society because of AIDS, poverty, mismanagement, and ignorance. This second narrative has not yet been constructed in a comprehensive fashion. We and our chapter contributors hope that this book will contribute to building such a second narrative, one that is more truthful, more transparent, and more politically realistic. Hopefully, at the next international conference, this second narrative will be told in the conference hall as well as in the hotel bar.

2

Ghana: The Politics of Entrepreneurship

Eric M. K. Osiakwan, William Foster,
and Anne Pitsch Santiago

THIS CHAPTER SURVEYS HOW the Internet industry developed in Ghana between 1994 and 2004. Four areas of negotiation among the government, the
National Communications Authority (NCA), Ghana Telecom, and the Internet
service providers (ISPs) will be studied:

- Establishment of international satellite gateways by ISPs.
- The legality of voice over Internet protocol (VOIP).
- The funding of Universal Access Provision.
- The development and management of an exchange point and national
  Internet backbone.

Other critical negotiation issues exist, but these four have been selected
because they had, and are still having, the greatest impact on Internet diffusion
(though not all of them are controversial). The critical negotiation issues
(CNIs) discussed in this chapter dovetail with one another, and so they need to
be examined in chronological order.

Between 1994 and 2004, Ghana drastically reformed its telecommunications sector. Previously, the government-controlled post, telephone, and telegraph (PTT) company had a virtual monopoly and presided over an inadequate
telecommunications infrastructure. Following reforms, robust Internet service
providers and mobile operators actively challenged the former monopoly PTT,
Ghana Telecom. Transformation was initiated under a plan called the "Accelerated Development Programme 1994–2000" (ADP), which was part of a
structural adjustment program sponsored by the World Bank. It called for the
separation of post and telecom services and their conversion into limited lia-
bility companies. Ghana Telecom became a partially privatized corporation
with a 30 percent share owned by the telecom's management team (known as

GCom, a consortium led by Telkom Malaysia). In addition, the ADP established the National Communications Authority (NCA) to regulate the communications industry. The NCA was legally established with passage by the Ghana parliament of National Communications Act 524 in 1996.

By 2000 the ADP had achieved an impressive increase in teledensity from 0.34 lines to 1.16 lines per 1,000 inhabitants, and in public phones from 0.001 to 0.16 per 1,000 inhabitants. A second national operator (SNO), Western Telesystems (Westel), was licensed, and numerous private FM radio and television stations were operating. Forty-eight ISPs were licensed, of which about twenty were still operating in 2004 (these ISPs consume a total Internet backbone bandwidth of 25 megabits per second [mbps] into and 15 mbps out of the country).

Low-cost Internet access at Internet cafes is available in most neighborhoods in the capital city, Accra. Five of the country's ten regional capitals have points of presence (POPs) established by ISPs to provide local Net access. The regional capitals also have a growing number of Internet cafes and community access centers, although their appearance is not as rapid as in Accra. Some business organizations needing Internet access have purchased dedicated connections. Wireless and satellite connections provide consumers with alternatives to the dedicated circuits supplied by Ghana Telecom and Westel, which are sometimes hard to obtain. Studies estimate that Ghana had about 300,000 fixed lines, 550,000 mobile subscribers, 400,000 computers, 20,000 Internet subscribers, and 300,000 Internet users in 2004.[1] With a population of about 20 million, Ghana can improve these statistics.

A diversity of private ISPs and mobile companies compete with Ghana Telecom (still partially government-owned) and Westel, but the latter do not always welcome competition. Michael Best of Georgia Tech has charged that when Ghana Telecom was associated with Telkom Malaysia, it was one of the most abusive telecom incumbents in Africa. In light of such accusations, the relationship between Ghana Telecom and private ISPs is worth exploring. ISPs are in fact able to operate their own satellite gateways to the global Internet backbone.

The 1995 decision to license an ISP, Network Computer Systems (NCS), as a value-added reseller was not especially controversial. However, the June 1996 decision to allow the NCS to operate its own international satellite connections to the Internet was controversial, because under the ADP plan, Ghana Telecom and the second national operator, Westel, were the only telecom operators with rights to the international gateway. The fact that the ISPs could bypass exclusivity is important, because it removed a key bottleneck by which the two telecom operators could have maintained control over the ISP industry and thereby stifled Internet diffusion, a strategy that was used by incumbent telecoms in other countries studied in this book. The Ministry of Transportation and Communications, led by Edward Salia, saw ISPs as value-added resellers of data services, meaning they could not provide voice. The ministry did not anticipate that in the 1990s the technology would develop and allow ISPs to transmit voice calls. Therefore, the ministry was surprised when ISPs began transmitting voice using VOIP.

The second area of negotiations we will focus on is VOIP—specifically, when and why it was judged as constituting an unacceptable threat to Ghana Telecom's foreign exchange earnings hence classified as "illegal" by the NCA. Certain ISPs had their equipment confiscated and owners were even jailed. Later, the courts ruled that there was no legal basis for these actions except for the fact that ISP licenses only granted them the right to provide data and not voice.

The Ghanaian government—the president, the Ministry of Transportation and Communications, and the National Communications Authority—all accepted Ghana Telecom's argument that it needed protection from competition by ISPs offering international calls. Ghana Telecom argued that only it could roll out infrastructure and provide access in underserved areas, particularly rural areas, thereby fulfilling universal access needs (in Ghana, universal access is defined as having a telephone line in every locality of more than 500 people). The VOIP debate needs to be understood in the context of negotiations on the funding of universal access. This issue forms our third CNI. The fact that a telephone infrastructure is needed to connect to the Internet, and the ISPs' argument that by allowing them to develop an Internet-protocol infrastructure they could deliver voice and data at a cheaper rate, makes this issue a CNI.

Negotiations on the question of universal access have broadened to include discussions of which organization should oversee the deployment and funding of an exchange point and national Internet backbone. The question under debate is whether Ghana Telecom should be involved in an Internet exchange point (IXP), and if so, whether its participation will be anticompetitive. The Ghana Internet Service Providers Association (GISPA), an industry coalition, is poised to establish the IXP. But can GISPA raise the funds to build a national backbone, or should the government take the lead in this "public good"? This question represents the fourth CNI, and it is still being negotiated. The establishment of a national Internet backbone and exchange infrastructure is critical to the integration and maturation of local applications, services, and platforms.

CNI 1: Establishment of International Satellite Gateways by ISPs

Nii Narku Quaynor established the first ISP in Ghana, Network Computer Systems, on 18 February 1988. The first Internet dial-up subscriber signed up with the NCS in 1993. The NCS applied to the Frequency Board, the precursor of the NCA, for a "value-added" services license so that they could resell international Internet connectivity directly. According to John Mahama, the former minister of communication, the NCS was granted a license because the trend toward convergence in the industry was not yet understood. Mahama pointed out that even in the developed countries of the West, convergence was still "futuristic and only in its infancy."[2] One key to NCS's successful application was that Quaynor's technical expertise and competence enabled him to negotiate an international gateway for the NCS.

The NCS originally utilized a dial-up connection provided by Ghana Telecom to connect to PIPEX, a British ISP. Users in Ghana dialed into the NCS and were routed via PIPEX to the Internet. In August 1995, following an increase in demand, the NCS migrated to a 14.4 kilobits per second (kbps) dedicated circuit from Ghana Telecom. The NCS then upgraded the Ghana Telecom connection from 14.4 kbps to 64 kbps. In June 1996 the NCS was granted a license to operate its own satellite connection to the global Internet. As noted, Ghana Telecom and Westel had been granted an exclusive international gateway until 2002. Quaynor maneuvered around the duopoly by negotiating with the NCA and the Ministry of Transportation and Communication for permission to implement his own international gateway. The primary rationale for Quaynor's request was that Ghana Telecom was not providing a reliable and efficient satellite connection to the Internet. The minister of transportation and communications, Edward Salia, wanted to encourage experimentation by an experienced Internet expert like Quaynor.

The NCS was convinced that it could provide better reliability to its customers if it could operate a separate international satellite connection. Because the government was a major user of the NCS's Internet services, it had an incentive to support the NCS's effort to establish a more reliable Internet gateway. Under an initial agreement, the NCS paid a bypass fee to Ghana Telecom. The bypass fee was fixed at the amount that the NCS was paying to the telecom for a 64-kbps dedicated circuit. Because the NCS was only providing a "data" service, Ghana Telecom did not perceive any threat to its "voice" service. This compromise was reached after intense negotiations.

It is important to note that Quaynor also served on Ghana's Frequency Board, the body charged with issuing international gateway licenses. Quaynor was entrusted with "this new Internet thing" by senior national management. Kwami Ahiabenu II, the executive director of AITEC, says of Quaynor: "one important and fundamental point about Nii, he was seen to be providing a developmental service; meaning NCS was seen as a literal ISP to the government and its agencies, rather than a private company."[3] Ghanaian policymakers equated voice services with Ghana Telecom and Internet services with the NCS. Ernest Wilson suggests that Quaynor's alumnus contact with President Jerry Rawlings was decisive: they both attended Achimota Secondary School, and this personal connection allowed Quaynor to successfully negotiate with the government. Such connections are important in Accra (and all capitals), and provide a social network that, to some extent, supersedes tribal identification.[4]

In 1996, two other companies, Internet Ghana (IGH) and Africa Online, established ISPs in Ghana. Originally, the IGH and Africa Online used international circuits provided by Ghana Telecom. Later, they obtained permission from the NCA to operate their own international satellite gateways. Africa Online received authorization fairly easily from the minister of transport and communication. According to Mawuli Tse, the founder and director of Africa Online, the authorization could be revoked at the ministry's discretion.[5]

A license for a very small aperture terminal (VSAT) was granted to Africa Online in late 1998 to connect to Teleglobe. Technically, the license did not include permission to operate an international gateway and Africa Online was required to purchase international capacity from Ghana Telecom.[6] Prior to this arrangement, Africa Online was using a leased line from Ghana Telecom and was making similar payments for bandwidth to the telecom. Establishing a satellite dish on Africa Online's premises meant that the physical infrastructure was different; contractually, nothing had changed. According to Mawuli, it took about a year to convince the NCA and Ghana Telecom to accept this arrangement.

No major contractual problems arose between Ghana Telecom and Africa Online over the leased lines. It took a long time for issues to arise, mainly because Ghana Telecom was not well equipped to provide the links. "Once we got the contractual green light, the technical team at Ghana Telecom was very helpful with the implementation. People like Richard Gyawu, Emmanuel Idun and Appiah showed a lot of dedication to the job," says Mawuli.[7]

The Ministry of Transportation and Communication and the NCA agreed to license ISPs as value-added service providers of data. Furthermore, they were allowed to establish international satellite connections that gave them direct access to the Internet. Former minister John Mahama noted that, due to the proliferation of satellite coverage over Africa, ISPs secured international connections for significantly less through alternative carriers than through Ghana Telecom's costly Intelsat service.

It became clear over time that Ghana Telecom and the ISPs were transcending their respective jurisdictions of voice and data. The telecom viewed the ISPs as a "threat" because of their ability to terminate international voice calls around mid-2000. This issue is explored further in the next section, which addresses the VOIP critical negotiation issue. The ISPs developed better and more reliable solutions than Ghana Telecom; hence, most multinationals and diplomatic missions chose to do business with an ISP for voice, data, and video connectivity. All the entities that had previously gone through Ghana Telecom now routed their voice, data, and video communications via an ISP, bypassing the telecom. As a result, Ghana Telecom lost revenue.

Still, Ghana Telecom had its friends at the NCA who were sympathetic to its plight. In fact, the telecom was a close ally of the NCA; some NCA employees had worked with the phone company when it was solely a government-owned entity. Although they now worked in a different organization, some NCA employees still favored the primacy of Ghana Telecom.

But the ISPs had their own constituency within the government. Because the NCA and the Ministry of Transport and Communication were receiving good service from the ISP industry, they wanted the ISPs to prosper. Minister Mahama expressed this sentiment when he said, "there was also a driving desire to promote the spread of Internet service in the country for socio-economic development."[8] It was also clear, however, that not everyone in the Ghanaian government was pleased with the idea of giving out VSAT licenses to anyone who wanted to launch an ISP. Ernest Wilson quotes a former government official who, when asked about ISPs and their international satellite connections, said that his colleagues "regret the decision to this day."[9]

By 1999, Minister of Communications Mahama made the acquisition of ISP licenses from NCA automatic. Mahama said he did this in response to complaints about undue delays by NCA in processing applications for ISP licenses. Mahama also said that he was convinced to implement this measure by the plight of ISPs who needed licenses to raise capital. The directive stated that applications should be approved once all requirements were met by applicants. Many licenses were granted, but most of them are not operational for several reasons. Once again, complex negotiations are ongoing between the NCA and the Ministry of Communications over the rights of ISPs.

Based on the precedent created by the NCS, Internet Ghana, and Africa Online, the NCA—under the ministry's goading—continued to allow ISPs to establish their own international gateways. By 2000 the NCA was granting separate ISP registrations and VSAT licenses to most applicants who met basic requirements.

In 2003, Ghana's parliament passed a law on national communications regulations. This law provides the legal structure of the telecommunications industry. Internet service is classified under the regulations as a value-added service. As such, ISPs must register with the NCA, but they do not need a license. Under the 2003 regulations, anyone who operates a satellite earth station must have a license. The new regulations also stipulate that providers of telecommunication services must make their networks available to value-added networks. The following question must be posed: Why do the regulations say little about Internet service if there has been so much conflict about the relationship between ISPs and Ghana Telecom? According to Kwami Ahiabenu II, the NCA is expected to enforce the regulations; thus it is not a lack of "regulations" that confuses matters, but a total inability on the part of the NCA to perform due to lack of adequate capacity.

By approving the NCS international satellite connection, the government initiated a series of decisions that enabled the ISP industry to bypass Westel and Ghana Telecom's control of international connectivity. In pursuing this course of action, the government made it possible for ISPs to offer voice calls (discussed below). More important, the breaking of Ghana Telecom's choke-hold on international connectivity allowed a new technology to flourish; consequently, a new paradigm in communications arose and Ghanaians were able to interact with the rest of the world at a fraction of the cost.

CNI 2: The Legality of VOIP

Many negotiations have been held on the question of whether Ghanaian ISPs can use their networks to support voice traffic. By 1996, technology began to appear on the market that allowed computers to convert "voice" into data packets that could be routed to another computer and converted back into voice. Thus the voice/data distinction was breaking down. Until this time, the government viewed the ISPs as data carriers and the telecom companies as voice carriers. Little did the government and the NCA know that the voice/data distinction was dying and that they needed to engage the reality of rapid technological evolution.

In an attempt to reduce the cost of calls to Ghana and increase their profits, certain phone companies outside Ghana routed calls more cheaply over the Internet through Ghanaian ISPs to the end-user in the country. These calls were carried over an ISP's international satellite connection. The ISP would then convert the "data" packets into voice and dial-out on modems to the caller's receiver. Although VOIP takes several forms, this "bypass" process was deemed as violating Ghana Telecom's exclusive voice license and as "illegal termination" by the government and the NCA.

Under the "settlements" system of international phone calls, Ghana Telecom terminated calls initiated by phone companies in other nations; in turn, those companies terminated calls initiated by the telecom. At the end of a business year, Ghana Telecom settled accounts with foreign carriers. Because the telecom traditionally terminated more international calls than it originated, it was paid an agreed rate for the difference. These payments were in hard currency and they were highly valued by both Ghana Telecom and the government. In short, international calling was a cash cow not only for the telecom but also for the government.

By 2000, however, Ghana Telecom found that the number of international calls it was terminating had dropped dramatically; profits fell as a result. The reduction in revenue was huge and could be seen very clearly on the balance sheets. Indeed the International Telecommunication Union (ITU) reports that

Ghana Telecom's revenue dropped from US$170 million in 1999 to US$89 million in 2000.[10] Ghana Telecom suspected that something was amiss. It soon determined that ISPs were terminating calls on their terrestrial network and collecting the hard currency that was Ghana Telecom's "due." Although the volume of international calls was increasing, this flow bypassed the telecom's gateway. Revenues were pouring into the ISPs. Ghana Telecom complained to the NCA, charging that the ISPs were stealing its revenue. In fact, some individuals and organizations that were not authorized or licensed ISPs were providing VOIP services. This group of illegal operators must be distinguished from the legitimate ISPs who held licenses and were providing a service that was consistent with their platform.

Ghana Telecom charged the ISPs with acting as Internet telephony service providers (ITSPs), and with causing the loss of year-end settlement revenues. Ben Adu, a consultant hired by the NCA, prepared a docket for the attorney general of Ghana. Adu also led a raid on Mac Telecom, Intercom Data Network (IDN), and Tin-Ifa Ghana Ltd., each a licensed ISP. Adu claimed that the companies were acting as ITSPs; with the help of the police, he confiscated their equipment and detained some of their executives. This action provoked a public outcry by customers and business partners of those ISPs. Tension ran high among various interests, including the ISPs, the NCA, the government, Ghana Telecom, the diplomatic community, and the general public.

The ISP owners who were thrown in jail petitioned the courts and logged a complaint against the NCA. The courts deliberated the issue and asked the NCA to justify its action. Surprisingly, the NCA could not provide the courts with tangible and credible evidence of wrongdoing by the ISPs. The courts ruled in favor of the ISPs and required the NCA to return all seized equipment. Furthermore, the NCA was ordered not to tamper with the ISPs provided that they decoupled the voice segment of their data operations. According to Mawuli Tse, the ruling points to the inability of Ghanaian courts to deal with technically complex issues. The NCA was slow in responding to the court decision because it wanted to appeal it. The IDN and Tin-Ifa bought new equipment so that they could restart their ISP business. Mac Telecom, however, went out of business.

The NCA changed position several times as it struggled to find a legal basis for their contention that VOIP deployment by ISPs broke the law. The NCA asserted that licenses issued to ISPs were for data and video traffic, not voice. When asked how to decouple voice from a video conference, the NCA reinterpreted this distinction. Some ISP customers were operating voice over their data networks as well. Indeed, the courts, the NCA, and the ISPs were grappling with the challenge of regulating VOIP, in general, and how VOIP was defined technically and legally. The essential difficulty was that the NCA had licensed ISPs to carry data, which includes VOIP. The situation was complicated because no explicit law declared all forms of VOIP illegal. Rather, the

NCA interpreted the law to suit its interests. It took the following position: it is not illegal for ISP customers to send voice over a private network, but it is illegal for companies to do the same on a commercial scale, terminating locally on the Ghana Telecom platform.

The NCA equated the operation of VOIP, which resulted in already noted revenue loss to Ghana Telecom, as "illegal termination." The telecom supported NCA's position. The key issue was whether the ISPs had the right to route international calls on Ghana Telecom's terrestrial network. The ISPs argued that because Ghana Telecom terminated traffic on ISP networks, the ISPs should have the right to use the telecom's network in the same way. The NCA's earlier acquiescence for ISP use of VOIP over private networks, which was made on the basis of incomplete information about a then infant technology, complicates the issue. ISPs had been granted rights to operate some VOIP services, but this decision was based on insufficient technical and legal knowledge, and insufficient definitions for adequate regulation. This should not be surprising, given that the ramifications of VOIP were not well understood either in Ghana or elsewhere in the middle to late 1990s. According to the NCA, during the five-year exclusivity period (until 2002), in which Ghana Telecom and Westel were entitled to exclusively operate the international gateway, such transgressions violated this entitlement. After 2002 the NCA began arguing that the ISPs did not have licenses to route international voice calls.

According to former communications minister John Mahama, "the whole problem was caused because at the time of the ADP and liberalization of the sector, the issue of convergence of voice and data services was not clearly understood by policymakers."[11] For example the gateway for transmission of data was therefore not viewed as a threat to exclusivity of the fixed operators. Hence at a point in time the ministry did not want to totally fault the ISPs as much as it did not want to take sides with Ghana Telecom.

Mahama's position was that VOIP technology had come to stay and could not be stopped. The Ministry of Communications hoped that Ghana Telecom would work with the ISPs within a framework acceptable to both parties. However, the telecom did not want to negotiate because it saw VOIP as a direct violation of its turf.

Frustrated with the NCA's inability to make a decision, companies such as Accelerated Computer Service (ACS) appealed directly to the minister of communications for permission to operate internal VOIP networks. ACS, a US company that provides business process outsourcing (BPO), was planning to establish a data processing center in Ghana with a thousand employees. It needed voice transmission to connect its Ghana and US offices, and was proposing a major investment that would create quality jobs. The minister of communications intervened and ordered the NCA to make a decision, within a week, as to whether ACS could use an internal VOIP network. Under such pressure, the NCA permitted the company to use VOIP for internal communications. This is another case in which the NCA's lack of understanding and foresight could have resulted in the loss of a major investment.

The ISPs perceived a need to deal with matters on a collective basis; hence they began meeting and eventually formed the Ghana Internet Service Providers Association in July 2001. Although the NCS did not attend the inaugural meeting of GISPA, it later paid the sign-up fee, attended subsequent meetings, and participated in the group's listserve. It took time and a significant effort before Ghana's ISPs trusted each other enough to work together in a common cause.

GISPA believed that technology was outpacing policy and regulations. Technological innovation was opening new possibilities, and ISPs felt that they should be allowed to experiment with VOIP to determine how it could be used to provide more communication infrastructure, even to the rural areas, and at cheaper rates. GISPA argued that Ghana Telecom's loss of settlement revenue was caused by other factors besides the termination of voice calls by ISPs. GISPA held that the whole telecommunications landscape was changing. Ghanaians were using e-mail, chat rooms, and Internet faxes to communicate, instead of placing expensive international calls. In addition, after 2002, consumers were receiving international calls on cell phones provided by mobile operators who bypassed Ghana Telecom's gateway and network. Finally, GISPA asserted that settlement rates and revenues were falling due to market pressures.

In March 2003, Ghana Telecom implemented another strike against its competitors. It set all ISP phone lines to a receive-only mode, thereby effectively shutting off the lines used to place calls to its switched network. When this stratagem was effected, the ISPs discovered that they could not place outgoing calls even using their administrative lines. The ISPs cried foul to all who would listen; they contacted their allies in the government and within a week Ghana Telecom backed off. It could have enabled only the ISPs' administrative phone lines, but there was such an outcry that all lines were enabled. Later, Ghana Telecom implemented another strategy to limit the outward calling capacity of certain modem lines.

At the time, the NCA initiated a study to quantify the losses that Ghana Telecom was experiencing due to illegal termination over its switched network. According to an article published on 1 October 2003 in the *Ghanaian Chronicle,* the NCA study identified thirty-two illegal unlicensed VOIP operators.[12] This activity, according to the article, cost Ghana Telecom US$15 million in 2002. The NCA wrote each of the thirty-two ISPs, demanding that they reimburse the telecom for lost revenue. The NCA also threatened prosecutions for nonpayment. It was later discovered that none of these ISPs had authorization to act as an ISP; they were not licensed and thus defamed the legitimate ISP community.

Instead of a comprehensive approach based on principles for regulation, the NCA reacted to issues in a scattered rather than a unified way. This was partially an inescapable result of regulating an infant technology. In many ways, these sets of negotiations and the failure to achieve a viable regulatory approach were significantly affected by the NCA's incremental regulatory approach, an approach punctuated by the NCA's decision to address issues in a piecemeal way. A series of NCA decisions based on incomplete technical and legal information and under pressure from senior government officials further muddled an already complicated policy environment.

Through negotiations held over the years, it became clear to all parties that voice could not be decoupled from data and video. Hence operators needed to establish a commercial framework that would allow this technology to grow. The acting director-general of the NCA, J. R. K. Tandoh, stated in a public forum that the NCA was developing a VOIP framework that would license operators separately.[13] An effort to develop a commercial framework for VOIP was also under way between Ghana Telecom and other operators, Tandoh added. A new framework is needed because Ghana Telecom and Westel's international gateway exclusivity has ended.

The arbitrage of international phone traffic has definitely funded the development of segments of the ISP industry in Ghana. Although only some ISPs have benefited from terminating VOIP calls over Ghana Telecom's lines, most ISPs sold leased lines connections to clients who then used those connections for voice calls.

CNI 3: VOIP and the Funding of Universal Access

To fully understand why the VOIP issue is so controversial in Ghana, one must understand the history of the debate over how to provide universal access in the country. Ghana Telecom claims that it needs the revenues generated by international voice traffic to expand access to telephones throughout the country. This claim, however, should not be accepted automatically. In fact, negotiations on how to provide universal access have been extensive and convoluted. This issue is essential because it creates the framework for Internet diffusion in rural areas; without a telephone infrastructure, rural communities may not be connected to the Internet. The most contentious issue, how to fund universal access provision, is complicated, because universal access is defined in several ways, and different operators hold competing positions on the question.

The ADP planning document cited universal access as a major concern. According to the ADP, universal access was achieved in two ways: first, all licensed operators were to develop infrastructure in their areas of operation; second, Ghana Telecom, Westel, and the mobile operators were to contribute 1 percent of their gross revenue to a universal access fund called the Ghana Investment Fund for Telecoms (GIFTel). This fund would be used to build rural infrastructure. In particular, GIFTel funds would be allocated to develop infrastructure in regions that lacked service. According to John Mahama, then minister of communications, the ISPs, as value-added service providers, had no obligation to contribute to this fund (as well as universal access provision in their license or authorization).

Ghana Telecom and Westel provided the ministry and the NCA with a list of areas in which they were to develop infrastructure per their license. Hence the ministry and NCA decided to license other companies to operate in rural areas not covered by Ghana Telecom, Westel, and the mobile companies. The NCA licensed the first rural operator, Capital Telecom, which, using GIFTel funds and its own resources, was committed to building rural infrastructure in the eastern, Volta, greater Accra, central, and western regions. According to Mahama, the NCA considered licensing a second rural operator but did not do so.

Although Capital Telecom secured a grant from the British government's Export Credit Development Guarantee (ECDG), the company soon folded. Capital Telecom failed because it purchased equipment that could not perform, lacked managerial expertise, and feuded with Ghana Telecom over interconnection and with Mobitel over spectrum. With the failure of Capital Telecom, the plan to achieve universal access evaporated.

Most operators defaulted in their GIFTel payments because GIFTel was not properly established. Therefore, part of the reason for Capital Telecom's collapse was that the company could not draw on the GIFTel funds. According to Mahama, the Ministry of Communications' top priority at the time was not GIFTel, but establishing the NCA board and launching an independent regulator. Furthermore, the NCA passively observed as Ghana Telecom undermined not only Capital Telecom but also the second national operator, Western Telesystems (Westel), by refusing to interconnect. Capital Telecom futilely demanded interconnection enforcement and the establishment of GIFTel.

Ghana Telecom and Westel both pledged that they would deploy services in their areas of operation, and the mobile operators wanted to achieve universal access in their own roll-out plan, rather than through GIFTel. This is the key point of contention: the operators did not want to contribute to a separate fund; instead, they wanted to achieve universal access by building their own infrastructure. Ghana Telecom deployed new telephony in some of its operating area, but Westel failed woefully. By the end of exclusivity in 2002, the NCA slapped noncompliance penalties of US$71.5 million and US$69 million on Westel and Ghana Telecom, respectively. Under the ADP program, and per their licenses, such penalties were to be imposed if Westel and Ghana Telecom failed to meet their universal access obligations. Naturally, the fines generated tension between the operators and the NCA.

Ghana Telecom and Westel argued that they could not pay the penalty and at the same time continue rolling out new infrastructure. The companies requested a grace period, as they were facing a huge financial burden. It was unclear, for example, how Westel could pay the fine and avoid bankruptcy. The NCA maintained its position, but as a result of intervention by the Ministry of Communications and the president, the fines were reduced and allowed to be paid in installments. In fact, the fines were still being negotiated in 2004, although some payments have reportedly been made. The companies still object and complain that they do not earn enough profit to stay in business, even without paying the fines.

After Ghana Telecom's management team from Telkom Malaysia (the GCom consortium) failed to meet their obligations in 2003, the government of President John Kufuor brought in a team from Telenor of Norway. The government negotiated with Ghana Telecom's new management team on an agreement to deploy 400,000 new telephone lines and to provide telecommunication services to each town or village having a secondary school. This agreement constituted a new policy strategy by the president to achieve universal access. Underscoring the importance of universal access, President Kufuor explained the strategy during his first State of the Nation address to parliament and the people of Ghana. He declared that his plan entailed use of broadband Internet. Ghana Telecom therefore began piloting Internet services. Plans have been drafted to provide broadband services at low cost; this will inevitably drive some ISPs out of business. Ghana Telecom continually argued that it could meet the president's goals only if it earned sufficient revenue from international calls.

GISPA, the ISP trade association, claimed that it was unfair for the government to cause the collapse of indigenous private enterprise. GISPA members argued that, although their licenses did not stipulate any universal access obligations, they had contributed significantly to the growth of the Internet in underserved areas. The ISPs further argued that if they were allowed to use VOIP platforms, then they could quickly provide voice services as well. Some ISPs had established POPs in four of the ten regional capitals (as far as the northern region), and were ready to support such services. Most ISPs cannot justify investing in infrastructure in remote areas, yet they feel the need to do so. GISPA's former chairman, Leslie Tamakloe, stated in a public hearing on telecommunications policy that "it cost more to drive an IP from Accra to Tamale (Northern Region) than to Nigeria so the fact that we are not funneling resources to Nigeria should give our government a cause to support us and not break our back."[14]

By pressuring the government, GISPA convinced authorities to temporarily halt the launch of Ghana Telecom's ISP. GISPA wanted Ghana Telecom's ISP to be a separate business entity without preferential treatment. The ISPs also wanted to receive the same government support and access to capital enjoyed by the telecom. Even without government financial support, some ISPs had extended service to underserved areas.

Under the national communications regulation law passed in 2003, the universal access fund designated to support a third-party rural telecommunications company was abandoned. A new strategy was put in place: each operator was to provide and extend its services to the entire geographical market that it was licensed to serve. All companies, including Ghana Telecom, Westel, the cellular operators, and new operators with national licenses, were required to build infrastructure in the rural areas. Russell Southwood, chief executive officer of Balancing Act Africa, took exception with the new strategy.

Under its Telenor management team (in place in 2003), Ghana Telecom is still making the case that it is best positioned to provide universal access in the country. The question Ghana Telecom faces is where will it obtain the funds to support universal access. The World Bank and other multilateral agencies are reluctant to lend or grant it the capital necessary for expansion. In 2000 the World Bank agreed to provide the telecom with a loan of US$100 million for the upgrade and expansion of its network. After the change in management at Ghana Telecom, this loan was approved but not disbursed. According to the Bank, the terms and conditions under which the loan agreement was reached had changed, and so the money would not be forthcoming.

At the same time, Ghana Telecom's new management had signed a contract with Alcatel to purchase equipment for network expansion. Additionally, Ghana Telecom secured credit with the Chinese government to finance equipment purchases from Alcatel China. Due to litigation between the Ghanaian government and GCom (the Malaysian-backed consortium that owns 30 percent of Ghana Telecom), a court writ was issued holding up disbursement of a finance agreement between Alcatel and Shangai Bell. The Ghanaian government is currently fighting the Malaysian-led consortium in court, and the minister concedes that obtaining an out-of-court settlement would have been preferable. The minister cites the high cost of court proceedings and denounces the Ghanaian members of the consortium who have sided with their Malaysian partners.[15]

It can be argued that Ghana Telecom's change of management was not properly implemented by former minister of communications and technology Felix Owusu Adjapong. As a result of the change in management, the World Bank loan was not disbursed and GCom took the Ghanaian government to court. As a result, it has become much harder for Ghana Telecom to raise funds. In addition, the telecom's strategy for achieving universal access has been hindered.

Until now, funds for ISP deployment have come from private sources. As the ISP community has become more sophisticated, more talks are being held between it and multilateral donors on the possibility of financing network expansion using Internet protocol.

The key question of Internet diffusion concerns how quickly market forces will drive the expansion of ISP networks throughout the country and into rural areas. A second question concerns whether Ghana Telecom will roll out Internet-protocol infrastructure in rural areas against the preferences of the ISP industry.

CNI 4: Development of an Exchange Point and National Backbone

Much debate has taken place on what kind of national infrastructure Ghana needs to support a vibrant ISP industry, who will build the infrastructure, and who will operate it. At the most basic level, Ghana's national infrastructure could take the form of an IXP located in Accra. At this Internet exchange, ISPs could interconnect and route traffic locally instead of through the US and other international backbones. At a more advanced level, a national Internet-protocol backbone could be established that would provide high-speed access to voice, data, and video (multimedia platform) for ISPs, telecoms, and mobile operators both within and outside Ghana. On paper, a national Internet-protocol backbone was to be implemented by the Communication Infrastructure Company (CIC), a private-public partnership that would combine all local infrastructures into one system. The government floated the CIC idea, but it never went far in terms of implementation.

The assumption that Ghana Telecom's circuit-switched infrastructure could serve as the basis for Ghana's telecommunications infrastructure is doubtful. Circuit congestion on the system is causing too many call failures and inefficiencies. By now, most of the copper that was used to build Ghana's telecom infrastructure is old and dead; those wires need to be replaced with new and better ones that can accommodate traffic demands over the long term. There is widespread skepticism that Ghana Telecom's bureaucracy is capable of establishing a reliable infrastructure.

Building an IXP in Ghana would be one step toward enhancing the country's telecommunications infrastructure. Ideally, an IXP will allow ISPs to route domestic traffic through other Ghanaian ISPs. An IXP can enhance response times and provide incentives for hosting websites locally rather than abroad. At one point, Ghana Telecom declared that it would establish an IXP. Later, the government sought to impose its position on the ISPs, but that did not happen. Meanwhile, the ISPs themselves where discussing how and where to establish the IXP.

The prospect of an IXP has been talked about since 1996, but one has not been built due to lack of cooperation in, and leadership of, the ISP industry. Previously, because the ISPs were isolated, it was impossible to implement an IXP. Beyond the technical aspects, creating an exchange point involves sociological and physiological challenges. In 2001, when GISPA was formed, discussions about a possible exchange point became more focused. The building of "trust" among the ISPs that compete against each other, however, has taken almost three years to accomplish. Only now has creation of a Ghanaian Internet exchange point become realistic. One issue of contention was finding a "neutral location" for the exchange. Initially, the ISPs wanted an ISP to host the exchange, but that did not work.

Eventually, the government supported creating an exchange point, but demanded that it be managed by Ghana Telecom. Most ISPs rejected this proposal. Ghana Telecom argued that because it had the most connections to the ISPs, it was in the best position to establish an IXP. The ISPs were skeptical of Ghana Telecom's neutrality, because the telecom was about to launch its own ISP. In addition, most of the ISPs experienced Ghana Telecom as hostile and unreliable, and so trust was lacking. In short, the ISPs did not want the exchange point to be placed under the control of what they believed to be an unreliable enterprise like Ghana Telecom. The ISPs favored placing control of the IXP in the hands of the BusyInternet Cafe (the largest Internet cafe in Accra, with a hundred personal computers in 2004); however, this proposal was withdrawn when BusyInternet began offering ISP services. The ISPs were also convinced that if the exchange point were controlled by an ISP, that operator would enjoy undue advantage. A consensus emerged that a non-ISP at a neutral location must oversee the IXP.

After the establishment of the Accra-based Ghana Indian Kofi Annan Center of Excellence in ICT in 2003, the government proposed that the center host the IXP. The center was designed as an autonomous, private training institution that did not aspire to be an ISP. With this second proposal, it became obvious that the government and the ISP community had agreed on the need for an exchange point. This consensus created a certain degree of understanding among the government, the NCA, and GISPA members. A series of meetings have been held on the establishment of a Ghanaian IXP under the auspices of the center. The center has offered to make a private room available for the exercise. The needed structures are in place and the exchange point will soon be launched.

An Internet exchange point will be an important first step, but Ghana's telecommunications infrastructure will be much stronger if it has a national backbone. Clearly, the current infrastructure does not allow for great expansion. Discussions are under way about what technology—wireless, VSAT, or fiber—is needed to create a new national backbone. A consensus seems to be developing around the idea of using fiber. Beyond the advantages of using fiber—speed, volume, and reliability—there is already fiber running through much of the country.

The government-owned Volta River Authority (VRA), Ghana's main power company, has a fiber network on its high-tension power towers. This network was the vision of Ghana's founding president, Kwame Nkrumah, who wanted the VRA to have an internal communication infrastructure. It is amazing that in the 1960s Nkrumah supported the use of fiber. The VRA realized the potential of its fiber infrastructure, and decided to develop it not only for internal communications but also in support of a national fiber optic backbone. To undertake this task, Volta Communications (Voltacom), a subsidiary communications company, was formed and licensed by the NCA with the concurrence of the Ministry of Communications.

The Voltacom fiber network runs from Accra through Cape Coast, to Takoradi, to Kumasi, and back to Accra to form a loop. Voltacom's services, however, were priced beyond what the market would bear. Only six companies, mostly ISPs and mobile companies, signed up for Voltacom's services.

The VRA could not support Voltacom with more money because its resources were dedicated to sustaining its main operation, namely power. Nevertheless, Voltacom rejected an offer by a foreign concern to buy a stake and to raise additional credit. Thus, while an existing viable national backbone potentially exists, it has not come to fruition. According to former minister John Mahama, the VRA was overly protective of Voltacom. Others believed that Voltacom did not know what it was doing because, as a government parastatal, it had no commercial strategy. In 2004 the government still had not forged a vision for Voltacom, but there were plans under way to "privatize" the company to encourage its expansion.

The second element needed for a high-speed national backbone is connection to the international Internet. In 2004, Ghana connected to SAT-3, an offshore undersea cable running along the west coast of Africa to Portugal. Some have proposed connecting SAT-3 with Voltacom to form a national fiber backbone. Not much cooperation exists, however, between Ghana Telecom, which controls the SAT-3 landing, and Voltacom. Because Ghana Telecom has maintained that it needs to develop its own fiber backbone, there is an effort to duplicate Voltacom's southern sector fiber network. Voltacom has activated its own fiber network, by itself, to the north. For a while, this provoked a standoff, but the Ministry of Communications and the NCA have established a committee to find a way for these two entities to cooperate on creating a single infrastructure for the national backbone.

An alliance between Ghana Telecom and Voltacom has not yet emerged. Yet it seems logical that an alliance will emerge on a fiber backbone, because it is simply too expensive for both companies to finance development of separate infrastructures. Significant parts of a high-speed national backbone exist. Such an alliance, however, will depend on strong leadership by the government. In 2004 a committee composed of representatives of all the parties began discussing how to move forward on a national fiber backbone. The government favors bringing in an outside strategic investor. The International Finance Corporation (IFC) has sent experts to Ghana to facilitate ongoing talks in Accra. The government has a major stake in both Ghana Telecom and VRA, so it should be easy to decouple their respective fiber entities and create a new enterprise. A general consensus supports creation of a new fiber company that would establish a national backbone. This backbone entity would sell circuits to various operators so they can focus on providing value-added solutions to their customers.

The inability of the government, Voltacom, Ghana Telecom, and the ISPs to implement a national backbone has slowed the geographical dispersion of the Internet in Ghana. Therefore, ISPs have not sprung up in regional markets. A few ISPs have built their own national backbones, but these have been confined to several regional capitals. Thus, Internet diffusion has been centered on Ghana's capital, Accra.

Conclusion

The rapid evolution of the Internet in Ghana between 1996 and 2000 can be explained, in part, by the fact that the ISPs were able to bypass the Ghana Telecom–Westel duopoly. The ISPs did this by operating their own international satellite gateways. Thus, ISPs were able to provide reliable, low-cost service. Ghana's Internet infrastructure was partially funded by arbitrage of expensive international voice calls. Some of this arbitrage was done legally, when customers ran voice traffic over their data networks. Some of this activity, however, was illegal in the eyes of the NCA. Specifically, some ISPs terminated international calls using Ghana Telecom's local exchange network.

In 1999, Minister John Mahama made access to ISP licenses automatic. This reform encouraged many to enter the market. By 2000, heavy competition had driven down the cost of Internet access from US$100 to US$25 per month. Internet subscriptions rose rapidly, as any study of Internet diffusion in Ghana demonstrates. The end of Ghana Telecom and Westel's exclusivity encouraged both companies to roll out new lines, which made acquiring Internet access easier for ISPs and their customers. Finally, rapid growth in Internet use can also be attributed to a growth in purchasing power by Ghanaian consumers.

The major attack on the ISP industry over the issue of VOIP drove ISPs into a coalition. It took almost three years for operators to build mutual trust. As a result of this new spirit of trust, a consensus emerged on the need for an Internet exchange point. Once GISPA was formed, other stakeholders—namely the government and the NCA—saw that they would now have to deal with a corporate body. The ISP industry had gained a better image and bargaining positioning.

The difficulties of achieving universal access have also affected Internet diffusion. Lack of local telephone loops in much of the country has limited the spread of ISPs and their ability to connect rural areas. Some ISPs even have trouble acquiring phone lines for their POPs in regional capitals. Ghana Telecom's new management has pledged to provide telephone and Internet access to all communities that have a secondary school. In order to fund universal access, Ghana Telecom insists that its international calling revenues must be protected against competition from ISPs. There is an Ashanti saying: "If I cannot get ahead, I will not let you get ahead." This saying is often represented by the image of a two-headed alligator, with both heads pulling in an opposite direction. Such lack of trust has prevented the establishment of an Internet exchange and a national backbone. The ISP industry in Ghana has been able to develop thanks to the decentralized nature of the Internet. Despite conflicts among ISPs, between ISPs and Ghana Telecom, and within the government, the Internet has indeed made remarkable progress.

Over the years, the negotiation of CNIs has evolved. Today, the various stakeholders prefer to discuss issues openly rather than resorting to other means. Some discussions do not lead to consensus, but the process of negotiating must be applauded. In the late 1990s and early 2000s, few negotiations were held. Ghana Telecom's plan to enter the ISP market, for example, prompted several discussions mediated by the Ministry of Communications and the NCA. However, there is still a need for more interaction, inclusion, and consensus building, so that issues may be seen in the broader context of the entire industry.

If further development of the Internet is to take place in Ghana, an open communication policy must be created. Such an environment would encourage more inclusion and interaction among stakeholders, as well as facilitate the signing of interconnection agreements between various kinds of networks. Clearly, the CNIs discussed in this chapter demonstrate that the enforcement of interconnection agreements is critical. It is essential for the NCA to establish a process under which ISPs can sign interconnection agreements with Ghana Telecom and other operators (such as mobile companies). The VOIP issue demonstrates that the ISPs that used Ghana Telecom to terminate VOIP calls should have been required to have an interconnection agreement with the telecom. In 2001 the Ghanaian courts rightly declared that no rules or regulations existed that made what the ISPs were doing illegal. The only violation found by the courts was that the ISP licenses were for "data" rather than "voice" traffic, a distinction that is tremendously difficult to make, since voice traffic is in fact data traffic.

The NCA needs to help establish an interconnection regimen between Ghana Telecom and ISPs that stipulates what settlements are due when either party uses the network of the other to terminate calls. In addition, the NCA needs a framework to enforce such interconnection agreements. Although Ghana Telecom is required to interconnect with the mobile operators, it has not allocated enough bandwidth for this purpose; as a result, many calls between Ghana Telecom and the mobile operators are dropped.

A convergence is occurring between ISPs and mobile operators. Users can now send e-mail messages to mobile handsets equipped with a short messaging system (SMS). It is only a matter of time before mobile users will be able to send e-mail or voice-mail to personal computers via the Internet. Ghana Telecom and mobile networks should not be allowed to impede convergence by refusing to negotiate interconnecting agreements with ISPs.

Developing and implementing market-based interconnection agreements that facilitate convergence will require an open policy environment. To achieve such an environment, the NCA must develop regulations that are farsighted and allow technology to evolve. It is clear from the CNIs discussed in this chapter that regulatory uncertainty and biased interpretations of existing regulations have hampered Internet growth. It is also certain that the lack of a definite communications policy has caused many problems for the telecommunications industry. In most developing countries like Ghana, restrictive laws and an untrustworthy regulatory process thwart the ability of local entrepreneurs and outside investors alike to supply the markets with new technologies that contribute to building the communications infrastructure.

In many developing countries, governments restrain or prohibit new information and communications technologies (e.g., VOIP), restrict unlicensed wireless fidelity (WiFi) and other wireless standards, impose crippling ISP licensing requirements, and limit access to fiber optic cable connectivity. Often, such restrictive policies derive from the government's close (and often corrupt) relationship with traditional, state-owned monopoly telecoms.

Elimination of existing (and emerging) legal and regulatory obstacles to deployment of an open communications network could significantly boost private sector investment and Internet growth in Ghana. This is not simply a choice between old-fashioned telephony and newfangled Internet technologies—it is a choice between two ways of structuring government and society. The old telephone network model is closed, centralized, controlled, and top-down; the new paradigm, like the Internet itself, is open, decentralized, competitive, and technology-neutral. If growth of the Internet in Ghana is to be fostered, then a truly forward-looking set of laws, policies, and regulations is needed. Communications networks and information technologies will thrive under an open communications initiative.

3

Guinea-Bissau: "Pull-and-Tug" Toward Internet Diffusion

Brian Michael King

AMID HEATED DISCUSSIONS OF politics and society in Bissau, one will often hear the Kriol expression *djunda-djunda*. The term, expressed in a synthesis of Portuguese and several indigenous languages, can perhaps best be rendered in English as "pull-and-tug." The evolution of communications policy in Guinea-Bissau has been a complex story of *djunda-djunda,* and this pull-and-tug dynamic has produced sparse Internet diffusion in the country.

The growth of the communications sector as a whole has been equally unimpressive. The incumbent telecommunications company, Guine Telecom, has a capacity for about 12,000 fixed lines.[1] Given network disrepair and inconsistent service, the actual number is closer to 10,000, with approximately 8,500 of these lines in the capital city, Bissau. Digitalization of the national backbone infrastructure proceeded fitfully from 1989, and was only completed in 1999. The first wireless local loop in the country was installed and put into service in November 2003, making Guinea-Bissau perhaps the last country on the planet to roll out cellular technology.

Internet diffusion has proceeded with greater, if still modest, progress. Estimates from 2001, some five years after the introduction of the Net in 1996, put the total number of users in the country at 4,000.[2] In 2002, dial-up subscriptions were estimated at 250. An independent Internet service provider (ISP) competes with the incumbent for customers, though to date both of these have restricted service almost entirely to within Bissau.[3] In 2006 there were some thirteen cybercafes scattered around the capital. Both ISPs report having a circuit with a down-speed of 512 kilobits per second (kbps) and an up-speed of 256 kbps, though actual connectivity is probably much more. To date, there has been hardly any formal use of Web-based tools by private or public sector entities, although individual use of e-mail and Web research continues to grow.

There are many reasons to expect new, comparatively robust growth in the sector in the near future, however. The extractive Guine Telecom monopoly concession was rescinded in June 2003. Since then, two cellular operators have entered the market under a new, competitive regime, and a pioneering national company has formed itself into an operator capable of offering a full range of communications services via Internet-protocol technology. Voice over Internet protocol (VOIP) is poised to become the engine for extending Internet connectivity to rural areas.

The history of Internet diffusion in Guinea-Bissau resists examination according to a strict format of critical issues that are resolved as new ones arise. The most fundamental issues have tended to reappear in different forms. Although privatization and liberalization of the telecom sector have moved inexorably forward, for example, there are still strong tendencies toward monopolization and renationalization. Furthermore, the emergence of new negotiation issues has tended to increase layers of complexity and add new pressures for the resolution of preceding issues.

This process through which the Internet expanded in the country has been a negotiation in the broadest societal sense. Much has happened outside the dictates of policy, or in spite of them. When legal and regulatory regimes have been nebulous or restrictive, societal values, perceived needs, and economic incentives have often determined practice, which have in turn influenced (or become) policy. While there have been key negotiations among stakeholders, and formal policy developments have marked significant moments of consensus, disputes are rarely resolved completely. This enduring, vigorous pull-and-tug between policy and practice is the subject of this chapter.

I begin with an examination of power relations in 1987, as they existed before the emergence of the Net, and discuss four critical negotiation issues (CNIs): privatization, liberalization, licensing and regulation, and VOIP. Privatization of the state post, telephone, and telegraph (PTT) service was placed in the hands of a few politically powerful actors, who in 1989 gave control of the sector to a private, foreign-owned monopoly. Since that time, competent local technicians have struggled to gain a voice in decisions about the sector.

When the Net arrived in Guinea-Bissau in 1996, an intense dispute over the poor investment history of the incumbent, Guine Telecom, was under way. This dispute fueled calls for liberalization. While legislation liberalized Internet service provision, key policy contradictions complicated diffusion of the Net and delayed widespread liberalization of the sector. Under new legislation passed in 1999, a regulatory agency was established, but undue influence by the government and nebulous and inconsistent policies muddled its mission. Thus, licensing and regulation became a significant obstacle to the expansion of the Net. The new regulator, the Institute of Communications, blocked VOIP licenses. Significant steps toward consolidation of liberalization of the telecom sector as a whole, however, ultimately opened the way, and a license for

VOIP was granted. VOIP is now poised to drive the expansion of connectivity into increasingly rural areas.

CNI 1: Privatization

Just a few years after Guinea-Bissau gained independence in 1974, the national communications infrastructure of the country was managed through a partnership with the Swedish International Development Agency (SIDA). The 1980 coup that installed João Bernardo "Nino" Vieira as president of the State Committee was followed by a gradual political shift away from this cooperative-based model to one oriented toward private enterprise. The first large enterprises were parastatals, private but with detailed supervision by the National Economic Planning and Coordination Commission, of which Vieira was also president.

In 1987, SIDA proposed the formation of a new parastatal company that would implement a new wave of network improvements. Key elements of the plan included a digital switching center in Bissau, digital backbone infrastructure for the interior network, service to regional capitals and isolated villages and islands, and building a pool of competent national technicians to manage the network. The Swedish government earmarked approximately US$700,000 for the project.

Some within the Guinea-Bissau government found the SIDA approach paternalistic and were unwilling to link a capacity-building plan to implementation of network digitalization. National technicians within the state-run PTT, however, apparently unanimously supported the SIDA proposal. Longtime PTT and Guine Telecom engineer Isidoro Rodrigues recalls that there was an intense debate on what equipment to buy: digital, which national technicians did not know how to manage; or new analog, which they could manage. Digital equipment was still relatively new and was very expensive. After much discussion, analog technology was chosen. The plan was to introduce digital equipment when project training and capacity building began to take effect. In Rodrigues's opinion, the new analog equipment was of good quality and was appropriate for use in Bissau at the time.[4]

The government moved ahead with its plan to form a new company. Potential strategic partners were sought through state-to-state contacts with Italy, France, and Portugal, the latter of which through Marconi, a public company that would later become part of the private Portugal Telecom Group. In 1987 an agreement with Marconi was signed for the routing of international traffic exclusively through Portugal for ten years. In exchange, Guinea-Bissau would receive training, equipment, and technical assistance to install a satellite earth station.[5] In November 1988, Marconi presented its proposal for the creation of a public-private telecommunications corporation in which Marconi would be the majority shareholder. The development plan specified US$22.5 million for investment in the national network and digitalization of its backbone infrastructure over the first five years.[6] The proposed monopoly concession was to last twenty-five years.

The National Economic Planning and Coordination Commission, which operated under the presidency, designated a task force, consisting of economists and lawyers, to review the Marconi proposal. The task force questioned the advisability of linking sector development to an exclusive concession of the kind Marconi proposed. An extraordinary meeting of the commission was called to discuss the issue. Manuel "Manecas" Dos Santos, minister of economic coordination, commerce, and tourism, chaired the meeting. Manecas was a sort of "superminister" with wide-reaching influence and power. He was a close personal friend of President Vieira, and he made it known that he was implementing the president's policy. The president had asked the task force to review the Marconi proposal "with the greatest brevity" and to make a decision. Dos Santos characterized the Marconi proposal as "serious and appropriate to the reality of the country"; he also called the task force's doubts "groundless." Mussa Djassy, minister of information and communications, was made the new coordinator of the task force. Apparently, the question to be examined was not if, but how, the Marconi proposal was to be implemented.[7]

A number of documents expressing doubts about the Marconi proposal are attached to the minutes of the commission's meeting. Concerns were expressed that the Marconi contract did not define precisely what Marconi's investment obligations were, that there were too few options for the government to terminate the concession, and that there were penalties if termination occurred. Jurists, economists, and engineers were pushed to the margins by the directors of the commission. While the Marconi negotiations were under way, a story (part rumor, part mocking joke) circulated that Communications Minister Djassy was brokering a deal under which he would personally receive an enormous sum of money. In the end, so the story went, all he received for his efforts was a lousy television. Thus a cloistered decisionmaking process determined policy for years, and its effects are still felt.

A few weeks after the agreement was signed in 1989, Marconi deposited US$1.7 million at Guinea-Bissau's national bank as its capital investment in Guine Telecom. Marconi now held 51 percent of the shares in the new company, leaving the government with 49 percent. Installation of the earth station and the central digital switching center quickly followed, but additional investment flagged.

Within a few years, Guine Telecom descended into chaos. The national directors of the company remember the early 1990s as a time of secrecy, distrust, and intrigue in their relations with Marconi. Proper records were not kept for critical items such as management indicators (including waiting lists and repair time data), reconciled reports on domestic and foreign bank accounts, and the minutes of board of directors and shareholder meetings.[8] Marconi officials made all important management decisions behind closed doors or out of the country. They discarded plans for network development made during the partnership with SIDA without suggesting alternatives. The yearly reports of the company became strangely laconic. The 1993 report, for example, merely stated that "the local networks included in the 1993 plan were constructed and remodeled, and plans call for total remodeling and modernization." The report continued: "Evolution of [phone] installations was very positive in 1993, exceeding predictions by 33%. It is apparent that this demonstrated demand is quite favorable."[9] It is difficult to imagine that Marconi management really doubted that a high demand existed for their direct-dial international telephony services. Many felt that the reports' limited attention to the interior network denoted complacency about meeting network build-out requirements specified in the concession contract.

"Guine Telecom works for Marconi!"

—Isidoro Rodrigues[10]

The years 1995 and 1996 were characterized by an intense dispute over the future of Guine Telecom. Displeasure with the opacity and complacency of Marconi's management had spread through the company, government, and society-at-large. A new union, the Telecommunications and Postal Workers Union, emerged in 1995. In March of that year, the union submitted a series of demands to the government and Guine Telecom, including extension of telephone access to villages of 500 inhabitants or more and the digitalization of automatic switching centers as specified in the concession contract. The union also called for representation by a national technician who would sit on the board of directors and participate in the day-to-day management of the company.[11] Initially these requests were denied, but after a two-day general strike the government promised to work toward the union's demands.

The strike initiated an intense period of negotiations among the union, the government, and Portugal Telecom International (PTI) (which had acquired Marconi in 1992 after Portugal began privatizing the sector) over the control of Guine Telecom. Each of these stakeholders attempted to regain control of the company, which already had a disastrous history. Portugal Telecom sent a new delegate administrator to diagnose the company's problems. In a November 1995 report, the new administrator noted the complete disintegration of administrative hierarchies, gross mismanagement of accounts payable, and indications that the previous administrator may have embezzled company funds.[12] The same year, the World Bank assisted the government with a comprehensive audit of the company that corroborated many of these observations.

Formal negotiations over the new management structure of the company began in mid-1995. The Guinea-Bissau delegation included longtime PTT and

Guine Telecom engineer Isidoro Rodrigues and economist Issufo Sanha. Both Rodrigues and Sanha had been on the task force that opposed the concession in 1989. The minutes of these meetings provide a detailed record of attitudes in the company. The technicians objected to the secrecy of Marconi's management and the poor performance in meeting digitalization goals. During the earlier negotiations with Marconi, the company had claimed that it was a capable manager of national networks, when in fact they were more experienced in international traffic. Even a superficial look at international traffic, tariffs, and investments demonstrated that the company was extremely profitable, but no clear formula was observed for dividing profits between the shareholders. Marconi appeared to be reaping enormous profits through Guine Telecom without reporting them to the government. Guinea-Bissau technicians felt that they had been forced to support this activity and had no voice in the company to effect change. Frustrated, Rodrigues declared during a meeting that "Guine Telecom WORKS for Marconi!"[13]

In July 1996, delegations representing Portugal Telecom and the government of Guinea-Bissau agreed on a new investment plan valued at about US$17 million. The plan included the universal access demands of the Telecommunications and Postal Workers Union and a new management structure in which a national administrator from within the company would sit on the board and serve as the government delegate. Rodrigues was given this position. Seven years after the conclusion of the initial concession contract, national technicians finally gained a formal voice in the company. The issue of privatization and national versus foreign corporate control of Guine Telecom was, for the moment, settled. All this occurred just a few months before the arrival of the Net, and the debates on liberalization were about to intensify.

CNI 2: Liberalization

The 1996 agreement did not end the dissatisfaction of some within the government with the pace of Guine Telecom's investment in new technologies. In September of the same year, Ansumane Mané, minister of transport and communications, sent a letter to Portugal Telecom asking that it allow a separate company to enter the market to provide cellular service. In response, Portugal Telecom sent José Manuel Briosa e Gala, the former Portuguese secretary of state for international cooperation, who now acted as a consultant for the Portugal Telecom Group, to negotiate.[14] Prime Minister Saturnino da Costa received Briosa e Gala alone, and President Vieira met with him personally at Briosa e Gala's hotel. President Vieira and Prime Minister da Costa promised to send Communications Minister Mané a message that he should "be more flexible."[15]

Within a few weeks, Mané traveled to Washington, D.C., for a workshop organized for African telecommunications ministers by coordinators of the Leland Initiative at the US Agency for International Development (USAID). Guinea-Bissau was not initially identified as a Leland Initiative partner, but it became one after lobbying by the USAID mission director and the representative of the UN Development Programme (UNDP). While Mané was in Washington, he signed a memorandum of understanding, affirming Guinea-Bissau's intent to participate in the initiative. In a follow-up meeting with a delegate from the US State Department, the prime minister of Guinea-Bissau reaffirmed his government's commitment to the Leland Initiative. A representative of Portugal Telecom International had signed the memorandum in Washington, but what was lacking was a signature from Guine Telecom, or more strictly a formal acceptance of the memorandum by the board of directors of the company.

For nearly two years the USAID mission worked to secure Guine Telecom's explicit agreement to allow competition and unobstructed access for ISP startups in exchange for technical assistance and equipment to establish a new, robust national gateway. Negotiating an enabling policy environment was the first objective of the Leland Initiative, second was installation of the gateway, and third was use of the Net as a development tool. While the first objective was stalled by negotiations over the memorandum of understanding, aspects of the second and third objectives advanced.

The Leland Initiative catalyzed discussion of information technologies in Guinea-Bissau. In October 1996, the same month that the Leland memorandum was signed, the UNDP hosted a subregional conference in Bissau on telecommunications. The UNDP paid Guine Telecom to operate a cybercafe with a 64-kbps Internet circuit. This was managed by a local firm, Sila Technologies (SiTec). For a full month, virtually anyone from government or civil society could enter the meeting room to get their first experience with the Internet. At the conference, Minister Mané went on record saying that the future of the telecom sector in Guinea-Bissau was "free and open competition."[16]

The conference provided a launch-pad for a pioneering national company to enter the Internet market. Sila Technologies, founded in the early 1980s by two German-trained engineers—Abdulai Sila and Amidu Sila—began offering satellite television services at a time when purely private enterprises were still looked on with suspicion. Subsequently, the company expanded into computer sales and service. Donors and international organizations generated significant business for the company. After SiTec managed the cybercafe at the UNDP conference, USAID contracted it to train hundreds of users from the agricultural, trade, health, and education sectors. Bolstered by these contracts, SiTec developed relationships with the foreign technical assistants brought in by the Leland Initiative. As a result of these activities, SiTec became a private ISP that operated a cybercafe using a line leased from Guine Telecom. SiTec employed its own trainers on-site, and they were ready to assist anyone who wanted to learn how to use a personal computer or navigate the Net.

Perhaps spurred by the rising prestige of the Net as a symbol of advanced technology, or by SiTec's cybercafe, in mid-1997 Guine Telecom opened its own cybercafe. A precarious competition emerged between the two companies, although in terms of policy virtually nothing had changed. Matters were about to intensify. At this time, SiTec's service was clearly superior to Guine Telecom's. In the public's mind, SiTec was the only national company capable of properly developing the new technology. Guine Telecom's concession, however, granted them exclusive control over all electromagnetic communications until 2009. Thus SiTec had virtually no legal recourse when Guine Telecom moved to block its access. But interruption of the SiTec leased line immediately caused a reaction among the community of donors, the media, and an ever-growing user base, which included influential members of government and civil society (many of whom were trained by SiTec). Guine Telecom's recent history of being subjected to intense scrutiny, and widespread customer discontent with the company, contributed to favorable perceptions of SiTec.

Throughout this period, the USAID mission in Bissau attempted to negotiate with Guine Telecom, but encountered poor responsiveness from the administrators of the company. Eventually, USAID asked Minister Mané to intercede. In response, Mané sent a letter to Portugal Telecom asking it to allow Guine Telecom to go forward with the terms of the Leland memorandum of understanding. In December 1996, Saraiva Mendes, president of Portugal Telecom International, responded that Portugal Telecom had already invested significant resources to bring the Internet to Guinea-Bissau. Mendes reminded Mané of the company's exclusive control granted by the Guine Telecom concession contract. Mendes further maintained that the Internet market in Guinea-Bissau was too small to justify further investment, because of the low number of personal computers in the country. He suggested that Leland assistance be used to address the shortage of personal computers rather than Internet access.[17] Many observers interpreted Mendes's letters as an example of PTI's complacency and underestimation of the Guinea-Bissau market; others thought he was lying outright about PTI's investments. In any case, Portugal Telecom seemed satisfied to retain total control of a lethargic market.

In the months that followed, the allure of information technology and issues of service provision began to fuel calls for liberalization of the sector as a whole. The Internet user base began to grow, and with it the perception that the Net was a necessary tool for national development. The SiTec cybercafe shared the same 64-kbps satellite link with Guine Telecom's cybercafe and Guine Telecom's incipient dial-up service. Users could wait as long as five to ten minutes for a single page to load, and service interruptions were frequent. It was becoming painfully apparent that 64 kbps was insufficient. Yet Guine Telecom did not increase bandwidth. Suspicion was growing that Guine Telecom was more interested in extracting donor funds than stimulating the sector, and some aid organizations began to support efforts to rescind the monopoly concession. The World Bank and USAID supported these efforts and were encouraged to do so by the new finance minister, Issufo Sanha, the same economist who opposed the concession in 1989 and who took Marconi to task for its mismanagement of Guine Telecom in 1996. Sanha appointed Paulo Gomes, a Harvard-trained economist, to head a committee to develop strategies to restrict or end the monopoly.

Policy reform was a politically sensitive issue. Monopoly concessions such as those for telecommunications and the ports were established under the close personal direction of President Vieira. Calling attention to the abysmal service and investment record of these concessions reflected poorly on the president. Direct confrontation with Vieira was still considered dangerous, but the political context had changed since he took power in 1980. The first democratic constitution was ratified in 1992, and the 1994 elections legitimized Vieira as president of the republic. In 1996, Guinea-Bissau adhered to the West African Monetary and Economic Union (UEMOA) treaty, Article 93 of which called for the gradual creation of a regional telecommunications market, and for member countries to begin instituting appropriate national legislation.[18] Guinea-Bissau's society as a whole was engaged in a complex and highly contentious process of democratization, and political momentum for liberalization was building.

Around this time, a Leland team traveled to Bissau to plan the installation of the Internet gateway and assess progress on Leland policy objectives. Minister Sanha scheduled an audience for Leland staff with President Vieira, hoping that they could help obtain the president's support for beginning a process of liberalization. The minister of social works, transport, and communications, and the minister of finance, attended the meeting, along with senior advisers including Paulo Gomes. The US delegation included Leland's chief field manager, Jonathan Metzger; the Leland Guinea-Bissau coordinator; and US ambassador Peggy Blackford. Metzger spoke about the potential of the Net as a development tool. The Leland Guinea-Bissau coordinator cited the recently liberalized fuel-provision sector, which had far exceeded growth expectations, and went on to emphasize how Portugal Telecom was inhibiting communications growth and abrogating the government's commitments to the UEMOA treaty and the Leland memorandum. President Vieira responded that he was unaware of resistance from Portugal Telecom. Ministers Sanha and Cardoso briefed the president on Article 93 of the UEMOA treaty, which called for creation of a regional telecommunications market, and on Article 11 of the Guine Telecom concession, which arguably obligated the concessionaire to adhere to treaties and national legislation. The overall thrust of the meeting favored reform, and near its end the Leland Guinea-Bissau coordinator asked the president to authorize the minister of telecommunications to send a letter to Portugal Telecom, informing it that the Guine Telecom concession needed amendment. The president nodded, indicating his approval. If the rumors heard around Bissau were true, the president had apparently just agreed to a process that could empty his own pocket.

In February 1998, Minister Cardoso wrote to Guine Telecom and Portugal Telecom International. He cited the UEMOA treaty, the worldwide explosion of information technology, as well as the poor record of Portugal Telecom in fulfilling its investment obligations. Portugal Telecom president Saraiva Mendes responded that PTI had in fact performed satisfactorily. Mendes recognized the right of the government of Guinea-Bissau to liberalize the sector, although he suggested that the first step was drafting national telecommunications legislation to which a new concession contract could conform. Whatever the outcome, PTI held, the concession contract guaranteed that its interests were protected. In Washington, D.C., Leland quickly identified a telecom lawyer from the Department of Commerce who could help the government of Guinea-Bissau draft telecommunications legislation.

On 20 April 1998, delegations of the government of Guinea-Bissau and Portugal Telecom International met in Bissau. Paulo Gomes headed the Bissau team. The PTI delegation was led by Briosa e Gala, a former Portuguese secretary of international cooperation who left government in 1995 and became a consultant for PTI. Though Portugal Telecom had formally accepted the process initiated by Guinea-Bissau, it insisted that the appropriate legislation should be passed before the concession contract could be changed. Gomes responded that it was not possible to implement telecom legislation while there was still exclusivity in the market, particularly in mobile and value-added services.[19] Gomes was reportedly very vocal about the right of the government to shape the future of the sector to meet development needs, regardless of the existence of the concession. According to two other people who were present at that meeting, Briosa e Gala responded, "that is not the position of your Government," called for a break, and made a courtesy visit to President Vieira. Reportedly, Gomes was later told to "slow down."[20]

Although the negotiations stalled, significant political and social will had been generated in favor of liberalizing the sector. In late May 1998, Guine Telecom sent a letter to the USAID mission signaling its agreement to allow community communications centers to operate as private, competitive businesses, and that it would provide these centers with unobstructed access to leased lines. This was needed reaffirmation of the memorandum of understanding, and Leland coordinators decided to proceed with the installation of the Internet gateway. The mission received the letter on 2 June.

On the morning of 7 June 1998, an attempted coup d'etat began a civil war that lasted several months. On 11 June, USAID mission staff and the Portuguese administrators of Guine Telecom fled the country on the *Ponta de Sagres,* a Portuguese container ship, along with some twenty-five hundred others. Six months later, President Vieira was deposed and went into exile in Portugal.

"It is a matter of national sovereignty."

—Carlos Schwarz Silva[21]

The civil war of 1998–1999 was devastating. Hundreds of thousands of people were internally displaced, and tens of thousands more fled to Portugal and neighboring countries. The modest economic growth achieved in the preceding few years was destroyed. The front line of fighting ran through the area of Bissau in which key telecom infrastructure (such as the earth station) and many embassies and international organizations were located. Several thousand active phone lines were lost, and many important telecommunications customers left the country.

Unenthusiastic about investing in an economy destroyed by war, Portugal Telecom never returned to resume management of Guine Telecom. After peace was restored, a transitional civilian government took power, acting with full legislative powers under a "transition pact." The government of national unity built on the momentum generated in support of liberalization before the war. In August 1999 a new policy declaration for the sector was issued, calling for "total liberalization and privatization" and the "gradual entrance of new operators in all segments of the telecommunications market."[22] The policy declaration stated that "parallel to entry into effect of the new Telecommunications Basic Law, the Government will conclude renegotiation of the Guine Telecom Concession Contract, to adapt it to the new legal norms." Some points marked for renegotiation were "the end of exclusivity; the obligations included in the concession; access to universal service; and interconnection for new operators and service providers."[23] The declaration concluded with the assertion that Guinea-Bissau would start the new millennium with cellular phones.

The 1999 Telecommunications Basic Law permits the free establishment and management of telecommunications networks.[24] It defines the "basic network" as the existing infrastructure used by Guine Telecom for fixed-line phones and telex. This network is a public good, and use of it may be obtained by means of a concession contract.[25] According to the law, international connection continued to be the exclusive right of the basic network concessionaire (Guine Telecom) until 30 June 2000.[26] After that date, international traffic would be open to competition. Under the law, Internet service provision is considered a value-added service and is explicitly liberalized. With private telecommunications networks and the capacity to carry international traffic legalized, in theory ISPs gained the right to install very small aperture terminals (VSATs) and to serve clients via wired or wireless solutions.

On 1 September 1999, Guine Telecom convened a shareholder meeting. During the meeting, Carlos Schwarz Silva, minister of social works, transport, and communications, presented Portugal Telecom with the new telecommunications legislation. Portugal Telecom was again represented by Briosa e Gala, who suggested that the new legislation was unconstitutional. He also lamented that PTI had not been consulted during the drafting process. Schwarz responded that a draft of the proposed legislation had been sent to Guine Telecom, to the attention of the delegate administrator. PTI had not been involved, perhaps, because it had resisted even naming an administrator. Ultimately, said Schwarz, it was a question of national sovereignty. PTI was of course invited to examine options for participating in the company under the new legislation. At the end of the shareholder meeting, new company officers were named. Briosa e Gala became president of Guine Telecom.[27]

While Guinea-Bissau's policy reforms were somewhat contradictory, they signaled a moment of opportunity. SiTec, for one, did not wait for further clarification. It installed a VSAT dish under a provisional license and began offering comparatively robust access to the Net, with a down-speed of 256 kbps and an up-speed of 128 kbps.

In the following months, general elections were held. Kumba Yalla took office as the new president of the republic and appointed new ministers. A few weeks into his tenure, the new minister of transport and communications, Carlitos Barai, received a call from Briosa e Gala, who reportedly asked the minister to suspend the Basic Law because it was unconstitutional.

"We cannot wait for Portugal Telecom for there to be telecommunications."

—João Frederico de Barros[28]

While the Telecommunications Basic Law tipped policy irreversibly toward liberalization, it also specified that Guine Telecom's concession had to be renegotiated. Formally, the monopoly concession was still intact. Portugal Telecom had in principle agreed to negotiate. But PTI sought conditions that would in effect maintain its monopoly, and would not compromise. Without resolution of this central contradiction, clear and consistent policy became impossible to formulate. Practice, however, continued to influence the process.

In 2000 the government of Guinea-Bissau and Portugal Telecom began renegotiation of the Guine Telecom concession. The government commission included representatives from the Ministry of Finance, the Institute of Communications, and the Ministry of Transport and Communications. The commission was supported, and almost entirely funded, by the World Bank. Reportedly, Portugal Telecom was difficult and unresponsive from the start. Due to scheduling delays on PTI's part, the first negotiating session was not held until July 2001.

The law firm that was advising the government, Gide Loyrette Nouel, proposed three possible strategies: negotiate with Portugal Telecom to rework the concession contract into a form the parties could agree on; modify the contract unilaterally; or unilaterally terminate the contract. The firm requested that the government detail every failure of Guine Telecom to fulfill its mission since 1989, with particular attention to management and investment practices of Marconi and Portugal Telecom. This preparation would provide background material for the negotiations and might help the government accomplish its goals without ending up in court.

The World Bank stated that it would not contribute in any way to actions that might lead to litigation. When options that entailed this risk were discussed, the Bank's position was consistent: more study was necessary. The government of Guinea-Bissau, however, was experiencing some of its greatest challenges amid adverse political circumstances, and a lack of human and other resources. Without foreign technical and monetary assistance, little could be accomplished. If Bank policy prohibited participation in actions that could lead to litigation, this approach clearly inhibited progress. Guinea-Bissau lacked resources to evaluate the full range of options. Portugal Telecom negotiators appeared to be keenly aware of the government's predicament, and stalled or canceled meetings in a strategy to outmaneuver the government's negotiating team. The government of Guinea-Bissau had to negotiate, but Portugal Telecom would not come to the table.

The next round of negotiations took place in August 2001. PTI reportedly sent representatives who did not have decisionmaking power. Following this unfruitful round, the Guinea-Bissau Ministry of Transport and Communications sent a letter to Portugal Telecom proposing a new timeline for the resolution of negotiations. There was no response from PTI. In October 2001, Carlitos Barai, minister of transport and communications, sent a letter that exhaustively detailed PTI's poor responsiveness. The letter also emphasized that development of the sector was "on standby" until the negotiations were completed. Portugal Telecom responded point by point, denying emphatically that PTI was stalling the process and reaffirming its commitment to reaching an agreement.[29]

The delegations, however, did not meet again until April 2002. According to the government, the long delay was due to repeated PTI cancellations. At this round of talks, Portugal Telecom insisted that the adjunct administrator position that the Telecommunications and Postal Workers Union fought to create in 1995 be eliminated from the board of directors of Guine Telecom. The Bissau delegation protested that this position had been an approved feature of the management structure of the company since 1996. Portugal Telecom challenged the delegation to prove that the position was actually approved by the shareholders of the company, and the government could not produce the relevant documents. Some progress was ostensibly made during this round. A verbal agreement was reached on a paper specifying certain build-out and quality-of-service requirements for Guine Telecom. Ratification of this document, however, was postponed until agreement was reached on other issues.

In the next round of talks, which were held in June 2002, Portugal Telecom attempted to reopen discussion of the service-quality agreement reached in the previous meeting. No progress was made, and further meetings were postponed. During a USAID-funded policy survey carried out in August 2002, it became apparent that a comprehensive investigation of the entire history of the relationship between the shareholders of Guine Telecom was urgently needed. Negotiations had reached an impasse, and Portugal Telecom appeared to be exploiting a lack of documentation and continuity on the part of the government, which, after all, had gone through a civil war. The August 2002 survey report suggested that a neutral technical assistant, not beholden to either side, go to Bissau to collect and collate primary documents of the history of the company. In this way, institutional memory of Guine Telecom and the Ministry of Transport and Communications could be reconstituted.

This effort began in February 2003 with support from USAID. The documents gathered together increasingly informed the government's strategy in what was becoming a delicate move-by-move exchange with Portugal Telecom. PTI's evasiveness made it increasingly likely that the government would take a unilateral action to resolve the impasse. A poorly considered action, however, could result in a high-profile lawsuit that the government would lack the resources to litigate. During the course of the research effort, it was discovered that Portugal Telecom had not paid any settlement payments for calls terminating in Guinea-Bissau since 1998. This was a blatant violation of the norms of the International Telecommunications Union, to which both Portugal and Guinea-Bissau belong. A USAID consultant, the chief of staff of the minister of transport and communications, and the Institute of Communications jointly drafted a letter designed to ratchet up pressure on Portugal Telecom to return to the negotiating table. The letter requested statements on Guine Telecom accounts managed by PTI. The letter also asked for a summary of settlement payments due for calls terminating in Guinea-Bissau since 1998, and referred to a request for the same information that had been sent a year earlier by the financial director of Guine Telecom. Portugal Telecom never responded to either request.

Government letters to PTI complained that the negotiation impasse was severely damaging the country. The Ministry of Transport and Communications pointed to its exhaustive good-faith efforts to avoid unilateral action, and suggested that such patience was drawing to a close. In what would be the final letter, Dionísio Cabí, minister of transport and communications, asked Briosa e Gala, president of Guine Telecom, to visit Bissau for a meeting. The letter invoked language from the concession contract on the company's obligation to provide quality service that "responds fully to the needs of the State, the People, and economic activities"; Cabí stated that repeated delays had prejudiced these needs. Briosa e Gala responded as he had previously: that once again, because of scheduling conflicts, it would be impossible to attend.[30]

It is necessary to describe the broad socioeconomic context in which these protracted negotiations were taking place. Since the elections of 2000, the government of President Kumba Yalla had presided over a period of severe social unrest. A near epidemic of hiring and firing at all levels had paralyzed every ministry. After a dismissal of a key official, no guarantees existed that the government's position on policy would remain the same or even be similar. Political repression intensified. With a moribund economy and new political pressure, independent media were progressively silenced. Only two local radio stations acted as independent broadcasters. One station experienced financial troubles and was forced to lease its transmitter to Brazilian evangelicals; the other was ordered off the air by authorities for "lack of pluralism" and was silenced for over two months. President Yalla continued to block a new constitution that included term limits. When sufficient political momentum had been built up in the National Assembly to ratify the constitution without the president's approval, he dissolved parliament and called early elections. Radio stations were silenced, but the Net continued to provide a link to foreign news agencies. Bissau residents tuned in to Radio e Televisão Portuguesa to hear reportage on national events and interviews with the political opposition. President Yalla denounced such news coverage as "neocolonialist," railed against "Internet politicians," and expelled the foreign news agency from the country. The majority of the public was left with access to little more than religious music and government communiqués. Rumors circulated that Yalla planned to repress use of the Internet, but this threat never materialized.

Election dates neared, but were postponed. Government resources were all allocated to the campaign, paralyzing the capacity of ministries to function. In this environment, the rapid deployment of cellular technology became a main generator of political will. In neighboring countries the introduction of cell phones brought governments tremendous political cachet. Government efforts in the telecom sector increasingly focused on the short-term objective of bringing in cellular phones before the elections.

The technical commission guiding the negotiations with Portugal Telecom was increasingly marginalized, branded as "political opposition," and charged with trying to subvert government efforts to introduce the new cellular technology. Rumors, eventually confirmed by the minister of transport and communications, circulated that the government was pursuing a deal with Sonatel, the monopoly operator in Senegal (a highly successful subsidiary of France Telecom), to introduce cellular service on an expedited basis. In technical terms, this would have been relatively cheap and easy since it only entailed an expansion of the Sonatel cellular network across the border. But in terms of policy it would have been illegal and potentially disastrous to grant a license to another operator before resolving contractual issues with Portugal Telecom. The World Bank continued to support the efforts of the technical commission to resolve the impasse with PTI, but the group no longer knew if it had a mandate to negotiate. The minister's chief of staff was a member of the commission, but even he rarely saw the minister, who spent his days campaigning for his political party, the Partido para Renovação Social. The minister reportedly changed his phone number and did not share it with staff. Faced with these worrisome developments, the commission drafted a memo listing recommendations for policy reform and steps to resolve the dispute with PTI. The commission also registered its concerns about the apparent listlessness of the process and requested that the president and Council of Ministers advise it as to whether its mandate was still in effect. No response was received from Yalla or the relevant ministers.

Apparently the memo never made it onto the agenda of the Council of Ministers, although at the urging of Minister of Transport and Communications Cabí the Sonatel deal was discussed. Reportedly heated arguments occurred at several meetings, and ultimately the council determined that there was no legal means to grant a license to Sonatel. Existing national code required an open public contest for a new operator. The statutes of Guine Telecom proscribed committing the company's infrastructure without the consent of the majority shareholder. Granting the license could conceivably place the government in court for issuing a fraudulent license. The ministers eventually agreed that a better course of action was to rescind the Guine Telecom concession, put new regulations in place, and hold a contest for the cellular license.

Perfectly timed for disastrous results, Portugal Telecom contracted Bissau lawyer Amine Saad—who was also the president of an opposition political party—to act as intermediary in discussions with the government of Guinea-Bissau. It was highly irregular for Portugal Telecom to recruit counsel other than lawyers identified at the beginning of the negotiations; Saad's political activities compounded the problems. Saad submitted a seventeen-page document outlining government faults, with the apparent intention of intimidating authorities by presenting well-collated proof of their wrongdoing.[31]

This maneuver only served as a provocation. A Council of Ministers decree rescinded the concession, calling attention to Portugal Telecom's nonpayment of international traffic fees, nonfulfillment of investment obligations, lack of transparency in management of Guine Telecom since its inception, and repeated attempts to subvert national sovereignty. A few days later, a delegation from Portugal Telecom finally appeared in Bissau. They visited Minister Cabí, who told them the official government position was that "the door was still open." Portugal Telecom was welcome to present a serious proposal for its participation in the sector, although it was to first provide clear information on foreign bank accounts and unpaid money for international calls terminating in Guinea-Bissau. Portugal Telecom told the international media that it was considering legal remedies against Guinea-Bissau because of its unilateral rescission.

GuineTel vs. Guine Telecom

Cancelling the Guine Telecom concession resolved the central policy contradiction of Guinea-Bissau telecom code, but the rescission also brought about a new period of confusion. A few weeks after the cancellation, the minister of transport and communications announced that a new company called Guine-Tel, in which the government would be a 90 percent shareholder, would "replace" Guine Telecom. The communiqué announced that GuineTel would be a cellular operator and have complete exclusivity over international telephone access for three years. The minister also announced that an open public contest would be held to grant a license to an additional private cellular operator, as required by national law.

In September 2003 a bloodless coup removed Kumba Yalla from power, and added yet another layer of uncertainty and nebulousness to the policy environment. All of the ministers appointed by Yalla were dismissed, with the exception of Minister Cabí of Transport and Communications, who remained in office by promising to introduce cell phone service within a month or two. President Yalla remained under house arrest for nearly six months. SiTec reported that Yalla opened an account, and that someone using this SiTec account spent much of his or her time online.

The employees of Guine Telecom, the minister of transport and communications, and the Institute of Communications maintain that the rescission decree effectively dissolved Guine Telecom. After a long delay, the statutes of the new company (GuineTel) were approved by the Council of Ministers, yet their promulgation was blocked by interim president Henrique Rosa, who called GuineTel an effective renationalization "operating on the margins of legality." The president of the Telecommunications and Postal Workers Union, Sello Camara, met with President Rosa to discuss the statutes. Rosa explained to Camara that a legal team had determined that, if promulgated, the statutes would create new policy contradictions. After his audience, Camara called a press conference to denounce the president as being "anti-development" and organized street protests against Rosa's alleged intransigence. Further complicating the climate, Portugal Telecom threatened to sue the government of Guinea-Bissau.

CNI 3: Licensing and Regulation

The 1999 Basic Law, which liberalized the telecommunications sector, also provided for the creation of a regulatory body, the Institute of Communications, which would be "administratively and fiscally autonomous" and of "juridical nature" while "carrying out its functions under the tutelage of the Minister of Telecommunications."[32] The functions of the institute are described as "assisting the Government in coordination and planning of the telecommunications sector, representation and regulation of that sector, and management of the radioelectric spectrum."[33] The statutes of the institute define its role as "coordination, supervision and planning the telecommunications sector, as well as representation of the sector and management of the radioelectric spectrum."[34]

While the regulatory function was notably underspecified in the actual statute, the Institute of Communications definitely emerged as a regulator. It requires that operators report for its reviews the specifications of all new technologies that operators wish to use. In instances of illegal competition, the institute has been asked to intervene. Nevertheless, it has struggled with its identity. Is it a consulting body representing the Ministry of Transport and Communications or an autonomous regulatory agency? The state is a shareholder in the largest company in the sector and exerts control over the institute. Directors on the institute's board are appointed by the Council of Ministers (under recommendation of the minister of transport and communications), and can be dismissed at any time by the council. This inherent conflict of interest has kept the institute from asserting itself and has confused its mission.

The institute bears a responsibility for regulating all communications within Guinea-Bissau and has approached the task in a particularly technocratic fashion. Before issuing licenses or deciding on regulation, the institute has sought to understand all conceivable technologies in virtually every way they may be employed. For example, the institute asked for donor assistance to survey the communications service needs of every city in the country and to draft a detailed plan that would serve as a blueprint for private companies to follow. Rather than stimulating the sector, Institute of Communications' approach has created a bottleneck of tight control, unclear regulation, and high licensing fees.

Immediately after promulgation of the Basic Law in 1999, SiTec installed a VSAT. Not long after the Institute of Communications was created, SiTec applied for a license to operate the dish. The institute responded with a lengthy document in French outlining all manner of technical information that SiTec would need to supply in order to receive a license. The company complied and was granted a provisional license valid for ninety days in August 2001. After ninety days, the company requested a new license, but there was no response from the Institute of Communications. A full year later, after several increasingly threatening letters from SiTec, the institute sent an even more exhaustive list of specifications it wanted from SiTec. The Sila brothers, the founders of the company, barely resisted the urge to start a public relations war, and instead gathered the requested (and redundant) information. In August 2002, SiTec was finally granted a license for the VSAT it had been operating since 2000. In December of that year, it was granted licenses to operate as an ISP and to have proprietary Internet-protocol networks. For nearly three years the company had been providing Internet access semi-legally. While SiTec persevered, this type of regulatory uncertainty has discouraged investment and undercut diffusion.

The 1999 Basic Law explicitly liberalized Internet service provision, and after the law was ratified, Guine Telecom and SiTec entered a phase of open, although often unfair, competition. In violation of the Basic Law Guine Telecom has refused to provide SiTec with sixteen additional phone lines needed for their operations. From 1999 until 2002, Guine Telecom was still repairing the extensive damage to infrastructure that occurred during the war; the company had run out of cables to repair the network and the wires needed to run phones to new clients. Though the Sila brothers and other partners had founded a new company called Eguitel Communications, the Eguitel lines had already been installed and approved by Guine Telecom technicians, and it was only a matter of activating them. A SiTec complaint personally offended the commercial director of Guine Telecom. In response, the director gathered billing information going back to 1997, when SiTec ran training sessions for USAID and the UNDP. Guine Telecom claimed that its denial of service for SiTec was based on unpaid and past-due bills. SiTec had actually left the communications business shortly after the Basic Law was passed in 1999. SiTec continued, but limited its operations to computer sales and service. Guine Telecom, therefore, was attempting to charge two separate accounts to one company. Eguitel responded to Guine Telecom's accusations of nonpayment with a complete record of payments for both the new company and SiTec, including invoices and receipts from Guine Telecom.

At the same time—and certainly not coincidentally—Guine Telecom drastically reduced its price for Internet access. Eguitel filed a grievance with the Institute of Communications, denouncing Guine Telecom's actions as a "provocation." The institute never made a determination, and Eguitel continues to operate without domestic phone lines.

The dispute with Guine Telecom spurred Eguitel Communications to find other means of reaching customers, many of whom were very loyal. In early 2002, Eguitel installed a broadband wireless connectivity solution capable of up to 11 megabits per second (mbps). The company formalized an agreement with the power company to run wires along power poles, and began extending service to corporate customers and international organizations via their own network. The company leveraged its continuing relationships with vendors that were originally consultants under the auspices of the Leland Initiative. Lyman Brothers Inc., a Utah-based company that provided Leland with connectivity solutions in many African countries, provided free technical assistance and a very reasonably priced dedicated VOIP link to the United States. Eguitel could now make direct contact with private companies and other partners, often for the price of a local call. The company quietly began offering US numbers to their corporate customers in Bissau via VOIP. The increase in the required bandwidth (up-speed of 1,024 kbps, down-speed of 512 kbps) was not reported to the Institute of Communications, whose bandwidth-linked tariffs would have bankrupted the company. Even in 2005, institute records showed that Eguitel had a connection of only 512 kbps, and Eguitel still listed a US number as its main telephone in its advertisements in the Bissau media.

Eguitel circumvented attempts to block its access to both bandwidth and customers, and emerged stronger and more independent. No technological fixes existed for the next obstacle that appeared, namely a rash of wire slashings that threatened to disable Eguitel's network. From experience, the ISP knew that it could not depend on the Institute of Communications to intervene, so it responded in an informal fashion. Eguitel allowed a rumor to circulate that if more of its wires were slashed, many more Guine Telecom wires might be cut in the near future. The vandalism stopped.

In 2003, as the impasse with Portugal Telecom dragged on, the Institute of Communications was increasingly subjected to political pressure. As the government moved ahead with plans to introduce cell phone service on an urgent basis, institute president Joaquim Albino was called before the Council of Ministers to comment on the proposed Sonatel cell phone deal. It was no secret that Albino opposed the deal, so it was not surprising that he expressed a negative reaction in his presentation. One week later, Albino was removed from the institute's board of directors and replaced by Anésimo Silva Cardoso. Cardoso favored the Sonatel deal and had better personal relations with Minister Cabí. In the months that followed, Cabí, Cardoso, and the adjunct administrator of Guine Telecom, João Frederico de Barros, together began crafting policy behind closed doors. Even after President Yalla was deposed in September 2003, this worrisome tendency continued.

CNI 4: VOIP

We challenge the Institute to identify the law they invoke to "mutilate" use of Information Technology in the country.
                    —From a 2002 open letter posted in Eguitel cybercafes

In the summer of 2002, Eguitel opened two telecenters in Bissau. In these telecenters, international phone calls could be made at prices much lower than those offered by Guine Telecom. As a result, the telecenters soon generated a brisk business. The Institute of Communications quickly ordered Eguitel to cease its telephony operations. Eguitel acquiesced, but also posted an open letter in its cybercafes challenging the institute to provide a legal justification for the order to "mutilate" use of Internet-protocol technology. The institute never responded, although, in private, institute president Joaquim Albino noted that the Guine Telecom concession contract was still technically in effect. Albino also said that VOIP would complicate negotiations between the government and Portugal Telecom.

In public, the fight continued. Eguitel vigorously lobbied influential members of the government, including Prime Minister Alamara Nhasse and

Minister of Transport and Communications Domingos Simões Pereira.[35] To sensitize the public, Eguitel began sponsoring public radio debates on the progress of sector liberalization, and the potential of Internet-protocol technology. The company also sowed rumors that it was planning to take the Institute of Communications to court.

In an unexpected development, on 6 October 2003 the Institute of Communications granted Eguitel a ten-year license to offer VOIP services without limitation. In terms of policy, the institute's action was not contradictory. The language of the Basic Law liberalized all international telephony as of 2000, and with the rescission of the Guine Telecom concession, VOIP was made legal. Guine Telecom, the Institute of Communications, and Minister Cabí, however, had formed an alliance that appeared to effectively block getting new licenses. Eguitel administrator Abdulai Sila maintained that the license was obtained for a variety of reasons, including the existence of a key rumor that put pressure on the Institute of Communications.[36] Guine Telecom was involved in negotiations with a foreign vendor to install a wireless local loop, a new VSAT, and new VOIP services. Sila maintained that the institute and Guine Telecom knew full well that Guine Telecom was about to launch these services illegally. Eguitel let circulate a rumor that if Guine Telecom were to begin to offer these services outside the law, it would do the same.

In 2005, Eguitel reopened its two telecenters in Bissau, and the company planned to open five more across the country by the end of the year. In April 2004, Eguitel increased bandwidth to full duplex T1 (up- and down-speeds of 1.5 mbps) in anticipation of increased VOIP traffic. VOIP is poised to be the engine driving Internet connectivity in rural areas. Donor support will likely be critical in this process.

Other Incentives: Portugal Telecom International

While this analysis of Internet diffusion in Guinea-Bissau has focused on the internal perspective, an analysis of perspectives from beyond the borders of the country can enhance our understanding. During the five-year period that the government attempted to renegotiate Portugal Telecom's participation in Guine Telecom, it met with poor responsiveness or no response at all. Portugal Telecom accepted the most fundamental aspect of national policy—namely liberalization—but insisted on reinstating its total control and the opacity that had prevailed before the 1996 reforms. Portugal Telecom's intransigence and unavailability left the liberalization process to government initiative, which would be slow and chaotic due to the conditions noted in this chapter. Some analysts thought that Portugal Telecom was stalling until a new and more sympathetic government took power. Other observers, like those within the World Bank office in Bissau, felt that Portugal Telecom was waiting for rule of law to be established so it could challenge the validity of certain policies and thereby regain its control of the market.

Data gathered from outside Guinea-Bissau suggests that Portugal Telecom may have been motivated by other factors. Since the installation of the satellite earth station in 1990, Marconi and Portugal Telecom had enjoyed complete control over international telecom traffic entering and leaving Guinea-Bissau. Traditionally, payment for this traffic is calculated by dividing charges per minute of traffic between the operators sending and terminating the call. In countries with low income per capita and astronomical phone rates, incoming calls tend to outnumber outgoing calls. Typically, telecommunications companies in such countries receive payment from the company originating the call. As provided in their concession contract, Marconi and Portugal Telecom managed all traffic settlement payments, using accounts they opened abroad in the name of Guine Telecom. When Portugal Telecom administrators fled Guinea-Bissau in 1998, settlement payments to Guine Telecom stopped entirely. The 1998 conflict caused significant damage to infrastructure, and many of Guinea Telecom's most important clients fled the country. The company's revenues plummeted. Because peace was restored in early 1999, a slight increase in payments could be expected as the economy recovered and some international organizations returned. Interestingly, Figure 3.1 demonstrates that US settlement payments increased dramatically in 2000, to more than double the 1996 peak. The dramatic spike in payments after 1999, at first glance, is difficult to explain.

Figure 3.1   US Annual Telecommunications Settlement Payments to Guinea-Bissau, 1990–2000

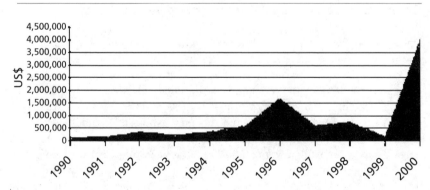

Source: FCC, 2003.

Before the equipment damage that resulted from the civil war, Guine Telecom and Portugal Telecom International collaborated to provide pornographic audiotext, or "phone sex," services. A block of Guinea-Bissau telephone numbers was made available for this service. The numbers were not actually assigned to any location within the territory of Guinea-Bissau. Inside the earth station complex, a bank of computers was dedicated to this service; these computers received calls from abroad and immediately transmitted them back out of the country. Guine Telecom's technical director, Malam Fati, recalls that the equipment was installed at about the time the company's new investment plan was finalized in 1996. Fati says that the money generated by this service paid for many subsequent network improvements.[37] The spike in 1996 payments represented in Figure 3.1 could have resulted from operation of the bank of audiotext computers at the Guine Telecom earth station. The decline in settlement revenues that occurred over the next year may have been due to competition, or a decline in interest after video became more widely available.

After peace was restored in 1999, Guine Telecom administrators began to suspect that something irregular was happening overseas with calls bearing the Guinea-Bissau country code (245). Suspicions were confirmed when a dissatisfied Spanish pornography user actually called Guine Telecom to complain about the service. Fati was alerted and discovered the existence of several Web pages that offered videotext. The pages appeared to target particular countries, and offered "free" access to live pornographic video without requiring credit card information. Interested viewers were instructed to call a number on the screen (dialing instructions from each country were included) to receive a password. These access numbers bore the 245 country code.

From outside the country, it would appear that someone within the territory of Guinea-Bissau was operating this service. The numbers listed on the sites, however, did not officially exist. Guine Telecom, the institute, and a consultant from the International Telecommunications Union all agreed that the numbers were not programmed within the territory of Guinea-Bissau. The Internet infrastructure of the country, furthermore, could not possibly support the graphic-intensive content and broadcast of the adult entertainment sites. At that time, Guine Telecom was more concerned with repairing its basic telephony infrastructure, which had been devastated by the civil war. According to the company's commercial director, Aliu Quinharé, as late as 2002 Guine Telecom had no new cables with which to repair its network and no wires for the installation of phones.[38] Approximately 50,000 people were waiting for service. Guine Telecom did not appear to be a company profiting from a brisk adult entertainment business, yet one was apparently operating in its name.

According to international numbering specialist Richard Cox, many major telecom companies engage in what is called "short termination" of calls nominally destined for a distant country.[39] Short termination is the practice of an international operator configuring its network to accept calls for numbers with a foreign country's prefix. Domestic calls to certain numbers bearing the foreign prefix may be routed to destinations on their operator's own domestic network. The operator, however, still collects payment for calls on the basis of its (foreign) number prefix, regardless of where or by whom they were actually terminated. Cox has investigated this practice for over six years, and says that it is notoriously difficult to prove or to prosecute. In many countries, such calls are treated as beyond the jurisdiction of national regulators, since they are nominally international. Telecom companies typically respond to anyone who complains that the calls were passed on to another operator outside their network, and are not their responsibility.

Short termination is very easy to hide and is very lucrative. Once such numbers are programmed, traffic is usually generated by making them available to intermediary companies, which sell them to producers of pornography. Keith Bernard, a consultant with Telecommunications Management Group (based in Washington, D.C.) and a former senior manager with a Hong Kong subsidiary of the company Cable & Wireless, confirmed that short termination is an industrywide practice.[40] It is much easier to conceal the practice if some aspect of the arrangement is legitimate. It is more viable, for example, if the Internet infrastructure of the country involved actually supports video-intensive porn sites. Alternatively, once an agreement is reached with an operator in a distant country, countless numbers can be programmed but only a part of the total traffic generated may be sent to the country in question. It is very difficult to track where the calls are actually terminated. An international operator can thus enjoy plausible deniability and can avoid the stigma associated with porn production by implicating another foreign company.

The possibility that Portugal Telecom is running a lucrative short-termination business suggests that the company has very different interests than may have been imagined in Guinea-Bissau. It appears unlikely that returns on investments in the national network would equal the tens of millions of dollars the company may have received in hidden revenue from short termination and the misappropriation of settlement payments. Portugal Telecom's unresponsiveness, legal posturing, and moves to sow confusion (such as contracting a lawyer who also happens to be the president of an opposition political party) suggest that the company may be trying to prolong its control over international traffic and protect hidden revenue streams from scrutiny.

Guine Telecom and the Institute of Communications collaborated to use the uncovered short-termination scheme to the advantage of the government of Guinea-Bissau. The institute verified on-site that the numbers programmed at the central Guinea-Bissau switch did not include the suspect codes verified on the websites. It then published the official national numbering plan that it had worked out with a consultant from the International Telecommunications

Union (ITU) on the ITU website. Next, a colleague in the United States called both the suspect numbers and genuine numbers while technicians monitored incoming calls in Guinea-Bissau. When they were put together, printouts of call logs from Guinea-Bissau and the phone bill from the United States proved that some of the calls originating in the United States were billed but were not in fact entering the national network of Guinea-Bissau.

Conclusion

Perhaps the most alarming lesson that can be learned from the case of Guinea-Bissau is that the incentives and interests that drive contentious negotiation issues are not limited to the borders of a country. Practices such as short termination perpetrated from abroad may be hidden, and without considering them, negotiators may be ignorant of the real dynamics of a situation. National regulators may have limited ability to deal with practices such as short termination, and the International Telecommunications Union depends entirely on the enforcement power of such regulators. Until legal and regulatory regimes are refined, countries like Guinea-Bissau may have little defense against short termination or consumer fraud carried out in their name. Donors and multilaterals should bring their international perspective to bear by facilitating responses to these challenges. Helping to build relationships between regulators across borders, and looking for ways to strengthen legal remedies, might provide enhanced protection. If a dispute arises, avoiding litigation enables donors to continue to assist with negotiations.

As the newly elected government of Guinea-Bissau begins to exercise power, technicians must overcome the maddening, persistent nebulousness of national communications policy. To do so, they will require a fresh mandate. Conflicting tendencies toward privatization and nationalization inherent in the Guine Telecom effort will necessarily—although not rapidly—be resolved. How this will happen vis-à-vis Portugal Telecom remains unclear. The World Bank and the government of Guinea-Bissau have agreed to reform the Institute of Communications to make it more autonomous and effective. The interests at play, however, suggest that this will be a long, difficult process. The only critical negotiation issue examined in this chapter that will probably be resolved in the short term is VOIP, and this is because prevailing practice will drive policy changes. With its enormous profit potential, VOIP is already becoming the engine driving the expansion of the Net to rural areas.

When the Net first arrived in Guinea-Bissau in 1996, it gained tremendous prestige as the symbol of "developed" technology. Many in Bissau may not have understood its importance, but the Internet was welcomed. Portugal Telecom's poor responsiveness and its underestimation of the demand for the

Net and other new technologies in Guinea-Bissau fueled calls for liberalization. In 2003, society's desire for cellular phones (and to a lesser degree VOIP) increased pressure for a resolution of the impasse with Portugal Telecom. Ultimately, the monopoly concession was revoked. In Guinea-Bissau, policy changes reflect significant moments of consensus; however, this consensus and real resolutions often take place outside formal negotiations. Favorable economic and technological conditions, rather than determining Internet diffusion, appear only to intensify societal pressure to resolve impasses that are holding up diffusion.

In Guinea-Bissau, an interesting parallel can be drawn between Internet diffusion and the spread of independent radio. The first democratic constitution, ratified in 1992, guaranteed freedom of the press. But the devil was very much in the details. Licenses for new independent radio stations would be granted via open public contest, the rules of the contest would be published in later regulations, and winners would be approved by the Council of Ministers. Contest rules, however, were never released. A few courageous, determined journalists did not wait for the regulations to emerge. They sought provisional licenses and opened the first independent radio stations.

The stations were extremely successful (particularly one that produced a biting, critical daily newscast in Kriol), and quickly found themselves enmeshed in a contentious, complex process of democratization. Conflicts with politically powerful actors were common. One station was literally toppled by bulldozers on government orders. A number of journalists received threats against themselves or their families. In all of these cases, neither the courts nor the police provided protection, and the stations could only depend on the support of society. "Society" in this sense means not just civil society, represented by merchant associations and the like, but society-at-large: the one that works, buys, argues, creates and spreads rumors, and clamors when it is displeased. When stations were shut down, it was public outcry that brought them back on the air. Once people are aware of their inherent right to self-expression, it can be very difficult to take it away.

Another salient and tremendously important detail that emerges from this analysis of Guinea-Bissau is that governments are not monolithic. There are always contradictions, complicities, and seductions at play in complex negotiations. SiTec, and later Eguitel, worked hard to recruit allies among competition-friendly members of the National Assembly and other government institutions, and this leverage helped them survive. The World Bank continued to assist the technical/negotiations commission of the government of Guinea-Bissau, even when it became increasingly marginalized. In spite of being branded as "opposition," the commission continued to give advice; it even did so when Minister Cabí was charging forward with a disastrous deal with Sonatel. Ultimately, the commission was asked to write the decree rescinding the monopoly concession, and it produced a document that resulted in a stronger and more uniform telecommunications code. Donors supported development of policies that they agreed with, even while overall transparency and democratic norms were lacking. This assistance helped resolve the primary policy bottleneck holding back the sector.

4

Kenya:
Diffusion, Democracy,
and Development

Mary Muiruri

IN THE LATE 1990S, Kenyans who enjoyed Internet access were thought of as members of an elite. The majority of Kenyans only knew about the Internet from television or from employees of international organizations who used the Internet as part of their work. Computers were expensive and therefore beyond the reach of most. Practically speaking, at US$200 per month for ten hours of access in 1996, the Internet was simply beyond reach. Countrywide, only 4,000 users could afford access.

Today the Internet touches the lives of many more people in Kenya's urban areas. Cybercafes can be found in many neighborhoods of Nairobi, secondary towns, and even small outskirts that previously had little or no access. Cybercafes are now full of patrons using the Internet for a whole range of purposes, including e-mail, searching for jobs and schools, chatting, conducting research, and enhancing awareness of HIV/AIDS. Although this chapter addresses key critical negotiation issues (CNIs), it also focuses on the relationship between Internet diffusion and the growth of democracy; this process culminated in the defeat of longtime incumbent president Daniel arap Moi in December 2002. The relationship between Internet diffusion and democratization has been one of mutual push-and-pull. The struggle to establish multiparty democracy in Kenya in the early 1990s created both opportunities and demands for Internet use. Furthermore, the Internet provided a relatively safe forum in which activists could express dissenting views against the government and its state-run institutions.

The former ruling party, the Kenyan African National Union (KANU), had been in power for thirty-nine years before it was defeated in the 2002 elections. KANU ruled through fear, and most of the citizenry was not organized to oppose the government. Kenyans had to accept whatever the government offered in the way of public sector services, and, not surprisingly, public education, security, welfare, and communications were dismal. The Kenyan Post and Telecommunications Corporation (KPTC) was tightly controlled by KANU for the purposes of spreading KANU propaganda and generating much-needed foreign currency revenue. The KPTC's duty to deliver adequate telecommunications service was overshadowed by its political loyalty to KANU; the latter determined the survival of the KPTC's top management.

With the opening of the political system in the 1990s, information technology (IT) pioneers—and Internet promoters in particular—were able to capitalize on political and technological changes and bring the Internet to Kenya. One of the rallying points for promoting democracy in Kenya, as well as the Internet, was demanding accountability from state-owned institutions. In December 2002 the opposition National Rainbow Coalition (NARC) won national elections by a landslide. Leading presidential candidates, including current President Mwai Kibaki and leader of the KANU opposition Uhuru Kenyatta, utilized the Internet extensively to communicate their platforms and policies to the Kenyan electorate, both at home and abroad.

The newly elected government was eager to privatize and liberalize the telecommunications sector. The discussion of multiparty democracy that follows demonstrates how the struggle for political reform had a major impact on Internet diffusion; similarly, we will see how the spread of the Internet influenced the political system.

Background

Kenya is located in East Africa and has a population of over 30 million people. In 1960, KANU, the party of independence, was formed from three existing parties: the Kenyan Africa Union, the National People's Convention Party, and the Kenyan Independence Movement. KANU was instrumental in uniting the country and negotiating with the British for the country's independence. When independence was achieved in 1963, KANU leader Jomo Kenyatta became Kenya's first president. Kenyatta was an African nationalist and supported independence and democracy for all African nations. His vice president, Daniel arap Moi, became head of state when Kenyatta died in 1978. Moi was from a small ethnic group and would have had a much easier time maintaining unity within the country. However, Moi consolidated his power by structuring his government around patronage ties. He ruled by divisive tactics that pitted different groups against each other.

In 1982, KANU was officially declared the only legal party in Kenya, a status it maintained until December 1991, when other political parties were legalized. The Kenyan government was under internal and external pressure to allow multiparty democracy. Such pressures were indeed prevalent throughout the continent at the beginning of the 1990s. The Moi government, however, continued to use its power to undermine the opposition, which remained fragmented until the 2002 elections. From the mid-1980s to late 2002 the Moi government was under increasingly acute pressure from an economy in dire straits (due in part to a global recession), loss of tourism revenues (exacerbated by the US embassy bombings), and significant cutbacks in donor funding.

During Moi's rule, political and civil freedoms, including access to information, were repressed. The political system thrived on limiting the citizenry's access to information, and as late as 1997 it was illegal for any government ministry to maintain an Internet connection. It was not until 1998 that the law was changed to allow government ministries to exchange electronic communications with other governments in the region.

Under Moi, most government-owned institutions, including the KPTC, were largely unprofitable and depended on government subsidies. The majority of state-owned institutions were headed by political appointees who owed their allegiance to the office of the president and paid little attention to maintaining sound business principles. During KANU's thirty-nine years in power, with KANU being the single party from 1969 to 1991, political patronage was the operative motivation for state enterprises. By the early 1990s, however, KANU lacked the revenue to distribute patronage as easily or as widely as it had in the past. Kenya's declining economy meant that the government was unable to underwrite unprofitable public enterprises.

With respect to Internet diffusion, this meant that only incremental progress could be made. The increasingly open political climate of the 1990s forced the KPTC and other government-owned parastatals to rationalize their operations and to address consumer demand for improved services. Each reform by the KPTC required the prior concurrence of KANU, and obtaining this required negotiations and pressure by Internet users for better services. Eventually, Internet diffusion affected ordinary people as diverse as arts and crafts entrepreneurs, students, and children. Amazingly, in 2004 it was not unusual to find third-grade students in Nairobi who had Yahoo accounts and who engaged adults in interesting discussions on key international events like the Iraq War. Without large-scale political liberalization, access to the Internet and freedom of expression and communications would not be the norm in Kenya.

Critical Negotiation Issues

The struggle to build multiparty democracy in Kenya coincided with the spread of the Internet in the country, and during this period four critical issues had to be negotiated before Internet diffusion could occur. The first issue was negotiating the initial Internet service provider (ISP) licenses, which eventually led to the formation of three ISPs. Prior to 1994 the KPTC monopolized the ISP market in Kenya. Between 1994 and 1998, three ISPs were licensed. The licensing process was regulated by the KPTC, and the ISPs were forced to pay the telecom excessive fees for access to leased lines. The three ISPs survived the KPTC's excessive access charges by using various tactics, as described below. Customers, in turn, paid higher fees, and smaller ISPs could not make a start in the industry because of high entry barriers. Between 1998 and 2000 the monthly cost of renting a 64 kilobits per second (kbps) leased line had decreased from US$12,500 to US$4,500, and cybercafes multiplied.[1] By 2004 the cost of renting a 64-kbps leased line decreased further to US$400 a month, and some sixty-five ISPs and Internet access providers (IAPs) were operating in a fiercely competitive market with a user base of 500,000.[2]

The second issue, negotiating new access costs, arose after politicians and businessmen realized the Internet's potential to create wealth. With the establishment of Jambonet, the national backbone, in 1998, the sector began witnessing tremendous growth, and new players expressed interest in profiting from the Internet.

Negotiating the telecommunications bill was the third, and probably the most contentious, issue. The telecommunications bill, passed in 1998, split the telecom monopoly into three entities and established an independent regulator as required by the World Bank's structural adjustment program. Telkom Kenya, the KPTC's successor, became the main and only supplier of Internet connectivity to ISPs in Kenya. Also in 1998, the Internet gateway, Jambonet, was established by Telkom Kenya, which paved the way for the creation of new ISPs. By 2000, licensing procedures were streamlined, thereby clarifying the requirements for entry into the industry.

The fourth issue, negotiating an Internet exchange point (IXP), came about as a result of the reforms that took place under the telecommunications bill. ISPs and cybercafe operators formed a coalition to negotiate for the IXP with the new regulator. This was a crucial negotiating issue, because Kenya does not have an international fiber optic connection. Thus the transmission of data between users who were a block away from each other potentially involved two satellite hops. The Kenyan IXP was licensed in 2002 and saved ISPs costly fees for transmitting domestic Internet traffic. KANU did not initially support the IXP, because it did not want to lose the advantages of its monopoly status.

CNI 1: Initial ISP Licensing

E-mail was first introduced to Kenya in 1989 by the Environment Liaison Center International (ELCI), which maintained a dial-up connection to GreenNet in London. Initial funding for early e-mail services was provided by international actors seeking to improve communications with their local partners. However, donors recognized that telecommunications issues were nested within a complex political landscape, and they rarely initiated the political negotiations necessary to improve access.

It was not until the mid-1990s that the Internet was readily available in Kenya. In order for ISPs to obtain licenses and access to the Internet, they had to accept the KPTC's terms; no bargaining was possible. When the first ISPs were licensed in 1994, the KPTC controlled the Internet, issued licenses, and regulated the sector. These were the powers typically held by telecoms across Africa. Until the late 1980s, the KPTC was an asset to the government, but by 1989 its financial situation had deteriorated due to inadequate collection rates on accounts receivable, especially from public sector institutions, poor pricing policies to offset inflation, a rapid rate of capital investment for rural infrastructure, and overstaffing.[3]

This financial decline coincided with a significant downturn in the Kenyan economy and with a US$377 million spending binge by KANU in preparation for the 1992 elections.[4] Thus, by the end of 1992, the government needed new sources of revenue. One strategy the government employed was increasing fees charged by parastatals. With respect to the Internet, the KPTC charged exorbitantly for Internet bandwidth—more than US$12,500 per month for a 64-kbps leased line.[5] At the same time, however, the Internet created a new information communication technology (ICT) market that would eventually demand an end to the KPTC's monopoly status.

In the mid-1990s, a handful of Kenyans created three pioneering ISPs: the African Regional Computing Center (ARCC), Form-Net Africa Ltd., and Africa Online. The process each followed to obtain licenses and bandwidth was somewhat different. Form-Net relied on its political connections, the ARCC on donor relationships, and Africa Online on overseas support.

At the time, the Kenyan government was skeptical about the Internet and concerned with controlling access to information. The three ISPs were allowed to function only because the government was desperate to obtain additional revenues. Thus, extraordinary fees collected from the initial ISPs by the KPTC outweighed the government's desire to stifle the flow of information. Still, the authorities remained suspicious of the ISPs and harassment was common. The ARCC served a particular niche within Kenya, while Form-net and Africa Online competed for the pool of customers who could afford the high cost of connectivity.

The ARCC

In 1994, Shem Ochuodho, a telecom engineer by profession, had just returned to Kenya after obtaining his doctorate abroad. In the course of his studies, he was exposed to the ISP sector. Prior to returning to Kenya, Ochuodho successfully sought support from the Overseas Development Agency (ODA) to establish the ARCC, the first Kenyan ISP. The ARCC's goal was to provide Internet services to nongovernmental organizations (NGOs).

Ochuodho knew that negotiating with the KPTC for an ISP license would be difficult. On the other hand, he also understood the political and financial difficulties the KPTC was facing and knew that the ODA grant gave him some leverage, since he could afford to pay for access up-front. In short, it was unlikely that the KPTC would turn down his offer. Yet Ochuodho frequently received intimidating letters and telephone calls from the head of the civil service threatening him if he persisted in his attempt to provide Internet services to the NGO community.

In the end, however, the government's desire for revenue outweighed its desire to keep the Internet out of the country. The KPTC unilaterally declared that the ARCC would pay the exorbitant fee of US$14,500 per month for a 64-kbps leased line. Under this arrangement, the KPTC retained US$12,000 and expended only US$2,500 to cover international frequency costs. In addition, the KPTC demanded that the ARCC pay approximately US$4,000 to obtain an ISP license; the ARCC was also required to make an annual payment of US$1,600 to the KPTC.[6]

The ARCC's costs were outrageous by African standards. By way of comparison, ISPs in Madagascar were paying approximately US$1,500 per month for a 64-kbps leased line. It was only a matter of time before pressures within and outside the country resulted in liberalization of the sector. Yet the KPTC was able to collect fees from the ARCC, and its two fellow pioneering ISPs, for several years. Despite the exorbitant costs the KPTC was charging, it provided very poor service to the ARCC; Ochuodho, in fact, questioned whether he was receiving the 64-kbps bandwidth promised by the KPTC.

Form-Net

The second ISP in Kenya, Form-Net Africa Ltd., was founded in 1995. Form-Net was the first fully commercial ISP in the country. The company was led by Yazim Nanji, who had just returned from the United Kingdom, where he had operated a number of hotels. When Nanji entered the ISP market, he was widely perceived as fronting for a powerful politician close to President Moi. This perception was confirmed later when Nanji broke with the politician in a dispute that was widely publicized in the Kenyan press. In interviews, Nanji gave the impression that he was not involved in any negotiations with the KPTC over licensing.[7] Furthermore, he assumed that negotiations took place between his backers and the KPTC.

Nanji expressed frustration over the exorbitant licensing and access charges imposed on Form-Net by the KPTC. He noted that ISPs faced many barriers, including additional fees of approximately US$1,000 for every category of equipment needed to run an ISP, as well as large amounts of time to process paperwork. He was also unhappy that the ARCC paid for the high costs of access by means of ODA subsidies. He believed that the ARCC's ODA subvention allowed the KPTC to establish high rates that others would also have to meet. Nevertheless, Form-Net was able to pay the KPTC's rates.

Africa Online

The third company, Africa Online, was established by three young Kenyan students who were studying in Boston.[8] Ayisi Makatiani and Karanja Gakio joined with Amolo Ng'weno to launch Karisi Communications. Karisi was the holding company for the e-mail network KenyaNet, which had been founded by Makatiani in 1989 as a news and communications platform for the Kenyan diaspora of Boston. The company changed its name to Africa Online in 1994 and became a commercial ISP in 1996.[9] It has since become the largest ISP in Kenya, with thirteen points of presence (POPs); it also operates in eight other African countries.

Initial funding for Africa Online was provided by Prodigy, a US-based ISP. Prodigy, however, was soon bought by another company, which had no interest in serving Africa. About the same time, while in Nairobi, Makatiani chanced to meet a former schoolmate, Kamande Muiruri, and immediately recruited him as the technical manager of a soon-to-be-established local operation.[10] This venture was initially based in the kitchen of Ng'weno's Nairobi apartment. In 1996, upon obtaining its Kenyan ISP license, Africa Online quickly established itself as the leading ISP in the country. By June 1996 the company had 2,000 Internet subscribers and 1,000 e-mail subscribers in Nairobi, and a few others in Mombasa. The company also had customers in Ethiopia, Burundi, and Tanzania.

Africa Online paid US$12,500 a month for a 64-kbps leased line that included International circuit charges.[11] According to Muiruri,[12] the KPTC dictated the licensing terms and fees and simply sent letters to the ISPs specifying the licensing fees of US$12,500 and thereafter the greater of 2 percent of annual revenue or US$4,166.[13] Africa Online was denied the opportunity to meet with the KPTC's management to negotiate more affordable rates. Like the ARCC and Form-Net, Africa Online had no option but to accept the KPTC's demands.

Kamande Muiruri confirmed that Africa Online did not enjoy any political patronage. The company survived by business acumen and by pushing the KPTC to recognize the importance of the Internet services it was offering.[14] In Kamande's view, Africa Online proved to Kenyans that they could do business in Kenya even without political backing.

Negotiation by Edict

The Internet became a lucrative market for the KPTC; the company earned a minimum of US$36,000 a month and regained the confidence of the government. At the same time, the KPTC's relations with the ISPs remained difficult, because the company feared losing its monopoly status. Despite their differences as competitors, the ISPs decided they had to forge a common strategy for negotiating with the Ministry of Transport and Communications to obtain adequate and assured bandwidth, appropriate charges for services, and lower licensing fees. The charges imposed on the ISPs for leased lines were unrealistically high and were perceived as a means of keeping new ISPs from entering the sector.

Because of the excessive access fees, Africa Online and Form-Net charged extraordinary rates to individuals and businesses for Internet access. Such costs excluded most Kenyans from using the Internet. Yet because of its ODA grant, the ARCC was able to serve even small NGOs working in the slums of Kenya, and this had an effect on access and prices. In the absence of the ODA grant, the NGO community in Kenya would not have enjoyed any Internet access.

After the initial fees were set by the KPTC and accepted by the ISPs, the battle over pricing continued. From 1994 to 1998, the three ISPs and their customers struggled to afford high Internet fees. The ISPs knew that they could not sustain their businesses unless the KPTC lowered its fees, which in turn would allow them to reduce charges to the general public and attract more users, thereby widening their profit margins.

The ISPs began to gain some negotiating leverage with the KPTC because of growing interest in the Internet on the part of educational institutions and the general public. The ISPs had spent a great deal of money on advertising. The KPTC, in turn, became slightly more responsive to consumer needs as a result of aggressive lobbying by the ISPs. Africa Online, for example, constantly used the media to educate users on the implications of poor and inefficient service delivery by the KPTC. Meanwhile, another dynamic was taking place within the KPTC. Senior management was losing its political patrons, and so the company began to cater to the needs of its customers. In addition, the technicians and middle managers who ran the company were quite competent and could operate the business efficiently when they were free of political interference. Thus the key to Internet diffusion in Kenya was the confluence of the ODA grant, the KPTC's desire to earn huge monopoly profits, and demands for better information services by private ISPs.

Although the ISPs tried to negotiate with the KPTC during the 1994–1998 period, they were completely unsuccessful and at the mercy of the monopoly. Two developments began to change the status quo. First, ISPs and educational institutions joined forces to negotiate affordable Internet access and streamlined licensing procedures. Excessive fees barred educational institutions from securing connectivity through the ISPs. This alliance resulted in the establishment of the first national backbone, Jambonet, which became operational in 1998. Second, international pressure for liberalization and privatization mounted, and an initiative by the US Agency for International Development (USAID) aimed at bringing Internet connectivity to Africa catalyzed further policy reform.

CNI 2: Establishing a National Backbone

The 1998 establishment of Jambonet, the national Internet backbone gateway, greatly benefited the ISPs. Although still a monopoly and a full subsidiary of the KPTC, Jambonet provided some relief to the ISPs. Jambonet, along with the Kenyan Education Network (KeNet), became negotiating issues under interesting circumstances. USAID's Leland Initiative had proposed giving assistance to the government of Kenya for the establishment of a national Internet gateway and backbone independent of the KPTC.[15] The KPTC rejected this proposal, developed Jambonet on its own, and proposed that USAID's assistance be directed to KeNet. Three years after this counterproposal, KeNet became a reality.

Jambonet

Jambonet was designed to support at least twenty-four ISPs. As a result of lowering entry barriers, Jambonet was expected to provoke serious competition among ISPs. Word quickly spread that competition in the ISP industry was under way and that many more Kenyans would soon be able to afford Internet access. Extended negotiations on bandwidth, licensing costs, and approval of new telecommunications equipment had to take place between the KPTC, existing ISPs, and aspiring ISPs.

The KPTC, which acted as the government's representative in the talks, viewed the Leland proposal to establish a backbone and gateway as a kind of diktat rather than a negotiation. During initial discussions with the KPTC, Leland negotiators emphasized that the optimum cost of a 64-kbps leased line should be about US$1,500 per month, and an unlimited dial-up account through an ISP should cost US$20 per month. At the time, ISPs were paying US$12,500 per month for a 64-kbps leased line.

After reviewing the Leland Initiative proposal, the government of Kenya opted to establish its own national gateway. Hence, Jambonet was launched in December 1998 by a local Kenyan company in partnership with a Canadian firm. Understandably, the prospect of reducing monthly costs from US$12,500 to US$1,500 (average cost of a 64-kbps leased line in other countries, like Madagascar) was great news to the ISPs. For end-users, costs would decrease from approximately US$200 to US$40 per month for unlimited access.

Jambonet seems to be a compromise measure designed to address ISP cost and quality-of-service issues on the one hand, and the strong desire to maintain a telecommunications monopoly on the other. Nairobinet, Insight Technologies, Net2000, and Telemedia Communications became new players in the industry. It is widely believed that senior Kenyan politicians were the real owners of most of the new ISPs, and that they had streamlined the licensing process as a result of self-interest.

The national Internet gateway backbone was eventually established at considerable cost, though the KPTC was able to retain its monopoly control over access to the Internet.

KeNet

Parallel to the KTPC-USAID discussions about Jambonet, both the ISPs and educational institutions were lobbying for better and cheaper access. It should be noted that the political environment in Kenya remained repressive; there was also widespread corruption during this period. As a result, beginning in the 1980s most donors shifted away from working directly with the government of Kenya to collaborating with local and international NGOs. A major priority of USAID was to encourage political reform through democracy and good governance. This translated into a major focus on strengthening civil society.

Proreform efforts were perceived by KANU and the government as undermining their political position. In turn, USAID judged that the Kenyan government was unwilling to implement telecom policy reforms, not only because of the vested institutional and personal interests already discussed. In the negotiations on the Internet, issues were not well defined, and both parties opted to avoid serious exchanges.

As noted, although the KPTC rejected the Leland Initiative's proposal for a national backbone and gateway, and while the KPTC completed Jambonet on its own, all sides appreciated the importance of bringing the Internet to the education sector. In 1999, of the twenty-three universities in Kenya, only the University of Nairobi and the US International University could afford to pay US$4,500 per month for a 64-kbps leased line. Other institutions could only afford dial-up services for their academic staff, and access was tightly controlled due to the high telephone charges associated with dial-up services. They were under pressure from the education sector but did not have, or were unwilling to allocate, resources to address this need.

Initially, Leland Initiative staff did have a strong interest in supporting the KPTC's counterproposal for KeNet. Though KeNet did not meet the initiative's primary mandate of encouraging policy reform, other dynamics were at play and the political climate in Kenya was about to change. In 1994, President Bill Clinton's Greater Horn of Africa Initiative (GHAI) made Internet access a USAID priority in the region. The US government identified Kenya as a key in the implementation of the GHAI.[16]

In the three years between the KPTC's rejection of the initial Leland proposal and USAID's acceptance of the KPTC and government of Kenya counterproposal, the Internet wave had fully hit Kenya. Still, the Kenyan government viewed the Internet with suspicion. Nevertheless, a way forward was apparent once Leland accepted that counterproposal. USAID could support Internet access in the education sector. At this time, champions who could support the education sector–USAID coalition emerged.

Among these champions were Stanley Murage, former permanent secretary of the Ministry of Transport and Communication, who played a critical role in negotiations by ensuring that they did not stall. Like Augustine Cheserem, former governor of the Kenyan central bank, Murage went into government service from the private sector. A land economist by profession, Murage understood the importance of the Internet to the country in general and to the education sector in particular. Murage is still cited by former employees of the KPTC as a champion of telecom liberalization in Kenya.[17]

Intense discussions took place between the Kenyan government and USAID; the US Department of State also participated. Negotiations focused on USAID's interest in enhancing Internet access for Kenya's education sector, the Department of State's interest in opening up markets for US businesses, and the Kenyan government's interest in having Kenyans play key roles. The crucial and mutual understanding was that the project would be locally managed and driven, and that USAID would act only as an adviser. The education sector would take the lead in articulating its own Internet needs and would design a network that was sustainable.

Also working quietly, but with great conviction, were members of the education sector. Most vice chancellors—the heads of universities, who are presidential appointees and thus politically connected—were quick to seize the opportunity and supported a process that would make access affordable.[18] Declining subsidies, higher expenses, and increasing tuition meant that most vice chancellors were under tremendous financial pressure. At the same time they were also under pressure from their faculty and students to provide Internet access, enhance sources of information, and improve the quality of learning.

Henry Thairu, deputy vice chancellor of the Jomo Kenyatta University of Agriculture and Technology, was a leading representative of the education sector. Thairu mobilized the educators to lobby the KPTC, Kenyan government, and USAID in support of KeNet. Thairu's education coalition was successful, supported by the Kenyan government, funded by USAID, and totally owned by universities.

In April 1999, leaders in the education sector met to discuss the need for collective negotiations with the government. The forum was attended by Francis Gichaga (vice chancellor of the University of Nairobi), Ratemo Michieka (vice chancellor of Jomo Kenyatta University), George Jones (former director of USAID in Kenya), Frieda Brown (head of the US International University), George Mbate, Lane Smith, and Mary Muiruri (all three of USAID), and Kelly Wong (with the University of Maryland). At this meeting the Kenya Education Network was formed with all represented universities as charter members.

Professor Ratemo Michieka was asked to solicit the participation of the entire university community through the influential Vice Chancellors Association. Michieka did not have any difficulty convincing his counterparts of the importance of the proposed memorandum of understanding. Every participant in this meeting was urged to contact colleagues in the government to lobby for the signing of the memorandum.[19] George Jones, former director of USAID in Kenya, became the principal liaison among the university dons. Jones's experience with USAID and Kenya, his wisdom, and the sensitivity with which he handled key issues were essential for maintaining the cohesion of the coalition.[20]

The unity of the university coalition and its ownership of the project finally convinced the Kenyan government that its restrictive Internet policies were denying students the opportunity to communicate and conduct research. The Vice Chancellors Association ensured that the Leland Initiative's memorandum of understanding was indeed factored into key discussions with all government officials. On 2 June 1999, after three years of negotiations, the Leland memorandum was signed, thus formalizing the relationship between the Kenyan government and the US government in the area of Internet development.

However, the lengthy negotiations resulted in a drastic reduction in project funding. The available Leland funds, about US$300,000,[21] were not enough to cover costs. Fortunately, another USAID initiative, the Education for Democracy and Development Initiative (EDDI), expressed interest in building on the Leland Initiative's work and allocated additional funds[22] for the network's roll-out and other related activities.[23] Within a few months, every educational institution voiced an interest in joining KeNet in order to be part of the collective bargaining process for better Internet access at affordable rates. Because KeNet infrastructure would eventually be expanded beyond the education sector, it was hoped that new markets for the private sector would emerge in secondary towns.

Interest Leveraging

Essentially, three elements accounted for the success of the negotations for a backbone gateway, an education network, and lower access costs. First, the strategy to support a wholly owned Kenyan network, the coalescence of the education sector as a stakeholder in the policy reform process, and EDDI's support and the funds it put on the table served as major negotiating tools and a catalyst for a successfully negotiated resolution. Some conditions had also changed: during the negotiations, inevitable privatization and liberalization of the sector rendered the KPTC and the government of Kenya more positively disposed to negotiate competitive access costs than they had been three years earlier.

Second, KeNet successfully argued that Telkom Kenya could increase its revenues by lowering prices and increasing its customer base. KeNet was able to make this argument because it was the biggest Internet lobbying group, it had financial commitments from USAID, and it exploited the political weight of the education coalition. KeNet members successfully argued that even though the twenty-three KeNet institutions could only afford to pay US$1,000 a month for a 64-kbps leased line, Telkom Kenya could increase its education sector revenues from US$9,000 to US$23,000 per month. To increase its negotiating weight, KeNet secured USAID's agreement to pay connectivity fees for one year in advance.

Third, KeNet assured Telkom Kenya that it was an important partner. KeNet would ride on existing Telkom Kenya infrastructure, and would not try to develop an independent education backbone.

Telkom Kenya and its negotiators reviewed KeNet's proposals with renewed interest. Telkom Kenya's sense of network ownership increased with agreement on the three elements discussed above. When Alex Maina, director of research and development at Telkom Kenya, became the telecom's lead negotiator, KeNet was pleased. Maina knew most of the telecom's concerns and was able to broker issues at the highest level. Helen Kinoti played a critical role by interpreting concerns and balancing expectations, and Mugambi Kinoti of the Office of Cost-Based Tariffs explained how Telkom Kenya formulated tariffs.

Telkom Kenya's negotiating team brokered a memorandum of agreement with KeNet that clarified issues of equipment ownership. The Telkom Kenya team even facilitated meetings with the Communications Commission of Kenya (CCK) to assign to KeNet certain frequencies reserved for research. As a result of these negotiations, access fees declined from US$4,500 per month to US$1,000 per month for a 64-kbps leased line for the KeNet institutions.[24] In 2000, tariffs for commercial ISPs were reduced from US$4,500 to US$3,000. These changes quickly attracted new ISPs, and within a span of eight months, cybercafes appeared in every corner of Nairobi and its environs.[25] Because of the reduction in monthly fees, some ISPs, including Nairobinet, could also afford to establish points of presence in secondary towns.

While the cost-based tariff negotiations were taking place, ISPs organized themselves into the Kenya Internet exchange point to aggregate bandwidth locally and to allow ISPs to lower charges. Generally speaking, Kenyans from all walks of life became very vocal in providing suggestions to the KPTC and the government on the optimum cost of Internet access and the value of implementing better Internet policies.

One other factor helped reduce the cost of leased lines in Kenya. This was a second cellular network roll-out, which occurred in 2000. The new infrastructure developed to support the cellular network gave ISPs the opportunity to provide Internet services in areas where Telkom Kenya's infrastructure was lacking. In addition, the telecom was forced to lower its rates for fixed lines because of competition from the cellular market. It also worked to improve its services to attract customers to the fixed-line sector.

With the national backbone established and prices for Internet access decreasing, the Kenyan government launched discussions on the liberalization of the telecom sector itself. Pressure from external sources like the World Bank was forcing governments throughout Africa to reform their telecom sectors;

particularly important were the encouragement of competition and the creation of independent regulators to oversee markets. In Kenya, the eventual breakup of the monopoly KPTC had implications for both the national backbone and KeNet.

CNI 3: Regulatory Issues

The Telecommunications Bill

On 14 March 1997 the government of Kenya introduced a draft bill to privatize and liberalize the telecommunications sector. The bill established the framework for launching Telkom Kenya Ltd. as a private telecommunication services company, created the Communications Commission of Kenya to regulate the sector, and assigned operation of the country's postal services to the Postal Corporation of Kenya. The bill was effective as of July 1999. Telkom Kenya Ltd. was licensed as the public telecommunications operator, given ownership of Jambonet, and provided with exclusivity for service in the Nairobi area. The longtime KPTC managing director, Jan Mutai, was replaced by Augustine Cheserem, who had been assistant general manager of the KPTC. Samuel Chepkonga, former KPTC legal adviser, was appointed to head the CCK.

Privatization and liberalization occurred as the democratic process progressed in the form of national elections. The public was generally dissatisfied with the government, as a result of a weak economy and practically nonexistent public services. Interest in the liberalization bill was generated, in part, by economic decline and high unemployment rates. Some believed that a liberalized telecommunications sector would spur economic growth, as it had in neighboring Uganda and Tanzania.

Three groups helped lead the liberalization of the sector, and also lobbied against replacing a public monopoly with a private one. These groups were the ISPs, the East Africa Internet Association, and a number of prominent women who had been at the forefront of telecommunications reform.

In Kenya, women have long been involved in advocating issues, including telecommunications reform. Betty Maina of the Institute of Economic Affairs, an NGO that facilitates the exchange of ideas, took the lead and organized lobbying groups to negotiate key aspects of the telecommunications bill.[26] Her efforts were directed at increasing rural access and highlighting the role of gender issues in communications policymaking. While Maina's aspirations to expand rural access to the Internet failed, she lobbied successfully for the inclusion of women on the CCK's board of directors.

Internet service providers met with parliamentarians to discuss the contents of the bill and to review how it would affect the economy. The ISPs emphasized how telecom monopolies discouraged investors. The strength of the

ISP coalition meant that they could not be ignored by the government. Lobbyists also mobilized civil society to challenge various sections of the bill that maintained the monopoly status of the KPTC.

Despite the best efforts of reformers, the final bill continued Telkom Kenya's monopoly. Although some issues raised by ISPs and others were incorporated in the final version of the bill,[27] the law was later amended to weaken these provisions. This experience demonstrates how civil society can be mobilized during the process of democracy building; it is also an example of how civil society's influence can have only a tenuous effect on transitioning states.

The CCK

The Communication Commission of Kenya was responsible for implementing the major aspects of the telecommunications bill, including issuing licenses, regulating prices, establishing interconnection principles, approving equipment, and managing the radio frequencies spectrum.

Samuel Chepkonga, the former legal adviser of the defunct KPTC, was appointed to head the new regulatory body. His history with the KPTC indicated that he was a friend of the monopoly, and this made many doubt his role as an independent regulator. While he spoke firmly about his independence, his favorable treatment of Telkom Kenya cast doubts on his claim. The first issue that gave reformers pause was the maintenance of the Internet monopoly in the form of Jambonet. Additionally, the CCK closed the offices of the Telecommunication Service Providers Association of Kenya (TESPOK), charging that it was operating an Internet exchange point. It appeared that Telkom Kenya had pressured Chepkonga to take this drastic action. For its part, TESPOK insisted that it had received a verbal license from Chepkonga to operate the local exchange point. In response, CCK director Chepkonga remarked: "Too bad. Next time make sure you get us to put it in writing. We were shocked to learn Telecommunication Service Providers of Kenya launched the new service without applying for a license."[28]

The Internet Exchange Point

The negotiations that led to the launching of the Kenyan IXP were among the most contentious of all. In part, tensions were caused by the tremendous growth of, and competition between, ISPs. Entry barriers had been drastically reduced, and there were as many as forty-seven ISPs operating in Kenya in 1999. In addition, a changing political culture brought about by democratization meant that Kenyans were more freely expressing dissatisfaction with dismal public services. Popular ire was directed at the public KPTC monopoly cum private monopoly (Telkom Kenya) and the new regulatory agency, the CCK.

Although the ISP industry initially supported Jambonet and was cautiously optimistic about the effects of sector reform under the telecommunications bill, ISPs quickly realized that neither would address their priority: a high monopoly tariff structure. Focus quickly shifted to the IXP issue. Because there was no in-country route for local Internet traffic (the function of an IXP), ISPs routed traffic between each other over an international satellite link, a highly expensive procedure. This, in turn, meant that Internet tariffs were being used to fund the costly international circuit operated by Jambonet.

Telkom Kenya opposed establishing an IXP. If local traffic would no longer have to traverse the expensive international circuit served by Jambonet, Telkom Kenya's revenues would decrease. Thus the main beneficiaries of the proposed local exchange point would be ISPs and their customers. Figure 4.1 reports the dramatic cost differences between the two systems.

Under an IXP system, each ISP pays for its circuit and router into the IXP datacenter. Local area network (LAN) technology is used to interconnect each ISP's router. TESPOK organized the Kenya IXP so that each ISP was to pay an entry cost of US$2,000, which could be paid in installments. Furthermore, all members connected to the Kenyan IXP would pay a monthly charge of US$266, irrespective of how much bandwidth they had.[29] Each ISP would also provide a router at both ends of the connection and pay the monthly charges by Kenstream, Telkom Kenya's data service provider, for a link to the Kenyan IXP. Because an IXP is in one sense a LAN, and in another sense a "closed user group," the Kenyan telecommunications bill could be interpreted as permitting TESPOK to operate the IXP without a license. To confirm this interpretation, TESPOK held several meetings with the CCK. The regulators

Figure 4.1   International vs. Domestic Leased Lines, Kenya, December 2000

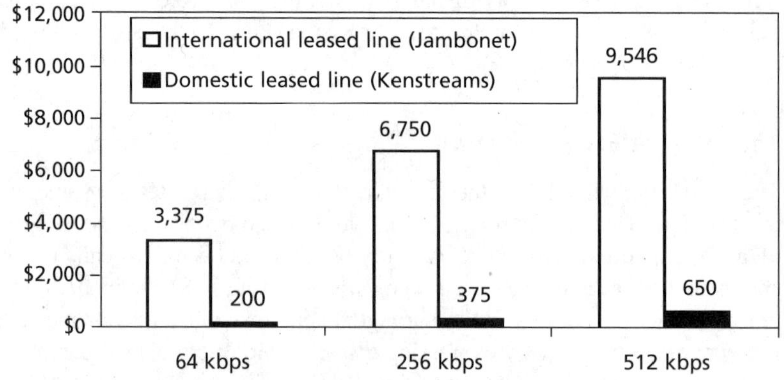

Source: Longwe, 2003.

agreed that the IXP did not need a license. According to TESPOK, if indeed ethernet LANs required licenses, then by definition every corporate office, government office, and educational institution was breaking the law by operating unlicensed LANs. However, Telkom Kenya appealed to the CCK, which declared the initial launch of the IXP to be illegal. The Internet exchange point was shut down for over a year. The battle for affordable, local exchange of information had begun.

TESPOK Negotiations

The Telecommunication Service Providers Association of Kenya was launched in 1999 as a nonprofit association representing value-added telecommunications services, including ISPs. The organization's objective was to grow Kenya's telecommunications industry. When TESPOK was established, the market had grown from three ISPs in 1997 to forty-seven licensed ISPs in 1999.[30] About half the ISPs were breaking even or profiting; the others were losing money. TESPOK was initially dominated by six major ISPs: Africa Online, Nairobinet, Net2000, Inter Connect, Swift Global, and Paging Services. It was chaired by Richard Bell, a former UN employee and the managing director of Swift Global.

Negotiations to establish an IXP began in August 1999 during a meeting among ISPs that had expressed interest in establishing a trade association. The first task of the association was negotiating with the CCK and Telkom Kenya for an exchange point. Allowing ISPs to transmit Kenyan Internet traffic through a local exchange point would save bandwidth costs and reduce demands on international circuits, thereby improving the efficiency of Internet communications. Satellite hops, besides being costly, increase traffic and cause latency for more interactive Internet applications, such as Web browsing. Statistics in Kenya indicate that between 20 percent and 30 percent of Internet traffic is local.[31]

In a letter sent to the Communications Commission of Kenya in July 2000, TESPOK confirmed that discussions on the IXP issue had been held with the commission's director-general, Chepkonga. The letter stated, in part, "TESPOK's chairman met with the CCK's general manager, Telecoms Development, and went into the details of the KIXP proposal. During this meeting CCK's Director General gave every assurance that KIXP did not require a license and did not in any way infringe upon Telkom Kenya's monopoly."[32] The TESPOK letter also asserted that a second meeting, this time with the CCK general manager, confirmed TESPOK's legal position.[33] However, the CCK's opinion was not stated in writing.

Within a week or two of its initial launch in February 2001, TESPOK received a letter from the CCK "instructing them to close down the KIXP and also instructing Telkom Kenya to disconnect all ISP links to the KIXP."[34] According to TESPOK, when the Kenyan IXP was launched in November 2000, there were "four ISPs exchanging traffic. The growth was so dramatic that within seven days all ISPs were forced to upgrade their links, while a further six ISPs applied to join the KIXP."[35]

The CCK asserted that the IXP infringed on the monopoly rights of Telkom Kenya. Equipment was disconnected, completely crippling the operations of the exchange point. It took about a year to sort out the dispute and restore the facility. TESPOK believes that the exchange was shut down at the request of Telkom Kenya. Ironically, TESPOK leaders affirm that the telecom was approached to host the exchange, but that it showed no interest in the proposal.

The CCK ruled that the exchange was illegal in the first place because it lacked the required license: "The KIXP was established without first seeking the necessary license from the CCK in keeping with the Kenya Communications Act, 1998, section 24 (1),"[36] the CCK said in a statement. The closure of the IXP caused anxiety within the ISP sector, but the media played a critical role by providing consumers with continuous updates on the importance of the exchange point. As a result of media attention, the director-general of the CCK was put on the spot; the CCK's verbal agreement on the validity and legality of the IXP was not denied.

According to a memo dated 2 July 2001 from Richard Bell, TESPOK chair:

> We filed an appeal with the Appeals Tribunal (as layer [*sic*] down under the act). Through the mediation of the First Secretary Commercial from the British High Commission we agreed to try and negotiate a settlement without forcing the issue through the courts. A settlement was agreed whereby the regulator gave an undertaking that if we applied for a license, it would be granted. So as not to prejudice our TESPOK case with the tribunal (ie. that it does not actually require a license) we applied for a license using a separate entity. Three weeks later a letter was received from the regulator refusing our license application. We subsequently went to the regulator and asked that the application be gazetted, which they agreed to do. Telkom Kenya now has 60 days (from 21st March) to object to the license, something they have indicated they will do, at which point we believe the regulator will then refuse our application.[37]

Had the closure of the IXP occurred during the days of one-party rule, Kenyans would have remained silent. In democratic Kenya, however, the industry quickly sought arbitration from the CCK. After heated negotiations, TESPOK was finally licensed to operate the IXP as a legal entity. Ironically, the IXP was officially relaunched on 18 April 2002 by CCK director-general Chepkonga. In his speech at the launch event, Chepkonga remarked, "TESPOK Chairman, Mr. Richard Bell, the Internet community in Kenya, distinguished guests, ladies and gentlemen, I am delighted to be here this afternoon to preside over the official launch of the Kenya Internet Exchange Point (KIXP)."[38]

The Kenyan Internet exchange point was the first IXP in the sub-Saharan region outside of South Africa; it has sparked similar initiatives in Nigeria, Uganda, Mozambique, Ghana, and Tanzania. In 2005, ten companies were connected to the facility. There are plans to connect the Kenyan IXP to other regional exchange points within East Africa once they are operational, as well as with other national IXPs in Africa.

Apart from the savings they receive from operating through the Kenyan IXP, members have enjoyed scalable speeds from 64 kbps and upward. Because bandwidth is not restricted, members can upgrade as often as needed, and the upgrades do not affect their monthly costs. Users have benefited from increased speed and reliability of data transmissions, and reduction of data packet loss and download times. The Kenyan IXP has reduced traffic latency from an average of 800–900 milliseconds to 60–80 milliseconds. Reliability and increased speed have also led to improvements in international transmissions, which are now less jammed. Thus, greater potential exists for e-commerce transactions.

Conclusion

Collective bargaining can be a powerful instrument. The Kenya case clearly demonstrates that under a democratic system, citizens can assert their collective will for the good of the nation. The Kenya experience also illustrates that, contrary to the belief that nothing happens in Africa without foreigners and multinationals, the majority of Africans do understand the politics of telecommunications issues and are better placed to resolve conflicts than are foreigners. The entire Internet diffusion process is credited to Kenyans who clearly understood their government, the value of the Internet, and the best way of implementing telecommunications reforms.

Strong-willed Kenyans like Shem Ochuodho, Amollo Ng'weno, and Kamande Muiruri took the initial step of applying for licenses, although they were forced to pay exorbitant rates for bandwidth controlled by the state monopoly. Kenyan politicians were motivated by self-gain. Nevertheless, they played an important role in pushing the government to liberalize the telecommunications sector. The benefits reaped by politicians through this process also helped the general public.

The Kenyan education sector flexed its muscle and successfully negotiated lower tariffs without antagonizing Telkom Kenya or the CCK. The lesson here is the importance of utilizing established building blocks. KeNet could have sought to establish an independent network, but instead it opted to utilize Telkom Kenya's infrastructure to build its capacity to support KeNet's needs. In so doing, KeNet helped Telkom Kenya to realize the power of strategic partnerships.

Women like Betty Maina, Muthoni Wanyeki, and others seized the opportunity to educate the public on the importance of the telecommunications bill and its implications for the delivery of telecommunication services. They even targeted parliamentarians and organized two workshops to enhance the capacity of opposition legislators to contribute to the debate on the bill. As a result, during the crucial second and third readings of the bill, lawmakers were able to make substantive proposals on provisions of the law.

Finally, Sammy Buruchara, Kamande Muiruri, and others worked to create the Kenyan Internet exchange point. They devoted long hours to negotiating with the CCK and Telkom Kenya for the IXP. As a result of the establishment of the exchange point, ISP businesses now operate in a well-regulated and competitive market. Many Kenyans continue to benefit from the negotiations on the Internet, as do foreign and domestic businesses, which can now establish ISPs in a streamlined industry.

The benefit of moving from a single-party to a multiparty democracy is the overarching theme of this case study. Without the democratization process, telecommunication services would remain a monopoly in Kenya, citizens would still be scared to dissent from government policy, and the Internet and mobile phones would only be available to the elites.

For countries facing stringent circumstances like those in Kenya in the 1990s, the lesson is simple: keep negotiating Internet issues. Davids *can* exist in a telecommunications environment controlled by Goliaths who are ready to crush anyone who stands in their way. African children and grandchildren must be allowed to enjoy the economic opportunities that are available through Internet use in developed countries, opportunities for e-commerce, e-marketing, e-learning, telemedicine, and communication. African countries can utilize the Internet to help jump-start their stagnant economies. Through the Internet and larger plans for economic development, Africans can end the cycle of poverty that continues to afflict so much of the continent.

5

Rwanda:
Balancing National
Security and Development

*Albert Nsengiyumva and
Anne Pitsch Santiago*

SINCE 1998 THE GOVERNMENT of Rwanda has been working to define the information communication technology (ICT) sector and its role in the country's development. The resulting national ICT policy was adopted by the Rwandan cabinet in early 2000. It describes a vision and the strategies for transforming Rwanda's predominantly agricultural economy into a knowledge-based economy through the development of ICTs.

By the time the genocide ended in 1994, there were at most a handful of operational phone lines in the country. Telephone lines were quickly repaired and just two years later there were about a thousand operating lines. In 2004 there were 32,000 lines. The ICT sector in Rwanda faces two major obstacles: first, the general state of poverty and scarce electrical telecommunications facilities; second, the lack of human resources.

In January 2002 the country established the Rwandan Information Technology Authority (RITA) to facilitate national and sectoral ICT strategies.[1] By 2003 a multisector regulatory body, the Rwandan Utility Regulatory Authority (RURA), was established. RURA has jurisdiction over several market sectors, including energy, transportation, communications, and waste management. This new agency, however, does not yet have the human capacity needed to serve all the sectors it oversees, including the growing ICT market.

From a policy perspective, the founding of RITA and RURA is significant because the Rwandan government owns the major telecommunications company, Rwandatel, which provides fixed-line telephone services as well as Internet connectivity (see Table 5.1). The Ministry of Infrastructure oversees Rwandatel, and until January 2003 was responsible for issuing new licenses for all telecommunications services. By 2003 the process of privatizing Rwandatel was under way, and a new private sector firm, Artel, had come online and was providing fixed telephony over very small aperture terminal (VSAT)

85

Table 5.1   Rwandatel Charges for Internet Connectivity, Rwanda, 2003

Technology	Setup	Monthly Charge	Subscribers
Dial-up	US$25	US$25	3,000
Wireless	US$25	US$254	80
Leased line	US$25	64 kbps: US$1,000	
		128 kbps: US$1,600	
		1 mbps: US$5,000	80
ISDN	US$25	US$254	500

Source: Rwandatel, 2004.

satellite, mainly in remote areas. Artel is not a competitor to Rwandatel, but rather complements the incumbent, because it provides access in remote areas where lack of infrastructure has handicapped telecommunications.

Since about 90 percent of the market for Internet usage is located in the capital (Kigali), and the balance is in six towns (Butare, Ruhengeri, Cyangugu, Gitarama, Gisenyi, and Kibuye), diffusion of telecom infrastructure to rural areas is extremely limited. Fifteen broadband VSATs are operational in Rwanda. The major owners are international organizations, Internet service providers (ISPs), and institutions of higher education

The state-owned company Rwandatel is also the major ISP, but four other providers also exist: Mediapost, Artel, Terracom, and the Kigali Institute of Science, Technology, and Management (KIST). In December 2003 the country was estimated to have a hundred cybercafes (see Table 5.2), about 60 percent of which were located in Kigali, with the remainder in several secondary cities.

Internet usage within the government, mostly by higher-ranking officials, is limited, though growing. There is no interconnected network within the government, but some ministries have Internet access and networks internally. As stated above, the government sees great promise in promoting the Internet as a tool of development and has actively worked to advance this policy.

A number of policies have been implemented by the government of Rwanda to ensure access to telecommunications facilities, especially by underdeveloped areas. A universal access fund is supported by two sources: 2.5

Table 5.2   Cybercafe Penetration and Fees, Rwanda, 2004

Number of Cybercafes[a]	100
Highest charge per hour	US$1.70
Average charge per hour	US$0.67
Lowest charge per hour	US$0.45

Source: Rwandatel, 2004.
Note: a. December 2003

percent of Rwandatel's annual revenue, and allocations from the government's annual budget. Rwanda is working to decrease the distance that must be traveled to access a phone line, from fifteen to three kilometers by 2009. In addition, the government has decided to exempt all ICT equipment (including electrical equipment, generators, and solar panels) from import taxes.

By 2009 the education sector will be the major beneficiary of ICT access. The government's plan is for each primary school to receive at least one computer with Internet connectivity. Each secondary school will receive ten computers with Internet connectivity, and each tertiary school will enjoy Internet connectivity through the Rwandan Education Network (Rwednet). In schools located in remote areas where electricity is lacking, Internet access will be supported by solar energy panels. Distance learning and instructional technology as a whole are major concerns of public institutions of higher education, such as the National University of Rwanda (NUR), KIST, and the Kigali Institute of Education. These institutions receive major support from the US Agency for International Development (USAID), the Department for International Development (DFID) of the United Kingdom, and the Swedish International Development Agency (SIDA). The private sector's use of ICT lags behind that of other sectors, but a number of new ICT service providers are emerging. In Kigali, computer retail companies have opened stores that sell computer equipment and network and maintenance services. Banks and some individual businessmen utilize the Internet for their transactions.

The Internet in Rwanda

Despite the minimal infrastructure available in 1996 (two years after the genocide), certain members of the government and individual entrepreneurs were determined to restart essential services and bring the Internet to Rwanda. In 1995, Patrick Ngabonziza, a returnee who had lived in the United States and Europe for many years, became the first entrepreneur to attempt to bring the Internet to the country. He established a company in Kigali and tried to work with the telecom monopoly, Rwandatel, to obtain fixed lines through which to run his service.

Although he was supported by the minister of telecommunications, Charles Muligande, Ngabonziza struggled against Rwandatel's manager, Sam Nkusi, who was opposed to competition. Muligande was a scientist and a former researcher at Howard University in Washington, D.C. He later became the vice chancellor of the National University of Rwanda, then the secretary-general of the Rwandan Patriotic Front (RPF), then the minister of foreign affairs and regional cooperation. Like so many others who returned to Rwanda after the genocide to help rebuild the country, Nkusi had lived in exile during the repressive years of the regime of Juvenal Habyarimana (1973–1994). Before returning to

Rwanda and taking the post of minister of state in charge of energy and communications, Nkusi worked in Canada as a telecom engineer.

Rwandatel's position in support of a monopoly was endorsed by senior members of the military. Military officers opposed independent companies that provided telecommunications services, for fear of security breaches. After all, radio and other forms of communication were actively employed as tools of the genocide in 1994, and the military was determined to prevent a recurrence of such abuses. Unfortunately for Ngabonziza, his attempts to establish the Internet in Rwanda could not overcome official opposition. After working to launch his company, Ngabonziza left the country for South Africa in 1996. In South Africa, he set up an Internet company, Mediapost, in order to establish a basis for his eventual return to Rwanda. In the end, Rwandatel and those opposing competitive Internet access could not prevent the arrival of the Internet, or the rise of competition.

Building an Internet infrastructure took place against the backdrop of the genocide and devastation. Eventually, after a lot of politics, bringing the Internet to Rwanda became a key objective of the government, the aid community, and private individuals. All these groups championed the Internet as a tool for reconstruction and economic development.

In 1994–1995, Lane Smith, coordinator of USAID's Leland Initiative, worked with various African countries to establish the Internet (see Chapter 8, which describes this general process). At that time, a high connectivity speed in the majority of sub-Saharan Africa was 256 or even 128 kilobits per second (kbps). Rwanda was included as a "Leland country" by chance. In 1995, Niyibizi Bonaventure, who then worked for the USAID mission in Rwanda, was in Washington, D.C., to attend a series of non-ICT-related meetings. He met Smith at the latter's office by happenstance, and they discussed the Leland Initiative. Bonaventure asked Smith if it would be possible to include Rwanda on the list of beneficiary countries, and received a positive response. A few months later, the first Leland mission to Rwanda was organized. Its objective was to contact the proper authorities to discuss the options for bringing the Internet to the country. Bonaventure later became minister of commerce and industry, then executive secretary of the Privatization Secretariat and chairman of the board of the newly formed Rwanda Utility Regulatory Authority.

Traditionally, the Rwandan government held 99 percent of the shares of Rwandatel, the monopoly telecommunications company. In 1995, Rwandatel negotiated its ascension as an Internet service provider with the assistance of the Leland Initiative. In exchange for its agreement to open the telecommunications market, Rwandatel was to receive the equipment needed to establish Internet service in the country. After the Leland Initiative delivered the materials to Rwandatel, however, the company refused to respect the agreement to open the market to competition. Furthermore, Rwandatel claimed that the equipment it had received was inadequate. It should be noted that the monopoly was very lucrative; Rwandatel assessed charges for both fixed-line and hourly Internet access through a modem hookup. The first major Internet-related conflict in Rwanda had begun.

Jim Lowenthal, an executive of Morocco Trade and Development Services and a former senior USAID official, was tasked with discussing the equipment issue with Rwandatel. Relations between USAID and Rwandatel broke down, because Rwandatel would not compromise on its monopoly status by issuing VSAT licenses to education institutions. Nkusi of Rwandatel refused to meet with Lowenthal for several days. Unfortunately, the meeting that finally took place between Nkusi and Lowenthal ended in a heated verbal exchange. It appeared that little hope existed for a resolution to the conflict. The government minister in charge of the telecommunications sector did not have the authority, or ability, to force Rwandatel to relinquish its monopoly, to open the sector (even at the ISP level), or to use cost-based tariffing. In addition, the absence of an autonomous regulator made arbitration impossible (according to Nkusi, Rwandatel was the regulator of telecommunications).

Supporters of the Leland Initiative, within and outside Rwanda, pushed Rwandatel and the Ministry of Telecommunications to guarantee the opening of the sector to competition. Proreform actors believed that competition and open markets were essential to the development and diffusion of the Internet in Rwanda. In contrast, Rwandatel, and in particular Nkusi, believed that the sector had neither the capacity nor the means to offer Internet service. Those opposing reform were not prepared to end Rwandatel's monopoly.

It was only after some years of negotiations that ISPs were granted licenses and allowed to compete for customers. Earlier ISP competition theoretically would have led to lower prices and greater Internet diffusion. Yet any new ISP would have had no choice but to rely on Rwandatel for its connectivity, and so it is likely that the positive effects of competition would have been muted as long as Rwandatel remained the monopoly supplier of fixed lines and connectivity.

Two significant elements that characterized this early period of Internet diffusion should be emphasized:

1. The country had just emerged from the terrible events of 1994, including the death of nearly a million people. A large part of the population was in exile in neighboring countries, and insecurity within Rwanda and its neighboring countries was high. Furthermore, a great number of old caseload refugees were attempting to return to their country of origin.[2] All these factors contributed to a humanitarian emergency within Rwanda. Thus the principal preoccupation of the new government was to organize vital services.

2. Like most countries in Africa, Rwanda receives a significant amount of income from the telecommunications sector. Given the postgenocide

context and the desperate need for funds, it is not surprising that Rwandatel, the monopoly telecom, tried to maintain its status as long as possible.

A relatively small number of people were involved in negotiations over Internet diffusion in Rwanda. Few Rwandans were able to comprehend either the technical issues or the potential impact of this new communication tool. Additionally, the institutions necessary for the development of the telecommunications market in general, and diffusion of the Internet in particular, were either weak or nonexistent. Institutional weakness delayed and frustrated negotiations. Ultimately, conflicts and negotiations over Internet diffusion were personalized.

Three of the four critical negotiation issues (CNIs) described below took place during the 1995–1999 period. This period in Rwanda, as well as in most of Africa, was generally characterized by an absence of local expertise in the field of ICT, exacerbated in Rwanda by the loss of human capital during the genocide, the domination of a state-owned monopoly telecom in the sector, and an illiberal telecommunications market. In general, during this time African countries did not have widespread telephone service throughout their territories; naturally, they also lacked multiple, private ISPs, and even lacked national policies to regulate and utilize the growing field of telecommunications. Rwanda was even worse off than most African countries because of the genocide. The fourth CNI, development of an Internet exchange point (IXP), took place at the turn of the millennium and was resolved in 2004.

CNI 1: Access to the Internet Gateway

As noted above, the two key issues of Internet diffusion in Rwanda during the second half of the 1990s were security and the monopoly status of Rwandatel. These concerns were pushed by powerful figures in Rwandatel and the Ministry of Defense. Precisely because the telecommunications infrastructure was damaged in the wake of the genocide, the military feared that ICTs could be used to foment insecurity and that no countermeasures could be taken. The reasonable concern that ICTs could be used to incite violence, as was radio during the genocide, led the military to support state control over the airwaves and all other forms of communication. Instability was still occurring within the country until the late 1990s. Genoçidaires, those who had participated in the massacres of 1994, were still attempting to regain power. They mounted occasional incursions into Rwanda from neighboring Zaire (now the Democratic Republic of Congo). Thus the military became a natural ally of Rwandatel's management, which wanted to maintain its monopoly status for reasons of profitability.

Interestingly, the minister of telecommunications, Charles Muligande, was a champion of the Internet and favored a competitive market for the telecommunications sector. He encouraged the private sector to apply for ISP licenses. This put Muligande at odds with Nkusi of Rwandatel. Rwandatel was able to maintain its monopoly status for some time by simply denying fixed-line access to the independent ISPs. Nkusi also enjoyed the support of the Ministry of Finance, which had relied on the monopoly's lucrative revenue. All parties in the negotiations understood the need for continued government revenue from Rwandatel.

During 1995 and 1996 the minister of telecommunications contacted Rwandatel several times on behalf of Patrick Ngabonziza's company, Computer Technologies. Ngabonziza was seeking phone lines through which to provide Internet service. Rwandatel responded that no more phone lines were available. Unfortunately for Ngabonziza, negotiations that could have resolved the impasse did not take place, because policies and regulations did not exist under which the minister of telecommunications could force Rwandatel to comply with the request for service. In fact, Rwandatel itself played the role of telecommunications regulator within the country, and thus it had the political power to protect its monopoly status. Ngabonziza, after waiting for six months for service, decided in 1996 to cut his losses and move his venture to South Africa. He returned to Rwanda in 2002, when conditions had improved, and opened a company called Mediapost.

The opening of the Internet market to competition finally occurred in 2001. Still, the personal intervention of President Paul Kagame was necessary.[3] One result of the slow process of transition was that between 1996 and 1999, Internet access was extremely limited. By the end of 1998, Rwandatel was servicing only 300 Internet subscribers. In late 1999, two major universities, the Kigali Institute of Science, Technology, and Management and the National University of Rwanda, the latter in Butare, received licenses to install VSATs. This development, achieved with the assistance of USAID's Leland Initiative (and discussed in greater detail later), led to a dramatic increase in Internet users. Rwandatel began facing competition when KIST began running a cybercafe on its campus; later, it offered dial-up access. The market really opened in 2002, when Ngabonziza was finally able to launch his new ISP, Mediapost. By the end of 2003, the Internet was available in most major cities, and four ISPs were operating.

Two significant facts emerge from this CNI. First, postgenocide insecurity within Rwanda was a major factor limiting access to communications, including the Internet. Because genoçidaires operated both within and just outside the borders of Rwanda, the government, particularly the military, was reluctant to open the communications market to free access. Additionally, the Internet was an unknown entity; therefore some members of the government were cautious about how it might be used by elements seeking to destabilize the country. A general fear also existed among the population that the Internet could be used for evil rather than good.

Second, the role of the diaspora was critical in the general development of the country and in Internet diffusion. A majority of returnees sought to use their experiences gained living abroad to invest in their country and take part in its reconstruction. It became imperative for Rwanda to create a welcoming environment for returning members of the diaspora. Unfortunately, the process took some time, and some returnees, like Patrick Ngabonziza, lost patience and went somewhere else to pursue their dreams. After all, frustrations are part and parcel of such endeavors.

CNI 2: Incumbent Wholesale Pricing

Before obtaining their own VSATs, universities in Rwanda were forced to pay Rwandatel's high fees for Internet service. The major expense was the cost of a leased line, at US$2,500 per month in early 1999. The National University of Rwanda obtained information on the cost of leased lines in South Africa and attempted to negotiate a better rate with Rwandatel based on that figure. Despite several requests, Rwandatel refused to modify its pricing scheme. The vice chancellor of the NUR called on the assistance of powerful politicians, including the minister of education and the minister of transport and telecommunications, in an effort to influence Rwandatel. But even with powerful actors working on the NUR's behalf, Rwandatel would not compromise.

Another problem experienced by the NUR was that although Rwandatel claimed to offer a connection speed of 64 kbps, in fact a speed of only 32 kbps was available for Internet access. Connection to the Internet was very weak, and technical assistance from Rwandatel was insufficient. The NUR, and other customers, paid high prices for poor service. For example, a line might remain disconnected for an entire week. In response to such poor service, the administration of the NUR at one point suspended payments to Rwandatel for several months in protest.

Negotiations between the NUR and Rwandatel over pricing did not go well. Nkusi was not willing to compromise on pricing, because he wanted to take advantage of Rwandatel's monopoly. The absence of an independent regulator favored Rwandatel. In this environment, the NUR decided to join other higher education institutions in a coalition to lobby for improved Internet access at better prices. As explained in detail below, public institutions could not afford to pay the high costs of Rwandatel's Internet service, so these stakeholders pursued other options, including the installation of VSATs by KIST and the NUR.

The NUR and other universities were never able to negotiate successfully with Rwandatel for lower rates. What the universities did gain from this process was added leverage with USAID and the UN Development Programme (UNDP). These organizations became sensitized to the problems the universities were experiencing when they tried to obtain Internet access through Rwandatel. The problems the universities faced with Rwandatel probably led to quicker negotiations later when they tried to obtain the VSATs. The dispute over pricing was not "resolved" until 1999, and for a three-year period little changed. As a result of security concerns, protectionism, and lack of human resources, reforms did not happen. Until the universities were able to obtain Internet access without the use of Rwandatel's leased lines, the diffusion of Internet access was extremely slow. The process accelerated after the universities were able to offer Internet services to their faculties, students, and the public.

Two major lessons emerged from this CNI. First, Rwandatel was incapable of delivering good service to its customers. As in most African countries, the incumbent telecom began offering Internet services to the public once connectivity had been established. The African telecoms, in general, viewed the Internet as a lucrative asset that required minimal additional infrastructure and investment. Naturally, they sought to maintain their monopolies for as long as possible. One of the problems that Rwandatel encountered, however, was that it lacked trained technicians capable of maintaining the new service. Because Internet technology is continuously changing, the technicians who maintain the network need regular training. Part of network maintenance is simply troubleshooting problems that arise, so practice is just as important, or more important, than theoretical knowledge about how the system works. The insufficient number of ICT technicians in Rwanda is apparent in the fact that Charles Semapondo, technical director of Rwandatel, is also in charge of Rwandatel's Internet services. Overseeing both systems is clearly too much of a responsibility for one person, especially in light of the fact that Semapondo does not have any specific training in Internet management.

The second lesson from this CNI is an obvious one: the high price charged by Rwandatel for leased lines caused universities to seek alternative means of gaining Internet access. It is clear that Rwandatel's fees for leased lines did not reflect its actual costs plus a reasonable profit. Rwandatel tried to take advantage of the NUR, which wanted fully half of the bandwidth available at the time. The NUR never received the bandwidth for which it had contracted. In addition, Rwandatel provided the NUR with poor service. It is likely that, had Rwandatel actually delivered the expected connectivity and provided adequate service, the NUR would have been satisfied with its arrangement with the telecom. The NUR needed Internet access, and would have paid excessive connectivity fees had Rwandatel fulfilled its obligations.

CNI 3: Authorization to Operate VSATs

Perhaps the most important actors in understanding the importance of the Internet and establishing it in Rwanda were the educators. In December 1998, a meeting on the development of the Internet took place at the UNDP office in Kigali. In attendance were representatives from the NUR, USAID, the UNDP, the Dutch cooperation agency, and local actors, including Nkusi of Rwandatel. The NUR officers were anxious to draw the attention of potential donors to the importance of the Internet for teaching and research. It was during this meeting that Rwandan stakeholders began to form an effective alliance, even if temporary and unintentional, to find an alternative to implement Internet access without relying on Rwandatel.

One of the major outcomes of the 1998 meeting was a renewed effort on the part of the NUR to coordinate its Internet efforts with those of other institutions of higher learning. The educators were convinced that the Internet could help rebuild the education system of Rwanda by acting as a multiplier of limited resources. Working together to define goals, the higher education institutions pooled their political clout to avoid duplicating their efforts. Silas Lwakabamba (vice chancellor) and engineer Albert Butare (vice rector for academics) of KIST and Emile Rwamasirabo (rector) of the NUR actively fought for the acquisition of VSATs. As explained above, Rwamasirabo of the NUR had signed a one-year contract with Rwandatel for a leased Internet line. The line was insufficient for the needs of the university, and Rwandatel provided mediocre service at best. The charge for this substandard service was US$2,500 per month.

A direct consequence of the December 1998 meeting was a visit to Rwanda in April 1999 by Lane Smith (Leland Initiative coordinator) and Kelly Wong (University of Maryland). Wong had attended the December meeting. The purpose of the Smith-Wong visit was to discuss the possibility of obtaining VSATs for the higher education institutions. At a meeting with university representatives, Smith offered VSATs to the educational institutions, thereby allowing Internet access without going through the monopoly, Rwandatel. Obtaining the equipment would be simple, because USAID, through its Leland Initiative, guaranteed delivery within ninety days. This guarantee, as we will see below, was a critical element that further galvanized the already strong university coalition.

The key now became obtaining official authorization (licensing) for the use of the VSATs. Rwandatel assumed the role of licenser, although the absence of a regulatory body meant that the Ministry of Telecommunications was legally entitled to grant such licenses. Rwandatel argued that the two educational institutions were not entitled to VSAT licenses, because they had no local technicians in place to maintain the systems. Rwandatel also argued that it would soon be able to offer the service at a reasonable price. In reality, Rwandatel feared that it was about to lose its monopoly. Technical and other problems arose from the beginning of Rwandatel's relationship with the institutions of higher learning. In October 1998, for example, the NUR had submitted to Rwandatel a list of materials it needed for installation of the Internet via a leased line, but Rwandatel had failed to provide adequate connectivity after the equipment was delivered.

Negotiations were taking place on several levels. The Leland team of Lane Smith and Kelly Wong, with the assistance of Christine Hjelt of USAID in Rwanda, were negotiating with the NUR and KIST for equipment delivery and maintenance. In November 1998, Christine Hjelt had called on Wong to attend the first meeting called to discuss the NUR's connectivity. Hjelt continued to be involved in the negotiations after the Smith-Wong visit of April 1999; in this way, she assisted the NUR and KIST in their negotiations with Rwandatel. Smith, Wong, and Hjelt also worked closely with the Ministry of Telecommunications, which, interestingly, supported the objective of granting VSAT licenses to the NUR and KIST. The USAID team also tried to negotiate with Rwandatel, but their efforts were blocked at every turn. At the same time, the NUR and KIST were also negotiating with Rwandatel, but they also made no progress.

A dramatic moment took place at the April 1999 meeting. Lane Smith stood up and said USAID would deliver VSATs to the universities and that they would be fully operational within ninety days after the licenses were issued. The silence that followed Smith's assertion was resounding. The university administrators knew at that moment that they had won their fight. Following the meeting, Nkusi tried to convince Smith not to send the VSATs. Nkusi argued that Rwandatel would be able to provide the necessary connectivity. Meanwhile, the university administrators increased the pressure they were exerting on Rwandatel to ensure that the licenses were issued.

Rwandatel asserted that the promised USAID equipment was inferior to the equipment that Rwandtel itself could provide. Nkusi still maintains that the equipment and bandwidth (256 kbps) offered by the Leland Initiative were obsolete and insufficient to launch quality Internet service.[4] He argued that new equipment would have to be added to that offered by Leland. Nkusi's stratagem was clear: preempt competition by asserting that USAID was donating inferior equipment. In response, Smith affirmed that the Leland equipment was the same that had been used in other countries with great success.

To resolve the impasse over the licenses, it was necessary to utilize the good offices of the Rwandan vice president, Paul Kagame. KIST invited Kagame to conduct a videoconference with Etienne Baranshamaje, the African virtual university coordinator at the World Bank in Washington, D.C. KIST wanted Kagame to see firsthand the problems Rwandatel was causing by blocking the licensing of the VSATs. Upon learning of Rwandatel's action, Kagame personally called Sam Nkusi and asked why the licenses were delayed. Kagame made it clear that he wanted the problem resolved immediately. In the face of such a directive from the country's vice president, Rwandatel could no longer obstruct matters and the VSAT licenses were granted in July 1999.

Kagame's intervention brought Rwandatel into cooperation with the universities. The new VSATs became operational in September 1999, eighty-seven days into the promised ninety-day period. The NUR and KIST now enjoyed Internet access. In the end, the two institutions had succeeded in their campaign to obtain VSATs. The universities saw their triumph as a step in building the national telecommunications sector.

The UN Office of Project Services (UNOPS) information technology team, led by Rafal Rohizinski, worked closely with USAID to install the VSAT unit at the NUR. Rohozinski, based in Kigali, had also supported the university VSATs, and together with his technical team he provided key assistance. In addition, logistical issues such as customs procedures and transportation were discussed, planned for, and closely coordinated. The international development organizations were firmly committed to helping the educational institutions obtain Internet access.

Having prevailed in obtaining VSATs, the universities now offer fast Internet access to their students and faculties. Given that Rwandan schools suffer from a lack of textbooks, access to the Internet is critical. The country also has many new teachers being trained for primary and secondary schools. The NUR's education faculty has prioritized distance learning, both to increase the knowledge of professors and to support them by facilitating their contacts with colleagues abroad. Rwandan professors can now work with organizations, such as the Multimedia Educational Resource for Learning and Online Teaching, that promote distance learning. In addition, partnerships with the University of Maryland, Michigan State University, Tulane, Swedish universities, and the Cisco Academy were made possible because of the NUR's successful negotiations. The NUR's education faculty recently established an instructional technology center that will facilitate the entire NUR faculty's use of technology in the classroom as well as instructors' use of Web-based opportunities for learning.

Beyond the immediate benefits of Internet access, NUR and KIST connectivity helped initiate a number of important projects, including:

1. A partnership launched in 1999 between the National University of Rwanda and the University of Maryland, with three areas of emphasis: distance education, computer science, and conflict management.
2. The Cisco Networking Academy Program, launched in December 2000 with support from the Leland Initiative and the University of Maryland, to teach technical skills in the maintenance and management of computer networks.
3. The African Virtual University, a distance learning project for short-term training and university degrees run by Western universities in the United States, Canada, Europe, and Australia for students in sub-Saharan African countries.

4. Free access to books and other materials, through a number of digital libraries worldwide, to facilitate teaching, learning, and research by Rwandan educational institutions.

Three major lessons arise from this CNI. First, the academic institutions played a vital role in pushing Internet liberalization in Rwanda. Academics and administrators understood better than others the direct role that the Internet could play in education and the complementary benefits it offered. The reduced state of the NUR was emblematic of the poor condition of higher education in Rwanda in the mid-1990s. The NUR had an insufficient number of professors, a majority of instructors did not have doctorates, libraries were poor and had outdated books, and textbooks and laboratories were ill equipped. The NUR's challenges called for alternative, creative methods of teaching and research at a time when the country lacked trained personnel at all levels. The universities fought for the Internet and, once they had won, utilized the Web extensively for many purposes: to access materials and libraries for use in the classroom, to partner with peers in developed countries, and to provide students with opportunities abroad.

Second is the significant role played by leadership. Paul Kagame's intervention in the negotiations illustrates how high-level actors were involved in bringing the Internet to Rwanda. Kagame advanced Internet liberalization by supporting VSAT licenses for KIST and the NUR, and demonstrated foresight and great appreciation of how the Internet could improve the education sector. In general, he has been a champion of ICTs as exemplified by Rwanda's Vision 2020 policy document.

Third was the need for the engagement of international organizations. Leland Initiative personnel, as well as those of other development institutions, provided key support in negotiating for VSAT licenses. Without the persistence of Leland director Lane Smith and his colleagues, the negotiations may have dragged on longer than they did. As it was, Smith visited Rwanda in April 1999, and by July a memorandum of understanding stipulating the terms for bringing the Internet to Rwanda via VSATs at the higher education institutions had been signed. By the end of September, the VSATs at KIST and the NUR were operational.

CNI 4: Lack of an Internet Exchange Point

In July 2004, the national IXP—or peering point—to facilitate in-country communication and information transfer became operational. As a result of negotiations, the ISPs, Rwandatel, and government regulators agreed on the importance of establishing an IXP. All parties also agreed that the Rwanda Information Technology Authority should take the lead in launching the IXP. The absence of an IXP had a negative effect on the diffusion of the Internet in Rwanda. The education system, in particular, had experienced problems establishing distance learning among campuses around the country. Such a program would support primary and secondary school teachers in remote locations. With the establishment of the peering point, this opportunity has become a reality for Rwandan educators. However, more coordination of ISPs is needed in order for the IXP to operate most efficiently.

In 2004 there were about ten VSATs installed in private and public institutions in Rwanda. Before the establishment of a peering point, all communications had to transit through a satellite to the United States, Canada, or Europe before returning to Rwanda. Thus, if two people within several miles of each other in Kigali sent e-mails back and forth, those e-mails might have traveled via satellite to a server in Europe or elsewhere before being sent back via satellite to the receiver. This process is inefficient and more costly than routing local e-mail traffic entirely within the country.

In addition to the education sector, the financial sector supported establishing a peering point, because it would facilitate financial e-transactions. Both Mediapost and Rwandatel also favored a peering point for business reasons, one of which is that a peering point can act as a backup server among the ISPs. One of the major barriers to establishing the peering point had been a lack of technical knowledge by Rwandatel and the ISPs of both how to install and how to maintain the system, and work on this front continues.

The rare state of consensus on an IXP was not automatic. When a peering point was first proposed in 1999, Rwandatel opposed the idea. Rwandatel's managers did not fully understand the advantages and were suspicious that a new technology could undermine the company's monopoly status. For a long time, Rwandatel controlled the telecommunications market without having to worry about quality of service or even the competence of its technicians. A new technology might challenge Rwandatel's technical knowledge and further spoil its reputation among customers. For a peering point to operate, an association of ISPs had to be established to ensure that the linking technology was working properly. A peering point also requires an autonomous body that is able to mediate among the member units. This also threatened Rwandatel, because an ISP association might erode its dominance and place more demands on Rwandatel's limited capacity to provide service.

The Rwandan Information Technology Authority is the executive body charged with coordinating and mediating between the ISPs and Rwandatel. RITA was founded in 2002 and began operations in January 2003. The body remains understaffed and not fully functional, because it has a staff of one (the executive director, responsible for multiple tasks). The Rwandan Utility Regulatory Authority, as noted previously, is also understaffed and has had difficulty recruiting personnel. There are few people in Rwanda who have the technical knowledge *and* diplomatic tact needed to establish and maintain a peering point.

Negotiations for a peering point occurred in several sessions, during which opposing views were expressed. The final success of the negations was due, in large measure, to Pius Ndayambaje, the interim executive director of RITA and an adviser to the Rwandan president on ICT matters. At first, meetings were dominated by Rwandatel technicians who lacked an understanding of peering points. Fortunately, Mediapost sent an expert from South Africa, Mark Elkins, who briefed the negotiators on the utility of the technology. These discussions made it possible for all stakeholders to understand the issues and formulate informed opinions. By the end of the meetings, everyone agreed on the need to establish a peering point within the structure of RITA. Mediapost was assigned responsibility for the technical maintenance of the peering point. Questions remained, however, over how to finance the peering point and how to obtain and install the necessary equipment. Additionally, technicians from the different participating institutions would have to be trained in its operation.

In October 2003 the Swedish International Development Agency, a major facilitator of ICT diffusion to developing countries in general and to Rwanda in particular, decided to support Rwanda's peering point. SIDA's assistance was coordinated by the Technical University of Stockholm, which has extensive experience in Africa and the Americas. Rwanda has fulfilled SIDA's prerequisites, namely the establishment of a neutral body to host the peering point, at least two independent ISPs, and an association of ISPs that can select technicians to be trained in the operation of a peering point. In February 2004, three computer science graduates from the NUR and one from KIST were sent to Sweden to undertake a two-month training program in order to fulfill the technical roles required by a peering point.

What can we learn from Rwanda's peering point negotiations? The advantages of an IXP were obvious, yet at first not all parties supported its establishment. After some discussion, however, even Rwandatel was convinced that a peering point would be advantageous. The costs of not having a peering point in the country certainly outweighed the costs of establishing one, and the negotiations needed to convince all stakeholders of this fact were relatively nonconfrontational. Not only does a peering point keep local traffic inside the country, but it also offers a capital advantage to ISPs by making it possible for backup of services. Therefore, establishing a peering point was viewed as a win-win proposition by all the actors involved, and the success of the negotiations resulted in the IXP being established in a relatively short period of time.

Other Critical Negotiation Issues

The four CNIs discussed in this chapter were among the most significant issues relating to Internet diffusion in Rwanda. However, they were not the only issues that arose. Another issue of particular importance for the country is its domain name (.rw). The domain is managed by the Swiss company Interpoint, so neither Rwandan ISPs nor RITA control access to, or use of, the name. It is clear that full control of the domain should rest in Rwandan hands. The International Corporation for the Assigned Names and Numbers (ICANN) has been asked to facilitate the return of the country's domain name back to Rwanda. It must be emphasized that local management of the domain name is critical to the creation of Rwanda-related websites. Local control will also affect socioeconomic development by raising Rwanda's profile on the Web. Before the domain name can be transferred to Rwandan hands, however, an association of its major users needs to be established, technical equipment should be obtained, and training needs to be undertaken by those tasked with maintaining the main domain name server (DNS).

Another issue that deserves attention is universal access as recognized by the International Telecommunications Union (ITU). Universal access, as defined by the ITU, means that all citizens should have at least some access to telecommunication media. Universal access is particularly essential in rural areas that have dispersed populations, poor or nonexistent basic infrastructures, and a scarcity of educational facilities. One reason universal access rules are important is that rural conditions are not conducive to attracting potential telecommunication investors. According to Rwanda's secretary of state for communications and energy, the government has begun applying a tax of 2.5 percent to each telecommunications operator.[5] This revenue is earmarked for a universal access fund that will be used to build infrastructure in underserved areas. As mentioned previously, by 2009 it is hoped that the distance anyone must travel to reach a telephone will be reduced from fifteen to three kilometers. If this objective is achieved, Internet diffusion and communications in general will be greatly facilitated.

Finally, another key issue has been voice over Internet protocol (VOIP). This technology has already been utilized in much of Rwanda, but its legal status is ambiguous, because no laws governing its use are in place. Certain cybercafes offer VOIP, whose customers rejoice in being able to call Europe and the Americas at a low price. VOIP has great potential to deny public telephone operators revenue from termination of calls. In addition to regulatory questions surrounding VOIP, technical questions also exist: how to improve the quality of VOIP and how to use more sophisticated equipment to expand services. Regulators need to divide the domains within which telephone and Internet companies operate. Until now the two domains were separated, but with the advent of VOIP the same technology can provide both voice and data services. An agreement is needed on the use and marketing of VOIP technology. Finally, lawyers and economists must join forces with telecom engineers to analyze the implications of VOIP and to formulate proposals for the spread of the technology.

Conclusion

By reviewing the various stages of Internet diffusion in Rwanda, we see that great progress has been made, despite the fact that access has not yet reached the entire country, especially rural areas. Compared with the other countries studied in this book, Rwanda is unique given the role played by high level officials in Internet negotiations. It seems that Rwanda's lack of institutions created a void into which stepped senior personalities. For this reason, negotiations on the Internet reflected the personalities of the primary actors, who were mostly younger yet experienced in the fields of telecommunications, academia, the military, and international development.

In terms of the various CNIs analyzed in this chapter, Rwandatel was omnipresent. The company sought to dominate the debate, but its arguments did not convince key policymakers and other stakeholders. Although Rwandatel had a very low level of technical capacity, the telecommunications sector itself was weak, and the government's main concern was solving the general insecurity in the country. Under these conditions, Rwandatel for some time was able to control the pace of Internet diffusion. In 1999, two institutions of higher education, KIST and the NUR, formed an alliance to protest against Rwandatel's dismal service. KIST and the NUR also fought to obtain VSAT licenses, and once they were obtained, Rwandatel's absolute power in the sector began to fade. The coalition gained additional strength through the support it received from international institutions such as USAID and the UNDP. By gaining powerful allies, the alliance of educators became strong enough to force a reluctant Rwandatel to grant its requests. In particular, Rwandatel was forced to respond to pressure exerted by the universities' champion, Paul Kagame.

The lessons that can be drawn from postgenocide Internet diffusion in Rwanda are multiple, but two stand out above all others:

1. *The role of leadership.* The Internet came to Rwanda during its period of maximum turmoil, a genocide that resulted in the death of nearly a million people. Given the breakdown of institutions, Rwanda is a case that calls attention to the role of individuals in promoting the Internet. Decayed institutions were not capable of creating policies to regulate the new technology; they lacked human resources, and they were forced to deal with other societal needs with a great sense of urgency. The Internet in Rwanda, even more so than in other developing countries, offered a gateway to and from the world. The Internet helped Rwanda gain recognition as it emerged from the dark events of 1994. The Internet offered a chance to overcome the evils and poverty of the past through education and general access to information.

2. *Diverse contributions of the diaspora.* The Internet came to Rwanda
    at a time when many people were entering and leaving the country, a
    time of great influx and outflow. After the genocide ended and the
    Rwandan Patriotic Front had restored order, Rwandans began rebuild-
    ing their country. Many members of the Rwandan diaspora, who had
    been living in Europe and North America for decades, returned. These
    returnees had great skills and knowledge in many areas, including
    technology, which they put to good use in developing the postgeno-
    cide Rwandan society.

Examining the future of the Internet in Rwanda, two issues must still be
addressed. First, the role of the Rwandan government's 2020 Vision policy
document must be defined. The document contains a number of initiatives to
transform the country from an agricultural economy to a service economy. It
describes four five-year plans built on the following pillars: human resource
development, use of ICTs in education, facilitating government administration
and service delivery, developing and facilitating the private sector, deployment
and spread of ICTs in the community, ICT infrastructure development, legal
and regulatory provisions and standards, and foreign direct investment in
ICTs. For the 2020 Vision to succeed, both the Rwandan government and international aid organizations will need to maintain a clear commitment to Internet diffusion and efficient utilization at a lower cost. Only such a commitment can guarantee that benefits will accrue to the masses and that the country
will move toward a sustainable and profitable information society.

The second issue that must be addressed is the need to increase human capacity within the regulatory body and among policy circles so that they can better formulate Internet policies. Policies need to reflect both short-term and
long-term goals of ICT diffusion in general and Internet diffusion in particular.

Finally, it should be noted that major projects are under way in Rwanda
to ensure greater access to the Internet and to promote use of the Internet for
socioeconomic development. In terms of access, three major initiatives exist:
a fiber optic network to link government institutions; a fiber optic link from
Kigali to Butare, the latter being the home of the NUR; and a new private company that will assemble computers. In the area of Internet applications, three
projects are supported by the Rwandan government: a national Web portal
maintained at the NUR by the Rwandan Development Gateway (a comprehensive ICT project for development run by KIST and the NUR); national geographic information center supported by the Regional Center for Geographic
Information Systems and Remote Sensing at the NUR; and a regional ICT
training center at KIST.

These projects highlight the government's support for ICTs as a tool of
development and its recognition of the role of ICTs in reconstructing postgenocide Rwanda. If the government continues to support ICTs, and if Inter-

net champions continue to push for access and development applications, the Internet will thrive in Rwanda. The hope is that new technologies will help the country advance both economically and socially. In this way, the background conditions that led to the genocide can be overcome and a new Rwanda can emerge as a regional, continental, and even global leader.

6

South Africa:
The Internet Wars

Charley Lewis

IT WAS AN ELEVEN-PAGE fax, unsigned, with a Telkom South Africa cover sheet, addressed to the Internet Service Providers Association (ISPA). And it confirmed the ISPA's suspicions. Things were coming to a head.

Only a few days previously, on 11 June 1996, Telkom South Africa, the country's giant, state-owned telecommunications monopoly, on whose networks the Internet and e-mail traffic of the entire client base of the Internet service providers (ISPs) depended, had finally entered the fray. The months of informal pilot testing, which the various private sector ISPs had anxiously been monitoring, had ended. A major new ISP for them to contend with had officially been launched. The South African Internet Exchange (SAIX) was now out there, in the market pioneered by the private sector ISPs.

Since Telkom's precommercial testing had begun on 1 October of the previous year, it and the other ISPs had talked of little else. An ISP operated by the incumbent could mean no-holds-barred competition for clients (particularly the profitable corporates, whose leased lines were rented from Telkom, making the telephone monopoly privy to their entire client database), including cross-subsidies and predatory pricing. Already, many of them knew of informal approaches to their own clients—and the carrot of cheaper prices.

Five ISP representatives had met to discuss the growing threat—Dave Frankel of Internet Solution, Jon Oliver of Global Internet Access, Mark Todes of Internet Africa, Steve Corkin of Sprint, and Internet activist Anthony Brooks. With the support of other ISPs, they had planned the formation of an ISP association (ISPA). The formal entry of Telkom South Africa into the ISP market was the final push needed to make ISPA happen. Their own public announcement of the launching of ISPA on 10 June 1996 had been deliberately timed to precede that of SAIX, throwing down the gauntlet. Individually, the private sector ISPs were vulnerable to retaliation. Together, in an industry association, they might prevail.

And now? For ISPA to receive a fax from the opposition was one thing. But its contents were even more startling. Someone at Telkom South Africa was clearly on its side. There, in eleven detailed pages, was the entire strategic plan for Telkom's entry into the dial-up market. And it clearly indicated that SAIX was the thin end of the wedge, that Telkom had long planned within months to launch its own dial-up ISP. This contradicted the declaration by SAIX chief executive officer Rikus Matthyser at the launch event, who promised no further inroads into the market of the private sector ISPs: "SAIX will not compete directly with its ISP customers."[1] It was time to move to the next step. Perhaps the occasion was now ripe for the formal complaint the private sector ISPs had discussed lodging with the Competition Board.

That fax and those watershed days in June 1996 were to scar the ISP landscape for years to come. The predicted "Internet wars" were about to begin.[2]

The South African Context

Despite its status as the most industrialized country on the African continent, South Africa in 1990 seemed an unlikely starting point for Africa's entry into the information age. By the end of the 1980s, just as the ferment in global computing that preceded the development of the Internet began, South Africa was a country gripped by crisis. Decades of racial oppression at the hands of a white apartheid oligarchy had led to diplomatic isolation and the imposition of economic sanctions and cultural and scientific boycotts. Domestically, popular opposition had risen to unprecedented levels, with an ongoing wave of mass protests against the backdrop of a growing armed insurgency led by the African National Congress (ANC). The economy was approaching terminal decline.

South Africa of the 1990s experienced a sequence of changes so dramatic and dazzling as to be beyond the most fanciful prediction. The growth and diffusion of the Internet in South Africa took place in a most unlikely context, amid the release of Nelson Mandela from prison after twenty-seven years, a tense and bitterly negotiated democratic transition to democracy, the triumphant fanfare of the country's first universal franchise election, and then the sobering and sometimes disillusioning work of forging a "better life for all"[3] as the ANC sought to translate its overwhelming electoral mandate into practical delivery of social development and economic growth.

In 1990, telecommunications in South Africa were governed by the 1958 Post Office Act, under which the state-owned company Telkom functioned as a telephony infrastructure and services monopoly. It was illegal to connect private equipment to the network, and third-party traffic was prohibited. All regulation fell under the Department of Posts and Telecommunications, which was responsible for telecommunications policy as well as the management of South African Posts and Telecommunications, also a monopoly. E-mail was new, its use restricted to a few thousand enthusiasts who embraced its revolutionary potential. The entire country boasted less than 5,000 users of bulletin board services, e-mail, FidoNet, and UseNet.[4] The wide webbed world of the Internet was an as-yet-undreamed-of future.

By 2004, dramatic changes had occurred. An independent, converged regulator, the Independent Communications Authority of South Africa,[5] now oversees the sector, ensuring a substantial separation of powers between policy and regulatory functions. Significant restructuring has transformed the telecommunications sector. Telecommunications and postal services have been separated and corporatized, and limited liberalization and partial privatization have been implemented. New mobile telephony services have surpassed the wildest projections,[6] with a roll-out well over double that of the 4.8 million (and shrinking) fixed-line user base.[7] The Internet and e-mail services market has become highly competitive, with some 270 companies ranging from backyard, shoestring operations to several commercial giants dominant in the sector. These companies provide a growing range of services to an estimated 3.25 million users and manage over 10,000 corporate leased lines.[8] Although no reliable estimates exist, South Africa also boasts large numbers of cybercafes, telecenters, multipurpose community centers, and school network sites.[9] The new democratic government makes extensive use of the Internet, and almost every government department, agency, and institution has its own website. A wide range of information communication technology (ICT) projects are active, including the Gauteng Online initiative in South Africa's second most populous province. Gauteng Online aims to provide computers to all state schools and e-mail addresses to their scholars. The Internet has also become a lifeblood of commerce and industry, with e-mail and e-commerce burgeoning. Dedicated legislation has been enacted to cover electronic transactions, online communications, and Internet security.

The Internet in South Africa presents a number of interesting paradoxes. Despite the relative international isolation incurred as a result of its racially oppressive apartheid policies, in the mid-1990s South Africa was nevertheless ranked far higher in Internet usage than most countries at comparable levels of development, such as Brazil or Mexico.[10] This is perhaps unexpected, given that South Africa was a society torn by fundamental social conflicts and undergoing a profound political and social transformation from a repressive racist regime to an open democracy. Nevertheless, during those years South Africa experienced its strongest and most robust diffusion of the Internet. While this paradox is not the subject of this chapter, it may serve to illustrate both the interest and challenge of South Africa as a case study in the dynamics of Internet diffusion.[11]

Critical Negotiation Issues

The history of Internet diffusion in South Africa is replete with conflicts and studded with clashes between powerful actors representing strong interest groups. In this process, there were moments when conflicts were settled, sometimes through negotiation, sometimes through force, before the development of the sector proceeded at a more measured pace. The story of that diffusion, of its clashes, and of the characters that people its events, is the subject of this chapter.

The following narrative is derived from the voices of its key actors as told through a series of interviews.[12] Although a process of interviews is subject to the limitations discussed in earlier chapters, it provides a richly textured vehicle to analyze events from the living perspective of the interests and objectives of its participants. In the case of South Africa, circumstances have limited the voices heard to selected participants. It proved far easier to secure interviews with private sector Internet service providers than with government providers. Only one representative from the incumbent telecommunications provider (and ISP), Telkom, which had been a key role player throughout, consented to be interviewed.[13] Despite considerable efforts to secure interviews with appropriate Telkom staff, because of the company's policies requiring clearance for "official" viewpoints, I encountered extreme reluctance of staff to talk on the record.[14] As a result, the story told here is, unfortunately, limited by the absence of a strong perspective provided by either the government or Telkom.[15]

Nevertheless, the story of the Internet in South Africa is unavoidably told under the long shadow of Telkom, the giant incumbent fixed-line operator whose monopoly over the provision of infrastructure for the Internet continues to provoke both conflict and calm. Telkom is at the same time both the monopoly provider of telecommunications infrastructure, the backbone upon which e-mail messaging and Internet traffic depend, and latterly an Internet service provider in its own right, competing against the very companies whose connectivity it provides. The ironies and paradoxes of this dynamic have shaped many of the conflicts in the Internet sector over the years.

Conflict is about power, but it is also about negotiation. The pages that follow describe a diffusion of the Internet that is at times evolutionary, at others fueled by conflict, but ultimately decided by negotiation. Those developments, conflicts, and negotiations have given impetus to the evolution of the Internet in South Africa. Sometimes they have held back the spread of the Internet, sometimes they have hurried it forward.

This chapter examines the interaction of the Internet actors, the conflicts and clashes of their differing sets of interests, and the outcomes of their disputes. It is a story in which a number of critical negotiation issues (CNIs) loom large. As described in earlier chapters, these are issues that are relevant to the diffusion of the Internet and over which opposing interest groups struggle. If left unresolved, these questions will impede the diffusion and development of the Internet in South Africa.

Most of the substantive issues center on fundamental building blocks of Internet diffusion. Many were resolved relatively amicably, allowing Internet development to continue. Others became the object of active struggle between the parties to such an extent that a delay in their resolution impeded further development of the Internet.

Based on a careful review of interviews conducted with leading actors, four CNIs stand out as having played a central role in South Africa since 1990:

1. *Anti-competitive behavior.* This was initially manifested through clashes between startup companies in the sector over market share, but subsequently appearing in disputes between Telkom's ISPs and those in the private sector over market dominance and ultimately commercial survival itself.

2. *Access to facilities.* Private sector ISPs sought to secure connectivity from the monopoly provider of infrastructure, Telkom, which in turn either delayed or refused to supply access, initially and largely through bureaucratic inertia and ignorance of what the Internet was, but later as a weapon in the anticompetitive behavior described above.

3. *Telecommunications liberalization, privatization, and regulation.* This caused intense debate over the shape, structure, and dynamics of the telecommunications market, questions that became mixed with the extensive policy reform that was embarked on in the years following the democratization of South Africa.

4. *E-commerce policy.* This, to a degree, is a special instance of the third issue, but one with direct and immediate implications for the development of the Internet.

There were indeed other critical negotiation issues, but these four were the most prominent.

Pricing, for example, has remained a key constraint on the development of the sector, and is frequently cited in interviews as a major ongoing brake on further Internet development. Mike Lawrie, founder of the national university network, describes access costs as "horrendous,"[16] while AT&T chief executive officer Peter Davies decries "the most expensive international bandwidth prices in the world," which he says "mitigates against ICT development."[17]

Similarly, the establishment in 1996 of, first, a local peering point and, subsequently, Internet exchanges in two of the country's major centers, dramatically affected both the speed and the cost of local access between ISPs. According to Mike Lawrie, it played a "significant role" in promoting "exponential growth" in local traffic volumes.[18] These sentiments are echoed by ISP chief executive officer Rob Fisher: "JINX had (and continues to have) a *huge* impact for my business!"[19]

Figure 6.1 summarizes the key critical negotiation issues that appear in the various country case studies and marks their period of relevance within the South African example.

The diffusion of the Internet in South Africa can be divided roughly into three broad historical phases. The first phase ran from before 1990 until about 1993, and was characterized by a loose community of individual Internet pioneers operating with enthusiasm and in cavalier disregard of the commercial possibilities of the new medium.

The end of this early phase was marked by the launch of the first commercial ISPs in late 1993. The second period, which lasted until 1996, saw early pioneers seizing on the commercial possibilities of the Internet. They did so by launching commercial ISPs that developed into fully fledged business entities with a full range of services based on evolving, workable business models.

The third phase of Internet development began in 1996. It was characterized by the implementation of telecommunications reform and the dramatic, and conflict-ridden, entry of the incumbent telecommunications operator into the ISP market.

Figure 6.1   CNI Framework and Timeline, South Africa, 1990–2003

	1990	1991	1992	1993	1994	1995	1996	1997	1998	1999	2000	2001	2002	2003
Telecom liberalization				■■■➤								■■➤		
ISP liberalization														
Telecom privatization					———➤									
ISP privatization														
Regulation				———➤								———➤		
Anticompetitive behavior							■■■■■■■■■■■➤							
Access to facilities	■■■■■■■■■■■■■■■■■■■■■■■■■■■■■■■■➤													
Monopoly pricing	————————————————————————————➤													
IXP							➤							
VOIP													———➤	
Universal access							————————————————➤							
E-commerce											■■■■■■➤			

Note: Thickest arrows are the most prominent CNIs.

The Early Years

The development of the Internet in South Africa began some years before the acrimonious "Internet wars" arose. In the early days, the pioneers of the Internet were a handful of bespectacled academics and barefoot enthusiasts for whom new technologies and tools were both a revelation and a passion. They connected to the Internet by dialing long-distance over static-ridden lines to their counterparts in the United States, using makeshift equipment belonging to South African universities. They were united by strong bonds of enthusiasm, sharing ideas, swapping software, and exchanging e-mail traffic.

The early years of the Internet in South Africa were characterized by a diverse ferment of activities undertaken by a loose community of enthusiasts who might perhaps be described as "Internet geeks." Internet pioneers like Lucio de Re, Mike Jensen, founders of the national university network Mike Lawrie and Francois Guillarmod, FidoNet coordinator Henk Wolsink, ISP founders Paul Nash, Alan Barrett, and Anthony Gerada, and of course Randy Bush, who played a central role from Oregon in the United States, all knew each other, either personally or virtually.

Much of the early Internet activity was centered around universities, many of which ran small, internal computer networks. Several academics had been exposed to the possibilities of bulletin boards and crude e-mail messages that were developing abroad.[20] Most enthusiasts were drawn in by the excitement of new and growing technologies and by the possibilities that these technologies were creating. Now looking like a slightly graying hippie with a ponytail, Lucio de Re still speaks animatedly of the "revelation of being able to exchange e-mail." He describes it as a "culture shock that is difficult to remember now." There was a real sense of community, a willingness to share, exchange, and assist, with "individuals being willing to put something back" on a basis of "dial me and I'll carry your data."[21] Many of the early pioneers remain active, some still as technological enthusiasts, others as chief executive officers.

In those early days, among that small band of enthusiasts, negotiation was unnecessary. Events, interests, and conflicts were among kindred spirits, and the reality of the high stakes that would define future negotiations was absent. As is frequently the case with pioneering efforts, things were different, and it was only later that people operated within a precommercial paradigm. "In the early days, it worked like this," says Mike Lawrie. "Randy Bush did me a favor. He accepted no money. I repaid the favor to someone else in Zimbabwe. The point was to keep the favor alive forever."[22]

But within a few years, by 1992, matters were already moving toward commercialization. The first such impulse came from Anthony Gerada's Digitec Online, which was established in June 1990 as a free bulletin board service to improve after-sales services to customers of his small distributorship of portable computers. By January 1992, claims Gerada, Digitec Online was the busiest such service outside the United States, with some 10,000 users.[23] Gerada constructed a special facility at his suburban home to cope with demand. He had twenty incoming phone lines and thirty more on order. To cover costs, Digitec Online introduced the first bulletin board access charge in South Africa at the princely rate of just over US$15 per annum.[24] Later in 1992, Lucio de Re, another enthusiast who had begun providing e-mail and bulletin board services, also began charging to cover the rising costs of servicing his growing numbers of users. De Re established pix.za (derived from Proxima information exchange) as the first commercial offering to the public of bulletin board and e-mail services.[25] At about the same time, in June 1992, the Council for Scientific and Industrial Research (CSIR) launched CompuServe Africa, which provided similar services, although at prices most customers considered prohibitive.[26]

The era of the e-mail junkie, soldering iron in one hand, keyboard in the other, was coming to an end. Although the Internet would never quite lose its sense of community and cavalier freedom, it was about to become a space where costs had to be recovered and where there was money to be made. And this trend would inevitably bring the Internet to the attention of policymakers and the incumbent operator. It would also, therefore, bring to the surface the kinds of issues and forms of negotiation relevant to this analysis.

The true commercialization of the Internet began with the establishment of The Internetworking Company of South Africa (TICSA) in late 1993. TICSA's founders were a group of young men who had gained experience working in the university network, UniNet. This group included former students Paul Nash and Chris Pinkham and former electrical engineering lecturer Alan Barrett.[27]

The idea of establishing a commercial Internet service provider had been brewing for some time. Toward the middle of 1993, Paul Nash and Lucio de Re, still wary of having e-mail fall foul of the legal prohibition on third-party telecommunications traffic, approached the state-owned monopoly, Telkom. They proposed establishing an ISP based on Telkom's infrastructure.[28] Telkom rejected the idea as "too undisciplined."[29] In other words, it was too far outside Telkom's ken to grasp. Thus Telkom lost its chance to become South Africa's monopoly incumbent ISP. "Telkom failed utterly to understand what the Internet could do for their business."[30] In fairness, though, it must be noted that a corporation the size of Telkom is structurally unsuited to early innovation, because it lacks the "potential for agility."[31]

Nash and de Re made a second attempt to forge an ISP partnership. This time they approached the Council for Scientific and Industrial Research. At a meeting attended by Peter Davies (then of OmniLink) and their CSIR partners, Nash and de Re made a second pitch to sell their vision of an ISP, this time using a more persuasive rhetoric of "bridges and funnels."[32] This attempt too was destined to founder, principally because of harsh partnership terms demanded by OmniLink[33] and probably because the CSIR was already marketing CompuServe Africa, which was allegedly "hemorrhaging money."[34] In the words of Lucio de Re: "The corporates just could not see the Internet coming."[35]

Stymied for the second time, Randy Bush advised Nash and de Re to "stop being enamored of the suits,"[36] to ignore Telkom, and to go ahead on their own and establish an ISP. By this time, Chris Pinkham, who had returned from spending a year working for Randy Bush in Oregon, and Alan Barrett, whose knowledge of Internet protocol was world-class, had joined them.[37] Thus, on 1 November 1993, TICSA was launched as South Africa's first fully fledged commercial ISP with a "voluntary, not-for-profit philosophy."[38] The vision of these Internet pioneers based in Cape Town was founded on an international gateway (via a line leased from Telkom) to the Internet with a connection speed of 64 kilobits per second (kbps). But TICSA and UniNet were not directly connected, and traffic between the two transited the United States. TICSA's initial customers included Vector Network Computers, Hewlett-Packard, Olivetti, The Internet Solution (TIS), and Proxima Internet Exchange (PIX).[39] In effect, TICSA was an Internet access provider (IAP), since it focused on providing access to corporate customers and other ISPs.[40]

By the end of November 1993, TICSA was supplying Internet connectivity to ten companies,[41] just short of its break-even target of sixteen.[42] In one fell swoop, the Internet in South Africa had come of age and become a competitive domain. Soon, however, bitter competitive rivalries would break out.

CNI 1: Anticompetitive Behavior

There has been some speculation about why Telkom allowed the ISPs to grow unimpeded during this period. Alan Levin, a founding senior executive of Intekom,[43] suggests that Telkom judged that its bottom line would benefit from Internet growth: "Telkom saw itself as a data carrier" and hence saw the ISPs as a "new revenue stream that at first appeared very unthreatening."[44] Others disagree, suggesting that Telkom failed to grasp the potential of the new platform and "didn't really understand . . . the potential impact of the Internet on their revenue."[45] Others have suggested that Telkom's decision was related to the impending transition to democracy. In the words of Soren Aalto, "What seemed to happen at that point was the message that with the '94 election and change of political regime coming up fast, Telkom folk had more pressing things to worry about than 3rd party traffic rules."[46]

Whatever was behind Telkom's lack of attention to the Internet, it allowed independent ISPs to emerge, albeit squabbling among themselves over market share. These disputes, although sharp and acrimonious, were small in scale. It was only later that the disputes encompassed the nature and structure of the entire market, taking on the David versus Goliath dimensions of a life-or-death struggle between the massive commercial weight and political power of the incumbent telecommunications monopoly and the emergent ISP entrepreneurs.

As such, the anticompetitive behavior of Telkom was to become the overriding negotiation issue that defined the character of the commercialization of the Internet, one that continues to cast a long shadow over the sector. Due to the centrality of anticompetitive behavior, I examine this issue at greater length than the other three CNIs.

In March 1994, six months after its founding, the partnership around TICSA fractured and collapsed, with one of its original customers, TIS, breaking away to set itself up as a rival ISP in its own right. Relations between TIS and TICSA had been uneasy for some time, in part due to a divergence of approach between the founders of TICSA, still imbued with a pioneering Internet-protocol camaraderie, and the hard-nosed, business-oriented MBA approach that Dave Frankel had brought to TIS.[47] Behind the impending breakdown lay a recognition by some of its pioneers that the Internet provided a lucrative platform through which substantial money could be made by selling access and services to companies and individuals. Comradeship was abruptly replaced by intense competition to dominate the small but profitable (and growing) market.

Relations between TIS and TICSA deteriorated rapidly. There were allegations of aggressive poaching of TICSA customers using underhanded methods, including falsified documentation. A defamation case was even lodged by TICSA against TIS, which retaliated by withholding payment of its TICSA bills. Finally, on 1 March 1994, TICSA disconnected TIS for nonpayment. TIS was quickly forced to secure its own leased line to the Internet.[48]

In recognition of the fundamental shift from camaraderie to commerce and profit, Lucio de Re wryly observed that "the biggest change has been the ownership of the Internet. That is what money has brought in."[49]

TIS was not the only ISP to fall out with TICSA. A few months later, Anthony Gerada's Digitec Online became involved in a dispute with TICSA, partly over service quality, but mainly over the change from a flat fee to a volume-based billing system. This dispute resulted in Digitec Online being cut off by TICSA one Friday at four in the afternoon. TIS, now TICSA's bitter rival, was only too glad to offer alternative connectivity. After working frantically through the night, Digitec was back online via the TIS backbone by noon the following day.[50]

Behind the acrimony and the infighting was a conflict over customer base, market share, and competing business models. The emergent commercial ISPs, and TIS in particular, were engaged in a bitter struggle for domination with TICSA. The areas of contention may have seemed like small squabbles for scant rewards between startup ISP companies, but they were a foretaste of things to come. The recognition of the Internet's profit potential seemed to have transformed a community of like-minded enthusiasts into a battleground for market share. The main actors at this stage were fledgling individual private sector ISPs who sought to commercialize the Internet: principally TICSA and TIS.[51]

However, the incipient Internet industry was soon shaken in an even more dramatic fashion by events that led to antagonisms and alliances that persist to this day. Starting on 1 October 1995, Telkom's precommercial testing of an ISP with nationwide Internet infrastructure, under the name of the South African Internet Exchange, was the first sign of a storm that would make earlier conflicts pale in comparison.[52] After years of ignoring the potential of the Internet, the incumbent was about to enter the fray.[53]

Telkom's entry into the ISP market was a break from its earlier failure to grasp the significance of the Internet. The company had over the years issued threats against activities that it perceived as undermining its exclusive revenue stream. Such activities included bulletin boards, which were viewed as competition to Telkom's own BelTel service.[54] But Telkom had hitherto failed to see the Internet itself as a potential source of business. Anthony Gerada, for example, describes Telkom as being "caught totally unawares by the whole Internet thing" and quotes its technical director as asking, "What is this Internet?"[55] Mike Lawrie ascribes Telkom's turnaround to the fact that Telkom had finally done "their sums" and recognized the "revenue stream from the universities" as easy pickings.[56] In Telkom's defense, former senior executive Alan Levin points out that "very few really understood the potential of the market." He also suggests that the belatedness of Telkom's entry was due to "the time . . . it takes . . . to establish strategic intent . . . in a very big corporation . . . exacerbated by the significant changes in management and shareholding that [it] were going through at the time."[57]

The ISPs had been aware of Telkom's precommercial testing since October 1995 and were quick to condemn the imminent establishment of SAIX as "unfair competition by the company that has the monopoly on bandwidth."[58] The ISPs recognized both the potential of Telkom to cross-subsidize its own ISP operations, thereby undercutting their pricing structure, and the potential for conflict of interest and even breach of confidentiality created by Telkom's access to their customer base. Telkom's Hendrik Bezuidenhout was quick to deny cross-subsidies, saying, "I'm not going to start a price war."[59]

The fears of the major ISPs were fully realized on 11 June 1996 with the public launch of SAIX. The new entity positioned itself as a provider of access and bandwidth to second-tier ISPs and to the lucrative corporate market. SAIX's tariffs undercut prices offered by other ISPs, and it enjoyed the added advantage of being able immediately to provide twenty local-access points of presence (POPs) throughout South Africa.

There have been suggestions that Telkom's pricing was based on a calculation error, but it is more likely that it was merely predatory.[60] Whatever the case, the pricing cut to the heart of the commercial viability of the existing ISPs,[61] and opened a bitter contest for survival that was manifested in the lengths to which the parties were prepared to go. A few days after the launch of SAIX, the first in a series of confidential "Telkom internal strategy documents that were leaked . . . by a secret ally" was faxed to the ISPs, revealing Telkom's plans to compete directly within the dial-up ISP market.[62] Further, allegations began to surface that Telkom's leased-line installation teams were actively trying to poach customers for SAIX.[63]

An Alliance of ISPs

Contestation breeds coalitions and alliances, and this critical negotiation issue was no exception. Although the advent of SAIX was the catalyst, a series of meetings of ISP chief executive officers to discuss common issues "including the future of the .za domain name, peering issues and influencing government policy" had already taken place.[64] These meetings were organized by Anthony Brooks using some degree of false pretense; they were convened under the banner of the African Internet Development Action Team (AIDAT) to prepare the ground for the establishment of an ISP association.[65] In the days preceding the formal public launch of SAIX, a series of meetings and phone calls initiated by Brooks secured the formal support of the ISP community for the launch of an umbrella body, the Internet Service Providers Association.[66] ISPA's own inaugural press statement of 10 June 1996 was carefully timed to steal Telkom's thunder by preceding the launch of SAIX by a single day.[67] Within a few days, on 15 June 1996, the ISPs retaliated further by announcing their intention to take Telkom to the Competition Board.[68] The gauntlet had been thrown down.[69]

The launch of SAIX persuaded the ISPs to move beyond their petty litigations and squabbles over market share, as the AIDAT meetings had already suggested they were capable of doing, in order to unite in the face of a common and powerful enemy. A further incentive behind the founding of ISPA was the creation of a platform from which litigation against Telkom could be launched without putting individual ISPs at risk of victimization or bankruptcy because of court costs.[70] But the effect of establishing ISPA went beyond combining for a fight against the incumbent. The meeting in which it was agreed to establish ISPA also addressed other common issues. An agreement "in principle" to establish a full, permanent peering point was made. This peering point itself had a key impact on the diffusion of the Internet by facilitating and promoting local traffic.[71]

The other association affected by the dispute between Telkom and the ISPs was the South African Value-Added Networks Association (SAVA),[72] a major user of leased lines. However, because SAVA operated in a different market segment and had at the time a "sensible and growing relationship" with Telkom "characterized by occasional skirmishes rather than outright warfare," it elected to stay out of the conflict in the early years.[73]

The other players engaged in the conflict were the bodies asked to adjudicate the dispute. After the early threats of litigation, ISPA formally lodged a complaint with the Competition Board, alleging anticompetitive practices by Telkom and SAIX. Thus the Competition Board was charged with resolving the dispute. In October 1996 the board reached an interim agreement in which Telkom pledged to "supply details of its business model to the Board as well as set up a neutral service desk to handle all digital line applications."[74]

Telkom Counterattacks

The victory for the ISPs was short-lived. In November 1996, Telkom launched a subsidiary, Intekom, specifically targeting the dial-up market. This confirmed the plan contained in the Telkom memos leaked to ISPA, and belied Telkom's public undertaking not to compete in this market.[75] Paradoxically, the launch of Intekom created a new ally for ISPA in the form of the number of "virtual" ISPs[76] that had sprung up on SAIX's backbone and bandwidth, initially to take over the 6,000 users who had signed up during SAIX's test phase.[77] They banded together into the SAIX ISP Action Group (SIAG), "claiming Intekom [had] an unfair advantage over them."[78]

Building on its earlier agreement with Telkom and still attempting to bring the contending parties together, in January 1997 the Competition Board initiated a process to define an agreed framework as a modus vivendi for the future of the Internet industry.[79] This draft agreement was called the "Internet Blue Paper."[80] Before long, however, the process was derailed. Having taken a full six months to start its digital line service desk, Telkom angered the Competition Board[81] by reneging on its undertaking of the previous year to provide "audit information" on the cost structures of SAIX.[82]

Shortly thereafter, Telkom rejected the jurisdiction of the Competition Board over the dispute with ISPA, and demanded that the matter be referred to the newly established telecommunications regulator, the South African Telecommunications Regulatory Authority (SATRA).[83] At this time, SATRA had barely acquired premises and staff, and was thus ill equipped to deal with such a major dispute. It is unclear why ISPA acquiesced to referring the matter to SATRA, save for the fact that the Competition Board process had proved ineffectual, and ISPA was hopeful that the new regulator, under whose jurisdiction the dispute seemed logically to fall, would be more effective.[84]

Once the ISPs had been persuaded to transfer jurisdiction to SATRA, Telkom immediately laid a countercomplaint, described by Anthony Brooks as a "clever chess move."[85] Telkom charged that the commercial ISPs contravened its monopoly and claimed that Internet-protocol services were within the sphere of its guaranteed telecommunications exclusivity under the terms of the 1996 Act.[86] Telkom asked SATRA to amend its license accordingly.

Short of skills and experience in this area, SATRA first handed down an interim ruling on 11 June 1997 (the anniversary of the launch of SAIX) that said: "Telkom could not claim exclusive right to Internet service provision."[87] SATRA then established an advisory commission, chaired by Anthony Brooks, to determine whether or not the Internet fell within Telkom's exclusivity. Based on the recommendations of its commission, on 14 October 1997, SATRA announced at a press conference that the provision of Internet services was open to competition and did not fall within the sphere of Telkom's exclusivity.

In the face of jubilation among private sector ISPs at the ruling, Telkom filed a legal challenge against SATRA's judgment, alleging that it had no legal basis and was marred by procedural irregularities. In a belligerent letter to *Business Day,* chief executive officer Mac Geschwind defended Telkom's right to the terms of its license and rejected interference by regulators or anyone else.[88] In December 1997 the Pretoria High Court upheld Telkom's challenge, finding a number of procedural violations in SATRA's process.

By this stage the bitterness and antagonism of a year and a half of legal wrangling had worn the contending parties down, and the matter remained in abeyance, with Telkom declining to proceed. In the words of one commentator, the "commercial stakes had become too high for either side to risk losing."[89] Telkom's complaint against the ISPs was never resolved.

A modus vivendi of sorts between Telkom and the ISPs has thus emerged. Both sides continue to compete in the ISP market, albeit in a manner characterized by mutual sniping and ongoing hostility. In January 1998, ISPA dropped its bar against membership by Telkom and Intekom, potentially opening the way to the inclusion of SAIX and Intekom within its peering arrangements.[90] However, antagonisms persisted, and neither SAIX nor Intekom, nor their successors, ever joined ISPA or connected to either of the Internet exchanges.

A year and a half later, in July 1999, Telkom began to turn its attention elsewhere: to the suppliers of value-added network services. A new chief executive officer, Tom Barry, sent the SAVA association an "infamous six-point letter" and initiated a series of attacks on, and attempts to close down, operators of value-added networks (VANs).[91] It was now the turn of the ISPs to "keep down in their foxhole and wait for the shelling to stop." They did this despite warnings from the SAVA about Telkom's "divide and conquer strategy."[92]

By 2002, matters had come full circle. Spurred in part by increasing overlap and convergence between VANs and ISPs, but also angered by Telkom's continuing behavior in the market, on 7 May,[93] ISPA and SAVA filed a joint complaint against Telkom with the Competition Commission.[94] The more substantial powers of this body, together with its jurisdictional agreement with the regulator,[95] may have offered the complainants greater prospects for success. The ISPA-SAVA complaint alleged anticompetitive practices, including refusal to peer with certain VAN providers, illegal cross-subsidization, and discriminatory pricing, and called on the commission to enforce accounting separation.[96]

In February 2004 the Competition Commission found that Telkom's conduct against the VAN operators had "abused its dominant position by engaging in a pattern of anti-competitive practices . . . to the detriment of the development and growth of the ICT sector."[97] The commission accordingly referred the matter to its enforcement arm, the Competition Tribunal, for a determination. According to the technology news site ITWeb, the commission further recommended the imposition of the maximum fine, US$500 million.[98]

Naturally the Competition Tribunal's ruling did not end matters. In May 2004, Telkom filed a High Court application to have the finding of the Competition Commission set aside on grounds that bizarrely echoed its initial dispute with ISPA: that the Competition Commission acted outside its powers in adjudicating a matter properly the province of the sector regulator, ICASA. Telkom argued that the memorandum of understanding between ICASA and the Competition Commission governing their concurrent jurisdiction in the sector was "unconstitutional,"[99] and alleged procedural irregularities on the part of the commission. This is a dispute whose bitter and litigious days are clearly far from over.

Greedy to Rule the Market

The struggle for market dominance of the lucrative Internet sector seems to have underpinned much of the negotiation, maneuvering, and tactical stratagems chronicled above. Paul Nash sums up matters: "You might just see a pattern emerging here—greed was a big factor in breaking a number of promising start-up activities, and slowing growth. Telkom was another."[100] Somewhat similar sentiments were voiced by an anonymous Telkom source who suggested that by entering the ISP market, Telkom's "retail greed [had] choked its wholesale business."[101]

The market-domination motive is also evinced by the suggestion that Telkom's entry into the ISP sector was a response, at least in part, to a perceived threat. Dimension Data, a major supplier of infrastructure equipment to Telkom, acquired TIS, one of the two major private sector ISPs. According to Alan Levin, one of Telkom's "strategic goals" was for Intekom to offer a stake in itself to a suitable information technology (IT) company with no Internet foothold, but that "the deal was vetoed [in 1997] by the Minister at the time, Jay Naidoo."[102]

What initially set the emerging private sector ISPs against each other was their divergent business models and conflicts over vital market shares within a small (albeit burgeoning) sector. Market shares could mean the difference between success and bankruptcy. Later, defense of hard-won viability against inroads from the incumbent became a priority. Defense had to be mounted against predatory pricing and customer gouging.[103] It became a fight for the very right to exist.

This series of disputes, and principally those between the incumbent operator and the ISPs, have left a legacy of mutual antagonism, mistrust, and bitterness that still colors relations in the sector. It is difficult to find anyone affiliated with a private sector ISP who has anything good to say about Telkom. Telkom itself tends to veer between defensiveness over its behavior and arrogance brought on by its size and domination of the telecommunications market.

Contradictory views exist about the impact of the disputes on Internet diffusion. Some have argued that Telkom's "regulatory intransigence is a key factor in the slowdown of growth in the industry."[104] Others have noted that the launch of SAIX and Intekom, and the consequent proliferation of "virtual" ISPs together with ready access to local POPs, was central to the rapid spread of the Internet outside the main metropolitan areas.[105] More indirectly, the launch of SAIX was a key catalyst in bringing the ISPs together under ISPA, which strengthened and unified the industry. ISPA precipitated the establishment of Internet exchanges in Johannesburg and Cape Town, with the consequent boom in local website development facilitated by quick access times.[106]

Looking further back, it can be argued that before the launch of SAIX, aggressive poaching of TICSA customers by TIS forced TICSA to take the Internet seriously—to treat it as a business rather than as a vocation. TICSA was forced to "either pack up or take TIS on—which was ultimately good for the industry, and led to aggressive network expansion."[107]

CNI 2: Access to Facilities

The internecine warfare between Internet players described above continues to characterize and shape the market. But another, related area of lower-grade conflict and protracted negotiation also spans the entire period. Also occurring was a struggle by physical ISPs, IAPs, and VAN operators to secure access to the infrastructure required to provide Internet services and content. The nature of those negotiations was determined by the market structure that governed the sector in 1990. This de facto monopoly on infrastructure still remains in place in 2006, despite substantial and ongoing changes in the policy framework. The structure is based on Telkom's continued retention of its monopoly on infrastructure provision, buttressed by the fact that resale and self-provisioning are illegal. This means that all providers of Internet and related services are required by law to purchase leased lines and other means of telecommunications access from Telkom[108]—which itself competes directly in the ISP, IAP, and VAN markets. This conflict of interest, together with the bureaucratic delays and inefficiencies common to many large corporations as well as Telkom's stubborn defense of its infrastructure exclusivity (and hence its revenue base), has created a secondary pattern of conflict between Telkom and ISPs.[109]

From the outset, the small group of enthusiasts experimenting with electronic communications ran into opposition, obfuscation, and delays from South African Posts and Telecommunications and subsequently from its successor, Telkom. Internet pioneers were frustrated in their attempts to secure access to the infrastructure and facilities they required. Requests for lines and physical connections were subject to bureaucratic delay and executive fiat. Major breakthroughs occurred when in 1987 IBM secured leased data lines to Holland,[110] and when in 1989 UniNet was granted permission to transmit data and e-mail messages because academics were considered a "common interest group" who could enjoy limited exemption from the ban on "third-party traffic."[111]

As noted above, a key issue of contention was the fact that the incumbent public switched telephone network operator, Telkom, enjoyed the exclusive right by law to supply all leased and dial-up telecommunication lines. The emergent providers of Internet services were therefore entirely dependent on a single company for all their connectivity. This made them acutely vulnerable to delays, disputes, and even arbitrary denial of service. The period after 1990 is thus characterized by ongoing complaints about the incumbent's foot-dragging over the provision of facilities, punctuated by active disputes and litigation.

The legally protected monopoly adopted a holier-than-thou attitude toward the emergent Internet sector. Telkom certainly saw no commercial reason to prioritize providing connectivity for a new set of services it neither understood nor appreciated. The approach of emergent ISPs and VAN operators toward Telkom oscillated between ingratiation and name-calling.

Throttling the Internet

The nature of the low-grade conflict between Telkom and Internet startups is perhaps best encapsulated by the dispute between the university network, UniNet, and Telkom. Having secured leased lines to other South African academic institutions in 1989, Rhodes University's 1991 application for an international leased line to connect with other networks in the United States was refused by Telkom. According to Telkom, the e-mail messages such a line would carry constituted prohibited "third-party traffic," for which there could be no "common interest group" exemption because there could be no such thing as an international "common interest group."[112]

Many early ISP entrepreneurs recall similar difficulties with securing the necessary infrastructure from Telkom. Anthony Gerada, for instance, describes persistent foot-dragging by Telkom in response to his request for an additional thirty phone lines to service the growing bulletin board business of Digitec Online. This incident led to a press outcry under the headline "Telkom Throttles the Internet."[113]

In part, the delays and poor service experienced by ISPs and VAN operators alike may be attributed to the bureaucratic mind-set and lack of customer responsiveness common to any monopoly. Dave Frankel of *The Internet Solution* described this phenomenon: "I spend half a million rand [US$80,000] with [Telkom] and don't get the service level that someone spending R 5,000 [US$800] a month gets from me."[114] In part the problem was also caused by deliberate attempts to obstruct potential competitors. But a gatekeeping, obstructionist mentality inherited from Telkom's role as an apartheid-era bureaucracy also played a part.[115] Mike Lawrie, for example, describes how "there didn't appear to be any channel to get Telkom to react. Rather than seeing how to meet customer requests within the regulations, it was a question of: how can we block this?"[116] Telkom's mentality may also have been a legacy of the apartheid "total onslaught":[117] as a bastion of employment for conservative Afrikaans-speaking whites, it had sought to preserve racial privilege in South Africa. Communications with the outside world by means of new technologies in the hands of "liberal" English-speaking academics were the object of suspicion. At the same time, in Telkom's defense, Lawrie also suggests that "investment fright" (caution about the high cost of investing in telecommunications infrastructure) may also have been a factor—"infrastructure is expensive to roll out. Telkom was worried about whether that investment would be recouped."[118]

Telkom vs. AT&T

Sometimes the conflict over access to facilities reached a boiling point. Mike Lawrie relates how, in late 1995, the management of UniNet, the university network, came within twenty-four hours of taking Telkom to the Supreme Court after a delay of more than a year in delivery of backbone circuits. Lawrie further describes a series of meetings held with three chief executive officers of Telkom that failed to secure better and more prompt access to facilities: "[UniNet] could get nothing special out of Telkom whatever."[119]

By July 1999 the relationship between Telkom and SAVA began to deteriorate following the appointment of Tom Barry of the Southern Bell Corporation (SBC)[120] as Telkom's chief operating officer. Telkom made a series of attempts to close down individual VAN operators for alleged license contraventions.[121] Perhaps the most protracted action against a VAN operator was Telkom's move against AT&T. On 1 September 1999 the formal postsanctions entry of AT&T into the VAN market in South Africa began. AT&T took over the VAN license originally awarded to IBM in 1994, in return for signing up IBM as its major customer.[122]

The entry of a major international telecommunications operator into the South African market, albeit in the shape of a VAN operator, seems to have set off alarm bells in Telkom. In the view of Peter Davies, chief executive officer of AT&T South Africa, Telkom perceived the "world's largest supplier of Internet services" as a substantial threat to its own share of both VAN and ISP markets.[123]

The following day, on 2 September 1999, Telkom sought to impose a list of five conditions on AT&T in exchange for the continued supply of services. Two weeks later, on 17 September 1999, Telkom stopped supplying leased lines to AT&T, which had refused the conditions. Following a protracted and intensive exchange of letters, in June 2000, Telkom finally agreed to limited, conditional supply of facilities. However, barely two months later Telkom reneged on the agreement. The dispute continued to escalate, soon moving to litigation. Three months later, in November 2000, Telkom filed a complaint with ICASA, alleging that AT&T's VAN operations contravened its monopoly. AT&T responded in March 2001 by filing a countercomplaint that Telkom's refusal to supply leased-line linkups between its customers was illegal and anticompetitive.[124]

When these disputes remained unresolved for nearly a year, there was an abrupt escalation. One afternoon in early 2002, SAIX disconnected its peering arrangement with AT&T, forcing all bilateral traffic between the two to travel via already congested international links. As a result, some third-tier ISPs, such as E Cape Net, switched from AT&T to other providers.[125]

In June 2002, ICASA finally ruled on the dispute, upholding AT&T's complaint that Telkom was illegally refusing to supply infrastructure. Telkom refused to comply with the ruling, however, forcing AT&T to file for a compliance order in July 2002.[126] An out-of-court settlement committed Telkom to supply fifteen requested services, including peering.[127] But the dispute did not end. With thirty minutes remaining before the deadline, Telkom filed a High Court motion to appeal the ICASA ruling.[128] The dispute was subsequently settled out of court several years later, in 2005.

Although the sharpest dispute over access to services was between Telkom and AT&T, it was a conflict that exemplifies claims by many VANs and ISPs that they continue to suffer at the hands of Telkom.[129] The dispute likely played a large part in the decision by SAVA to band together with ISPA and lodge a joint complaint before the Competition Commission alleging anticompetitive practices by Telkom. As described previously, this complaint alleged "discriminatory pricing, illegal bundling of services and cross-subsidization of competitive services."[130]

The consensus among both private sector ISPs and VAN operators is that Telkom South Africa denial, or delayed provision, of facilities over the years has had a considerable detrimental effect on the diffusion of the Internet in South Africa. Mike Lawrie, for example, has no doubt that South Africa "has been impeded."[131] Peter Davies describes Telkom as "100% motivated by intent to protect their monopoly at all costs," and points to the hampering of Internet development. Davies alleges that at least one prominent international firm has rejected South Africa as a low-cost ICT destination, principally because of the "unreliable environment" and increased risk of investment created by Telkom.[132]

CNI 3: Telecommunications Liberalization, Privatization, and Regulation

There is a debate about which milestone properly marks the maturing of the South African Internet market into its fully competitive phase. According to some accounts, the 1994 split between TICSA and TIS, despite occurring so shortly after the commercialization of the market, signifies the transition. Most analysts, however, view the 1996 ISP market entry of the giant state telephone monopoly, Telkom, as a key event signaling a new level of competition.

The year 1996 was a watershed period for the Internet sector in many respects, especially in the area of policy formulation. In July 1996 the restructuring of telecommunications policy drew to a close with the passing of the Telecommunications Act, which confirmed Telkom's exclusivity in public switched telephony and telecommunications facilities until 2002. The act also established a regulator for the telecommunications sector. Although the act, which was promulgated into law in November 1996, made no mention of the Internet, it did establish the legal and regulatory framework that continues to define the sector. The law's provisions dashed the hopes of many in the private sector for a rapid liberalization of telecommunications. Many felt betrayed by the process and were angry that their recommendations had been excised from the final legislation. Mistrust was created, which colored relations between the government and the private sector for years.

The unfolding drama of telecommunications reform in South Africa during the 1990s remains a negotiation issue of critical concern and importance to the diffusion of the Internet. This is true even though the Internet players themselves were relatively peripheral to the major telecommunications developments. The telecommunications infrastructure, of course, constitutes the foundation upon which e-mail and the Internet operate. The Internet is therefore deeply affected by the market structure of the telecommunications sector, through issues such as network roll-out, interconnection, bandwidth, pricing, access to facilities, and much more.[133]

In the mid-1990s, South Africa was only one of many countries in Africa grappling with telecommunications reform—market liberalization, partial privatization of the incumbent infrastructure monopoly, rate rebalancing (between local and international call charges), and the establishment of an independent regulatory regime. The country embarked on a process that illustrates how market forces must be balanced with social and political realities. Managing telecommunications change was a highly contentious process, largely because of the massive potential for foreign investment in, and the perceived profitability of, the sector. This is a common pattern in telecommunications reform in Africa and elsewhere. In the case of South Africa, however, an emphasis was placed on inclusive (and hence protracted) stakeholder consultation in conformity with South Africa's democratic transition. The discussion that follows, therefore, highlights both commonalities and differences between telecommunications reform in South Africa and other African countries.

The first step of telecommunications reform occurred in October 1991 with the Post Office Amendment Act, which initiated the separation of the Post Office from Telkom. Both were corporatized, and their regulatory functions were retained within the Department of Posts and Telecommunications.[134] Innocuous and elementary by current sector benchmarks, these initial reforms were based on a review of the sector initiated during the apartheid era under the former boss of Sanlam,[135] Wim de Villiers. The changes were fraught with the political tensions of the early years of apartheid reform and were subject to attack from both the right and the left of the political spectrum.[136] Nevertheless, the de Villiers review marked a key moment in shaping the direction of telecommunications over the next decade or more.

The National Telecommunications Forum (NTF) was launched two months later, in November 1993, as a stakeholder structure for the negotiation of telecommunications reform in an attempt to resolve political tensions around the issue.[137] Based on the stakeholder negotiations paradigm of the Convention for a Democratic South Africa (CODESA),[138] the NTF created strong expectations of an inclusive "win-win" outcome—hopes that were later to be disappointed. The forum initiated the first substantive negotiations to reform the telecommunications sector.

At stake in the NTF negotiations was nothing less than the future size and shape of the entire telecommunications sector in South Africa. Faced with external global pressures toward reform and deregulation, as well as with internal demands from the private sector for newer and more extensive services, the process promised a fundamental overhaul of the sector. The objectives, market structure, and regulatory and institutional framework of telecommunications were at stake.

At the heart of the debate was the question of whether—and, from the viewpoint of most stakeholders, to what extent—the sector should be opened to competition. Viewpoints varied widely, from those on the left (principally organized labor) who sought to retain a state-owned, service-delivery-oriented monopoly, to those in the private sector, who were hungry for investment opportunities and thereafter argued for a complete opening of the market. Debates raged around both privatization (either through the granting of an equity stake in the incumbent operator, or by listing shares on the stock exchange) and liberalization (the extent to which the telecommunications market, or sectors of it, would be opened to competition from additional entrants).

The very objectives of the telecommunications sector as a whole also came under intense scrutiny. Influenced by the momentum of democratic change, and by the social development priorities of the ANC's Reconstruction and Development Program (RDP), the balance between commercial imperatives and developmental priorities was debated. The institutional landscape was also the subject of debate and negotiation. The structure, design, and powers of the institutions required to oversee and manage the sector were contested, as was their degree of independence and subordination to governmental oversight and control. Together, these issues raised the stakes and made negotiations difficult, intense, and highly conflictual. The timing of the debate added to its intensity: a new democracy was being formed, and so the appetite for fundamental change was high. Furthermore, the new government mistrusted those who had served the ancien régime.

New Democracy, New Telecommunications Policy

The retreating apartheid regime had initiated the telecommunications reform process, but it was perceived by both the ANC and the trade unions to be engaged in "unilateral restructuring of state assets"[139] in order to undermine the ability of the new government to effect social transformation and the redistribution of wealth.

The first two telecommunications ministers of the new ANC government, Pallo Jordan and Jay Naidoo, and the ANC's sectoral policy think tank, the Center for the Development of Information and Telecommunications Policy (CDITP), headed by Andile Ngcaba (who was later to become director-general of the government department overseeing telecommunications), were key players in the reform process. Initially, ANC officials espoused the developmental priorities and public service delivery perspectives established by the ANC's Reconstruction and Development Program.[140] The ANC's position gradually evolved toward one of "managed liberalization" under strong ministerial control. Enormous and sometimes competing pressures were exerted from multilateral agencies like the World Bank and the International Telecommunications Union (ITU) in favor of wholehearted and immediate reform. Potential investors in the incumbent operator lobbied for a guaranteed monopoly or a period of "exclusivity."

Not unsurprisingly, the trade unions constituted a vehement voice against both privatization and liberalization of the telecommunications sector. Both types of reform had long been viewed with antagonism by the major union in the sector, the Post Office and Telecommunications Workers Association (POTWA) and its successor, the Communications Workers Union (CWU). The Congress of South African Trade Unions (COSATU), the labor federation giant, shared POTWA's perspective. On the one hand, the twin potential pillars of telecommunications reform were seen as inimical to core union interests: the creation and preservation of permanent, quality jobs at high levels of skills and remuneration. On the other hand, privatization and liberalization were antithetical to the socialist principles of the unions. Promarket reforms were seen by labor as undermining the extension of telecommunications services to historically disadvantaged communities by placing the imperatives of profit ahead of broad service delivery.

The private sector was also deeply engaged in the telecommunications negotiations. Almost unanimously in favor of liberalization, the exact positions of the various private sector players varied according to their perception of how liberalization and privatization best suited their particular commercial interests. Ultimately, the private sector was embittered by the slow timetable of managed liberalization embodied in the final policy outcome.

Positions, favored policy outcomes, and draft legislation changed considerably over the period of the negotiations. At the outset, the 1995 telecommunications policy green paper[141] posited a range of policy options, from the retention of Telkom's monopoly with minimal liberalization, to a rapid transition to full competition. The tensions described above suffused both the process and content of the green paper. Tensions continued through the National Colloquium on Telecommunications, held in November 1995. At one extreme were the trade unions, which were resisting reform at every step. At the other extreme was the private sector, baying for telecommunications reform with varying, commercially motivated degrees of fervor. ANC minister Pallo Jordan uneasily held the middle ground in the debate. The March 1996 telecommunications white paper reflected carefully crafted compromises. It set out a phased and managed liberalization over seven years under the oversight of an independent regulator. This negotiated accommodation enjoyed the support of most major stakeholders, and even the unions reluctantly acquiesced to a degree.

Furor over Legislation

The calm was soon shattered as the white paper moved toward legislative enactment under the direction of a new minister, Jay Naidoo, and the recently appointed postmaster general, Andile Ngcaba. Minister Naidoo had been appointed in a cabinet reshuffle that followed the demise of South Africa's government of national unity. The notorious fourteenth draft of the bill, which removed most of the independence and authority of the sector regulator and made the liberalization timetable subject to ministerial discretion, provoked a public furor and led to the resignation of Ministerial Special Adviser Willie Currie.[142] These late changes to the draft legislation may have been partly motivated by the ANC's desire to put its stamp of authority on the democratic transformation. They also seem to have been motivated by the desire of the ANC to secure more favorable terms for the partial privatization of Telkom.[143]

The Telecommunications Act, as finally passed in November 1996, was largely unchanged from the fourteenth draft. As such, it generated considerable acrimony. Behind the parochial issues tabled by most private sector companies lay a common chorus: charges of betrayal and allegations that the government was advancing the narrow interests of Telkom at the expense of the sector's development.

The sector regulator, the South African Telecommunications Regulatory Authority, was finally established in February 1997. In April of the same year, SBC and Telkom Malaysia were awarded a 30 percent equity stake in Telkom, whose new license gave it exclusivity over the provision of telecommunications services until 2002. By June 2000 the telecommunications regulator (SATRA) and the broadcasting regulator (the Independent Broadcasting Agency [IBA]) had been merged, into the Independent Communications Authority of South Africa.

2001 Policy Review

The year 2001 saw a public review of telecommunications policy as Telkom approached the end of its exclusivity period. The Department of Communications initiated another stakeholder consultative process. This involved a public policy colloquium, but it was much less extensive and transparent than the 1996 process.

In any case, the review was ridden with conflict and controversy. The telecommunications policy directions, unveiled by Communications Minister Ivy Matsepe-Casaburri in March 2001, proposed the introduction of limited competition to the telephone network through the licensing of a second network operator. At this time, much debate was taking place within the cabinet. Trade and Industry Minister Alec Erwin emerged as the victor, temporarily, in a push for broader liberalization of the market. A set of revised policy directions was released in July 2001, and included the proposed granting of two additional licenses to the Public Switched Telecommunications Service (PSTS), as well as broadband licenses. Following objections from Telkom and mobile holding company M-Cell, which experienced a market capitalization plunge of US$300 million following the release of the revised policy directions, an about-face occurred. In August, a third and final set of telecommunications policy directions were issued, which licensed only a single competitor to Telkom and dropped the licensing of broadband. Interestingly, and less controversially, all three versions of the policy directions proposed the introduction of an "e-rate" to facilitate Internet access for schools.

In November 2001 the Telecommunications Amendment Act was promulgated, legislating, inter alia, the introduction of a competitor to Telkom. Following a protracted process, often mired in difficulties, a license was only finally awarded early in 2006,[144] with the new operator only expected to commence operations toward the end of the year. Initially, selecting an appropriate equity investor for the license consortium was disputed; later, internal squabbling between the members of the agreed consortium slowed the process. The net result of the often troubled and frequently antagonistic negotiations around telecommunications reform in the country has been the entrenchment of Telkom as the sole provider of telecommunications—and Internet—infrastructure.

One result of maintaining Telkom's monopoly has been extremely high prices for Internet access. Since 1996, Telkom has dramatically raised the price of the local calls required for dial-up access. Although partly driven by the need for rate rebalancing between local and long-distance traffic, such high prices (leased lines are also expensive by international standards) are also attributable to lack of competition and regulatory weakness.[145] According to Peter Davies, chief executive officer of AT&T South Africa, the country "has the most expensive international bandwidth prices in the world," which, together with its unreliable regulatory environment, "mitigates against ICT development."[146] This is echoed by Mike Lawrie, who describes access costs as "horrendous."[147] The high cost of access is widely viewed as a major inhibitor of Internet development.[148]

Telkom's status and the licensing and regulatory protection it enjoys have promoted an aggressive mind-set (in the litigious tradition of its Texas-based strategic equity investor, the SBC) under which Telkom acts against any perceived threat to its monopoly or revenue stream.

CNI 4: E-Commerce Policy

The explosion of local connectivity after mid-1996 was mirrored in the growth of e-commerce.[149] The first local directory search engine, Ananzi, was launched in early 1996.[150] At the end of October 1996, the banking giant Absa announced, prematurely as it turned out, that it would offer limited home banking facilities via the Internet "in the next couple of days." Absa failed to deliver on this pledge, largely because of the absence of international secure transaction standards.[151] By March 1997, however, most of South Africa's main banks were anxious to provide services over the Internet, with Nedbank becoming the first to offer online transactions.[152] Banking was not the only sector to adopt e-commerce in fits and starts. In a *PCReview* article in February 1997, Arthur Goldstuck detailed the difficulties and failures of his attempt to finance a car purchase via the Internet.[153]

By 1999, Internet-enabled e-commerce had outgrown its teething problems and was flourishing. In July of that year the Department of Communications released a discussion paper on e-commerce policy, a measure preparatory to formal legislation.[154] The development of national policy and legislation on electronic commerce may be considered a sign of a maturely competitive Internet sector. Yet e-commerce, too, has provoked its share of acrimony and dispute. Like so many other processes in the telecommunications sector, it became another politically charged critical negotiation issue.

The process began simply enough with the formal launch on 30 July 1999 of an e-commerce discussion paper by Andile Ngcaba's Department of Communications.[155] After the discussion paper was issued, a series of stakeholder working groups were established in September 1999 along the lines of previous participatory policy development initiatives.[156] The working groups were charged with drafting e-commerce recommendations. They met over the next few months and finally presented their recommendations at an all-day colloquium. This, in turn, was followed by an e-commerce law workshop held on 19 April 2001. Arising from this process, an e-commerce green paper was formally issued on 20 November 2001.[157] Finally, an electronic communications and transactions bill was submitted to parliament on 8 March 2002.

Issues of Contention

The key issues of contention surrounding e-commerce were similar to those arising from the previous telecommunications reform process. Complaints about process—the dominance of a single actor, the inability of stakeholders to exert meaningful influence, grave concern at the wide-ranging oversight powers that the legislation granted to the government, and the significant number of issues left to the discretion of the executive (via the minister of communications or the director-general)—were salient points of contention. On the other hand, many in the sector were satisfied with how the electronic communications and transactions bill addressed commercial issues, and so they made only limited comments on those provisions. Still, there was considerable opposition to the wide-ranging, noncommercial aspects of the proposed legislation. These dealt with, among other things, the accreditation process for certification service providers, the registration of encryption providers, the registration of "critical" databases, the transfer of the South African Internet domain name (.za) to a new body, and the creation of so-called cyberinspectors.

Substantially, the most vocal opposition to the legislation centered around the proposed transfer of authority over the domain name to a government-appointed body. This dissent was voiced, principally, by private sector ISPs and VAN operators, who feared government control and felt that their own (and prior) efforts to create a successor domain registry body, NameSpace, were being undermined. Mike Lawrie, the incumbent domain registrar, and Michael Silber, an Internet lawyer and prominent mover behind NameSpace, were at the forefront of lobbying efforts. A number of academics and other individuals, as well as organized labor,[158] also expressed views on the content of the draft legislation.

Michael Silber has described the legislation as consisting of "the good, the bad, and the ugly."[159] While welcoming the bill's legal recognition of online contracts, signatures, and transactions, Silber was concerned about the poor wording of some sections and the proposed creation of the cyberinspectors. More fundamental was the private sector's opposition to the government's power to assume control over any database it deemed to be "critical." Also disliked were the bill's provisions requiring registration of all "cryptography providers."

An informal coalition arose, consisting of the Internet Society, ISPA, and the Communications Users Association of South Africa (CUASA).[160] These groups all held similar concerns regarding sections of the bill. However, each operated independently, and separately submitted alternative language.

The legislation was seen as a particular threat to the private sector's efforts to establish its own national domain name authority. This body, Name-Space, had been launched in September 2001 on an interim basis,[161] although control of the South African domain had not yet been transferred. The conflict between the private sector and the Department of Communications over control of the domain was what captured the attention of the public.[162] The incumbent registrar, Mike Lawrie, angered at being excluded from the relevant working group, declared that "the result that emerged was horrible."[163] Lawrie publicly stated his refusal to redelegate the domain to the Department of Communications instead of to NameSpace. The issue came to a head in June 2002, when Lawrie moved the primary files for the domain offshore,[164] amid rumors and speculation that they had been transferred to the Principality of Sealand,[165] a libertarian offshore platform in the English North Sea and site of the server hosting company HavenCo.[166]

In the meantime, Michael Silber, as chair of NameSpace, along with others, worked behind the scenes to achieve a compromise. An agreement was finally achieved after the appointment, in November 2002, of a compromise panel that included Mike Lawrie. The panel was charged with appointing a board of directors based on a process of open consultation. After some delays, the compromise body, known as the ZA Domain Name Authority, was formally registered with nine members in September 2003. Negotiations to effect a smooth handover from Lawrie to the new body are currently under way.[167]

Impasse Resolved

While the high-profile conflict over control of the South African Internet domain appears to have been resolved, some additional—and possibly equally worrisome—provisions of what is now the Electronic Communications and Transaction Act remain. Issues surrounding critical databases and cryptography providers have not yet been resolved.

To date, no regulations have been published on certification, encryption, databases, or cyberinspectors. Additionally, it seems that the much maligned cyberinspectors may not be introduced, or that they will be introduced on a much smaller scale than originally contemplated. The Department of Communications has commissioned a study to examine what databases fall within the category of "critical." The study will also determine the prevalence and distribution of such databases. Informal discussions are also proceeding on the question of the registration of cryptography providers. These talks have led certain international providers of cryptography algorithms to withhold them from South African developers due to fears surrounding possible registration requirements.

The furor over the South African Internet domain appears also to have overshadowed the potential impact of another piece of legislation related to the e-commerce policy process, namely the clumsily named "Regulation of Interception of Communications and Provisions of Communication-Related Information Act." This act, among other things, imposes onerous obligations on telecommunications service providers, including ISPs, in respect to the logging and archiving of "communication-related" information (as opposed to content). Such information includes e-mail headers, Internet access logs, and the like, as well as surveillance and decryption of traffic.

Conclusion

It can be argued that the maturity of the telecommunications sector in South Africa is reflected in the modus vivendi arrived at through the e-commerce policy process. Indeed, the Internet in South Africa has come a long way from its early days at the start of the 1990s. The early Internet enthusiasts, tinkering away in garages or on company time, have been replaced by an established sector consisting of several million users, hundreds of ISPs, a formidable infrastructure (even if it is still owned by a single company), considerable economic and social value, and specialized legislation.

The story of the Internet in South Africa, as told in this chapter, has revealed a kaleidoscope of interactions, negotiations, and conflicts involving a range of key actors. Certain critical negotiation issues stand out: What are the key trends that determine impasse, negotiation, or resolution? And how have these patterns affected the diffusion of the Internet in South Africa?

On one level, the period under examination witnessed a transition from "ponytails" to "suits," from those for whom the nascent Internet was a hobby and passion, to those for whom it has become an economic enterprise. Interestingly, this shift has been described in similar terms by two key figures at opposite ends of the spectrum. Lucio de Re, deeply involved in the development of South Africa's Internet, remains outside its commercial ambit. A shy, even diffident consultant with a craggy face and a graying, unruly ponytail, who commutes by bicycle, de Re remarks that "the biggest change has been the ownership of the Internet."[168] His words are echoed by Michael Silber, whose ebullient, bearded smile, rounded face, and twinkling eyes belie his status as one of South Africa's leading Internet corporate lawyers: "the individualists, the mavericks, the visionaries are no longer running the Internet."[169]

The early years of the Internet in South Africa may best be characterized as a precommercial phase. At that time, the Internet depended on interpersonal ·relationships and a shared passion for a budding technology and the exciting possibilities that it offered. The guiding principle was one of collaboration, and attempts to recover costs or make a profit were at best haphazard, and often disastrous.[170]

It was only after the Internet was stabilized as a platform that it became the focus of commercial exploitation. Among its early pioneers were those, like Anthony Gerada, who quickly grasped its commercial possibilities. Within a few months an explosion of ISPs mushroomed across the landscape. These startups engaged in highly competitive jockeying—often sharply antagonistic, and occasionally illicit—for commercial advantage and customer base. A new species of individual, armed with an MBA, a vision of the business possibilities of the new medium, and an aggressive commercial instinct in the mold of Ronnie Apteker of Internet Solutions, came to the fore.

Once commercial viability business models and revenue streams had been established, such a relatively stable, robust, and growing market could hardly escape notice by the country's incumbent telecommunications operator. The entry of Telkom into the market signaled a new phase of competitive maturity, but it also heralded the onset of a bitter conflict between Telkom and its rival private sector ISPs that had been first to occupy the market space. The Internet market has now stabilized, although it is still marked by litigation and hostility.[171] The maturity and stability of the market are demonstrated by the strong participation of Internet multinationals such as Tiscali/WorldOnline, UUNet/MCI, and AboveNet.

In a decade and a half, a fundamental transformation of the sector has happened. Corporate maneuverings, takeovers, and mergers have replaced the buccaneering approach of the early pioneers like Lucio de Re and his friends, who happily "borrowed" international dial-up access from an unused telephone jack.[172]

The development of the telecommunications sector in South Africa was by no means straightforward, nor without uninterrupted growth and steadily increasing benefits. It was a process of diffusion characterized by periods of sharp conflict and hiatus. Furthermore, the process was not driven by uninterrupted technological development and innovation. Clearly, the clash of personalities and contending interests played a major role in both forward movement and bargaining impasses. Finally, the nature of the conflicts, the delays, and the negotiated outcomes resulted in a situation of uneven, often patchy benefits and erratic growth.

The CNI approach illustrated throughout this book can be seen to underpin the negotiations described for South Africa. At bottom within each case lies a clash of interests between defined and more or less coherent groupings. The ability of different groups to benefit from the development of the Internet hinged on differing, even opposing, outcomes with respect to particular Internet policy issues. This state of affairs defines the relevance of each issue for the diffusion of the Internet.

Based on their differing constellations of interests, contending groups articulated and mobilized in favor of competing visions of Internet growth and development. At times, these differing visions provoked antagonism. This antagonism constitutes the degree of contestation manifested in each issue.

The resulting conflicts led to delays as each group sought to design an outcome under which it would be the major economic, social, or political beneficiary. If an issue went unresolved. it impeded the further development of the Internet. However, once a consensus had been reached or a solution imposed, the impasse was unblocked and diffusion proceeded.

The experience of South Africa is similar to that of the other countries documented and analyzed in this book. The South African case reveals a similar dynamic of critical negotiation issues, even though the actual fabric of issues and their specific content is highly specific.

One key difference, perhaps a defining difference, with regard to South Africa is that private sector entrepreneurs and ISPs were able to establish themselves within the sector before the monopoly incumbent, Telkom, grasped the potential of the Internet. This was partly due to South Africa's status as an early pioneer of the Internet. It was also due to distractions caused by South Africa's democratic transition. Finally, Telkom apparatchiks simply failed to recognize the wave of the future until it had broken over them.

South Africa's unique experience with the Internet made the struggle for access much less of a critical negotiation issue than elsewhere on the continent. In the early 1990s, access had already been conceded by the incumbent, although it was subject to bureaucratic obfuscation and delays. Afterward, access became a weapon used by the incumbent against the ISPs and the VAN providers in an ongoing struggle for market dominance and control. In South Africa, as elsewhere, the key conflict may be characterized as one between the incumbent Goliath and the emerging private sector ISP Davids. In South Africa, however, the Davids had already occupied the promised land, and the Goliath was forced to seek their eviction.

Several of the critical negotiation issues discussed in this chapter are far from resolved. The dispute over anticompetitive behavior is likely to continue to wend its way through various levels of litigation and counterlitigation. Regardless of whether the specific complaint is resolved or whether it is shelved in favor of some kind of modus vivendi, the tensions and conflicts of interest that underlie it are likely to remain. Perhaps the draft convergence bill, published for comment in December 2003, with a revised draft due in early 2005,[173] will become a new subject of contestation. The draft bill certainly has the potential to usher in a major restructuring of the market, with new (and as yet very unclear) horizontal categories of licensing. These could have major implications for the incumbent operator and ISPs alike. Certainly the September 2004 ministerial determinations, intended to liberalize the sector by permitting both self-provisioning and resale, and allowing the carriage of voice via any protocol,[174] are subject to very differing interpretations by Telkom and the ISPs and VAN operators.

There is no shortage of additional strife on the horizon. The sector is still characterized by bickering, complaints, and litigation. In March 2003, for example, ISPA filed a complaint accusing "Telkom of anti-competitive practices in the way it is offering a number of Internet products," including its discount SurfMore and BestFriends dial-up packages and its asymetrical digital subscriber line (ADSL) offering.[175]

The narrative and analysis presented here have demonstrated that, contrary to the conventional wisdom contained in much of the literature on Internet diffusion, the process is not a smooth, evolutionary, upward curve. This account reveals a highly contested terrain, one characterized by conflict and negotiated struggle. Furthermore, consensus is often both partial and temporary.

Interestingly, the divisions over Internet diffusion that emerged in South Africa had less to do with the racial polarization and political conflicts of the apartheid era than with more straightforward commercial imperatives of profit and capital accumulation, market power, and policy design.

This chapter has sought to identify, describe, and analyze four critical negotiation issues that were central to the diffusion of the Internet in South Africa. These CNIs were highly contested, and their resolution was meaningful. Certainly, these points of conflict were perceived as central by the players themselves, and their comments and reflections suggest that deadlock on certain issues impaired the diffusion of the Internet, while their resolution had the opposite effect.

The analysis presented here, although not comprehensive, has focused on how the diffusion of the Internet was perceived by key participants. This chapter has also examined how solutions were negotiated, and what effects those solutions brought about. Such an examination of the complex interaction of individuals, interest groups, and institutions is of relevance to policymakers as they seek to understand and manage similar transitions in other countries in Africa and other parts of the world.

7

Tanzania: From Padlocks to Payments

Jonathan Miller

IN 1990, ON THE eve of the information revolution, Tanzania stood out as the most socialized country in Africa. Tanzania's economy was in poor condition due to the failure of the economic policy known as *ujamaa*.[1] Today, despite continuing dependence on donor funding, the country is a multiparty democracy, has a free market economy, and, from its perspective, outperforms its neighbors in of the areas of macroeconomic stability, political stability, and social cohesion. Tanzania's profound political and social transformation has been accompanied by equally dramatic changes in its telecommunications sector. Previously, the importation of computers was prohibited, the phone system was decaying, and no data communications existed. Today, Tanzania enjoys a healthy information communication technology (ICT) sector, rapidly expanding national and international data communications, and significant public Internet access. Furthermore, the country is on the brink of fully liberalizing the telecommunications sector.

To understand Internet diffusion in Tanzania, the local context must be understood. Annual gross domestic product per capita was estimated at US$287 in 2003,[2] and half the population lives on less than US$1 a day. Seventy percent of the population lives in rural areas, although telecom infrastructure is heavily concentrated in urban areas, especially in the commercial capital, Dar es Salaam. Nevertheless, a range of public sector reform initiatives have been launched, and a poverty alleviation program enabled the country to enjoy substantial debt relief under the World Bank's Heavily Indebted Poor Countries (HIPC) program in 2001. These reforms have led to increased aid for development activities, and such assistance is likely to grow over the next few years, including to the telecom sector. The country's economic reform process, especially with regard to privatization and investment, is also changing the telecom landscape. Now, international firms are entering the economy and creating infrastructure.

Current Status

Tanzania has had at least rudimentary Internet access since 1990. Until recently, Internet use has been confined largely to Dar es Salaam, and, like in most African countries, only a small minority of the population enjoys access. Lately, however, there is evidence of quite rapid growth in access. For instance, international Internet bandwidth trebled from 2001 to 2002. At the same time, there has been a rapid expansion of the national network, which now includes virtually all first-tier geographic regions and some districts. Dial-up subscriptions have grown by a factor of six over the period 2001–2002, and cybercafes providing public access to the Web have proliferated.

Some observers estimate there are more Internet cafes—several hundred—in Tanzania than in any other African country. Most are located in Dar es Salaam, but some have opened in regional centers. E-mailing friends and family abroad is very popular, as is use of the Internet to find jobs and download music. Many customers also take advantage of voice over Internet protocol (VOIP) to make inexpensive international calls. Use of VOIP officially violates the government's policy of providing exclusivity to the monopoly Tanzanian Telecommunications Company Ltd. (TTCL), but the practice is tempting, with rates of US$0.30–1.00 for a ten-minute call to Europe or North America.[3] Equivalent rates via the TTCL and mobile operators are over US$3 per minute. Impressive as this may sound, however, the number of users remains small in comparison to rates of usage in developed countries.

Cybercafes first opened in Tanzania in 1996. Coastal Travel, the first cybercafe, had seven personal computers and a slow and very expensive Ethernet link (10 megabits per second [mbps]) to Bill Sangiwa's Cybertwiga, the first commercial Internet service provider (ISP) in Tanzania. In those early days, Internet users were mainly foreigners and travelers who read and wrote e-mails at US$2 an hour. Soon more outlets appeared, and some even offered food service. An early example was the Java Café, located at a famous Dar es Salaam meeting spot called the Cozy Café. A customer at the time recalls how young men flirted with both their girlfriends and the Internet.

Despite some impressive progress, until recently Tanzania lacked an Internet backbone and had no Internet exchange point. The country still lacks a direct landing point for the Internet. Data service providers connect to the Internet via satellite in countries as diverse as France, Norway, the United Kingdom, and the United States. Collectively, this bandwidth amounts to only a claimed 24 mbps. A subsidiary of the monopoly TTCL recently rolled out twenty or so 2-mbps national links to regional centers. This connectivity certainly offers opportunities for businesses, local government, and private citizens to gain access to the Internet, but as yet there is little traffic.

Aside from cybercafes and other public access points, Internet access is limited to several large companies, central government departments, and key government and parastatal agencies that have local area networks (LANs) and Internet connectivity. Access to the Internet by small to medium-size public and private institutions is severely restricted due to the lack of electricity, computers, and connectivity.[4] With the exception of the University of Dar es Salaam (which is a significant user and provider of Internet connectivity to the academic community and beyond), and more recently the Dar es Salaam Institute of Technology, there is minimal Internet usage in secondary and tertiary educational sectors. One exception to this trend is the Muhimbili University College of the Health Sciences (MUCHS), which was one of the earliest users of the Internet in Tanzania. MUCHS continues to make use of the Internet for telehealth purposes. In addition, the Aga Khan Hospital has a new facility dedicated to use of the Internet for limited telemedicine applications.

A vibrant Internet industry has grown in Tanzania. In addition to hundreds of cybercafes and emerging public call centers, there are now over twenty ISPs in the country, serving upward of 20,000 Internet accounts.[5] Alternative modes of public access, such as multipurpose telecenters, are scarce. One telecenter has operated in Sengerema since early 2001, and three more have been constructed in refugee camps near Bukoba in the north of the country as part of a recent agreement between the government and the International Telecommunications Union (ITU).[6]

With regard to Internet content production, there are now several hundred Tanzanian websites and two substantial country portals. Approximately 10 percent of the sites have Kiswahili language content.[7] Some clearly target local Tanzanians by offering chat rooms, sports information, slang dictionaries, and local humor. Most sites, however, are designed for non-Tanzanians with an interest in Tanzania, and for the Tanzanian diaspora. Little commerce is conducted via the Internet in Tanzania, although at least one online shopping portal exists—Watawetu—and some business-to-business e-commerce takes place as well.

How has Tanzania reached this stage of Internet development? Much of the answer lies in the relatively quick progress made in the early days before the Internet became a contentious issue. Under the championship of President Ali Hassan Mwinyi, and his senior ministers, wide-ranging telecommunications reform was achieved, including liberalization and partial privatization of most telecommunications services. Such progress was arrested when authorities deemed that the process had "gone too far."

The telecom field is a key sector and had been undergoing reforms since the early 1990s, including shifting balances between public and private roleplayers, moving from monopoly to competition, shifting from domestic to foreign ownership, and changing centralized to decentralized governance. In 1993, Tanzania established independent regulatory agencies for broadcasting and telecommunications, and agreed to the unbundling of the telecom and postal organizations. The latter took effect in 1994 with the founding of the

TTCL, the first "strategic" parastatal that the government attempted to privatize. In 2001 the government agreed to sell 35 percent of the TTCL to an international consortium, a move that generated considerable controversy. As discussed in some detail below, this issue was not resolved until 2004.

This chapter provides a detailed examination of the critical negotiation issues (CNIs) relevant to diffusion of the Internet and traces the historical events that have influenced the status of the Internet in Tanzania. It describes the push-and-pull of different actors over time, as well as the nature of their relations, and highlights important continuities as well as changes.

CNI 1: HealthNet and SatelLife

In 1987 the Tanzanian Media Women's Association (TAMWA) was founded and began offering perhaps the first electronic data communications in the country. TAMWA quickly entered the ICT arena when it obtained training for some of its members in desktop publishing so that they could produce the organization's magazine, *Sauti Ya Siti* (Voice of Women). Seeing the potential of modern technology, and despite the fact that Tanzania's telephone infrastructure at the time was poor, TAMWA installed a modem so that its members could use e-mail.

The late 1980s were a period of UN conferences and a time when women were mobilizing around issues of development, violence, and reproductive health. Commenting on those times, Fatma Alloo has written: "We decided to download messages, get them translated into Swahili, and let women know what was happening and how to mobilize around issues of concern before going to these UN conferences. The exercise proved highly innovative and had tremendous impact nationally and globally."[8]

Thus, many years before the Internet appeared on the agenda of policymakers, nongovernmental organizations (NGOs) and academic institutions were preparing for the revolution to come. During the early stage, negotiations were primarily about spectrum allocation and were not more significant than other negotiations on office or organizational resource allocation. It was not until the early 1990s that the long process of bringing the Internet to Tanzania began.

Thanks to the pioneering efforts of biostatistician Bill Sangiwa of the University of Dar es Salaam and the International Development Research Center (IDRC), two different three-year projects were launched in 1991. First, the Eastern and Southern African Network allowed researchers at the University of Nairobi, Makerere University, the University of Dar es Salaam, the University of Zambia, and the University of Harare to exchange e-mail with the rest of the world. Each node ran a suite of FidoNet software on an IBM-compatible aperture terminal with a 40-megabyte hard drive linked via a modem and a dedicated phone line to the existing (and very unreliable) telephone system. Second, the same universities were establishing the means to exchange health and medical information via HealthNet, a satellite-based communications service operated by the Boston-based NGO SatelLife.[9] Due to the overlap in the participating institutions, common sources of funding, and other areas of commonality, in 1991 the two projects were merged.

The objectives of the merged project were to reduce the cost of international calling and improve the speed and reliability of transmissions by use of satellites. A license was needed for use of the satellite frequency spectrum. In the absence of a regulator, the Tanzanian Post and Telecommunications Company (TPTC) and the Department of Communications in the Ministry of Communications were responsible for the licensing processes.[10] Licensing procedures were long and involved, and the incumbent TTCL had no desire to relinquish frequency allocation or see its revenue base eroded through the use of satellite transmissions that bypassed expensive international lines. The licensing situation for satellite data transmissions led to the first set of Internet negotiations.

The use of satellite technology was a new idea full of unknown implications. The monopoly TTCL perceived that the granting of licenses would result in the loss of exclusivity and lower revenues; it also understood the value of improved access for research and health-related projects. Because the technology was so new, the TTCL's opposition was weak compared to what it would be in later years. The director-general of the Muhimbili Medical Center and the Sangiwa-led University of Dar es Salaam contingent supported HealthNet-SatelLife and opposed the TTCL. In addition, strong international support came from the IDRC and the National Startup Resource Center at the University of Oregon.

Although there was no formal negotiation as such, Sangiwa describes how he worked "behind the scenes" on a person-to-person basis with government officials, enlisted contacts in the Ministry of Health to educate all the players, and presented the merits of the case to gain support. At the same time, he lobbied the TTCL to obtain their support for and approval of a spectrum allocation.

In due course, the Ministry of Communications supported the application and permitted satellite frequencies for transmissions by HealthNet and the Eastern and South African Network (ESANet). Usage was restricted to a "closed user group" of HealthNet and ESANet members. As a result of informal but successful negotiations, research and health professionals increased usage of ESANet and HealthNet with store-and-forward e-mail procedures via satellite.

Due to the newness of the Internet, and because this was the first negotiation on an alternative to the standard telephone system for national and international data transmission, there was relatively little conflict. These initial discussions established the context for future Internet policy, regulation, and legislation; they also set the ground rules for future negotiations. In 1992, with little effort, the National Commission for Science and Technology (COSTECH) and the University of Dar es Salaam Computing Center also began offering closed user group store-and-forward e-mail services, although in some cases the definition of "closed user group" was rather broadly interpreted.

The period prior to 1993 witnessed the first steps toward electronic data communications in Tanzania. These moves occurred well before the technology appeared on the political radar of policymakers. Data communications enthusiasts in the research and NGO communities pursued informal negotiations with the monopoly TTCL and the Ministry of Communications, and these informal talks benefited the emerging community of Internet users.

CNI 2: Sectorwide Telecom Reform

The initial negotiations reviewed above took place in parallel with three other telecom policy reforms. These reforms were to have a major influence on future Internet diffusion in Tanzania, for two reasons. First, they affected the physical structure upon which the Internet depends.[11] Second, they highlighted the relationship between ICT reform and the shifting balance between the public and private sectors. This second factor conforms to a general pattern witnessed in virtually all African countries.

Reform Programs

In the early 1990s, three reform programs were initiated. First, a new telecommunications act was drafted. The drafting committee received technical assistance from the World Bank and was chaired by Henry Mgombelo, a former electronics instructor at the University of Dar es Salaam and then a member of parliament. The act was promulgated late in 1993 and called for a division of the services provided by the TPTC. Furthermore, the Tanzanian Communications Commission (TCC) was established to regulate telecom activities.

The second reform was the launching of the Telecommunications Restructuring Program (TRP). The TRP was designed to overhaul the entire telephone network in Tanzania. Scheduled for implementation between 1993 and 2000, the TRP was a multidonor project led by the World Bank and the Swedish International Development Agency (SIDA). The TRP was conceived as a major catalyst for telecommunication and information technology (IT) development in Tanzania. It comprised major network rehabilitation and modernization and also policy, regulation, and institution-building aspects. The TRP brought in more than US$250 million to pay for a new, almost all-digital network.

The third reform was the establishment of the Presidential Parastatal Sector Reform Commission in 1992, which was assigned the task of overseeing the privatization of state-owned companies and assets, including the TTCL. It is noteworthy that state-owned companies constituted an estimated 80 percent of the economy at the time. Privatization would begin with smaller and nonstrategic assets before moving to larger assets. The privatization of the TTCL following its unbundling was the first large transaction involving a "strategic" utility.

The Parastatal Sector Reform Commission guided the government's partial divestment from the TTCL. In preparation for privatization, the TTCL was restructured and obtained separate licenses for different services. It entered the ISP and Internet cafe businesses via a wholly owned subsidiary, Simunet. It also transferred its 25 percent stake in mobile company Mobitel to the government, freeing itself to enter the mobile arena via its CelTel operation. The TTCL was severely criticized for unfairly favoring CelTel by providing network access and capacity. The TTCL was also accused of reneging on its interconnection agreements with Mobitel, unilaterally offering to settle for US$2 million although it allegedly owed US$20 million.

The promulgation of the Telecommunications Act in 1993 marks the beginning of a vibrant period in the evolution of telephony, data communications, and the Internet in Tanzania. For the first time, commercialization of many telecom services occurred. The act heralded a period of rapid and in some cases dramatic changes in the country's telecom landscape, including competition for telecom, courier, and local IT business. A pronounced increase in stakes also led to a series of conflicts and negotiations between public and private sector players in which the emergent telecom regulatory authority played a central role.

A key outcome of the 1993 act was the emergence of four new legal entities: the TTCL, the Tanzanian Postal Corporation, the TCC, and the Tanzanian Postal Bank. Adolar Mapunda, then managing director of Tanzanian Post and Telecommunications Company, supervised the changes that took effect on 1 January 1994. As of that date, the TCC was charged with regulation of the postal and telecommunications industries.

The president and the minister of communications and transport are credited with the privatization process and with understanding the need for an independent regulator to guide the sector. Extensive consultations and evaluations occurred before the president appointed Awadh Mawenya as the TCC chair. Mawenya was known as a distinguished professional with integrity. Similarly, the communications minister appointed a solid team of six commissioners for a three-year term. The work of the TCC was carried out by its director-general, Emmanuel Olekambainei, who was appointed by the president. It fell to the commission to guide and regulate the new and increasingly complex arena of voice and data communications.

The TCC established strict rules for its commissioners and staff, while re-munerating them well and in a transparent fashion. Director-General Olekam-bainei said that the "commission insisted on following the law and enforcing regulations strictly with transparency, consistency and accountability, without fear or favor so as to lay the right foundation and set the proper precedent."[12] Olekambainei placed a sign reading "You Are Now Entering a Corruption Free Zone" at the entrance to the commission offices, to impress upon everyone the importance of regulating the sector with integrity.

In May 1994 the TCC published conditions, guidelines, procedures, and fees for the licensing of service providers and frequency allocation. It also set licensing requirements for importers and distributors of telecom equipment and local contractors. While the TTCL was granted a ten-year period of exclu-sivity for national and international voice communications, the TCC encour-aged limited (regulated) competition in data communications services, paging, courier services, and mobile telephony.

The TCC decided at an early stage to allow retail suppliers to operate without licenses if their wholesale suppliers were licensed. Early Internet cafes therefore did not require any license under this arrangement. During 1994–1995 the commission, with the assistance of the World Bank, intensively trained its commissioners and secretariat staff on telecom and utilities policy and regulatory skills.

In 1993 the first mobile (analog) concession was granted to Mobitel, which was jointly owned by the TPTC (later the TTCL) and Millicom Inter-national. Mobitel began operations in 1994 and soon entered an extended dis-pute with the TCC over licensing and other issues. Mobitel claimed that it did not need a TCC license and objected to TCC conditions on geographic zones, migration to digital technology, and the required 35 percent local sharehold-ing. Eventually, its concession was converted into a formal license in 1995. Also that year, a second mobile license was awarded to Tritel through an open tender process during which the TCC, supported by the minister of communi-cations, had to fend off interference by a number of special interest groups, in-cluding some politicians. Competition led to a decline in mobile charges of ap-proximately 60 percent.[13]

As the first steps toward an open, competitive market in telecommunica-tions were taking place, there was a parallel open debate on telecom policy. Toward the end of 1995 (when national general elections brought in a new government), the regulator, the TCC, hosted a three-day forum for public and private sector players on sector liberalization. The forum marked the begin-ning of a process that resulted in the 1997 publication of a national telecom-munications policy. The new policy stipulated principles for continued sector liberalization and the government's continued divestment in the incumbent TTCL. The policy also emphasized the need to develop rural telecom services by means of a rural telecommunications development fund. This policy has yet to be implemented, but was slated for implementation in 2005.

In the three years between the inauguration of the TCC in 1994 and the publication of the national telecommunications policy in 1997, fundamental policy reforms were enacted, including liberalization of the mobile market (as manifested by the existence of a second mobile operator), bifurcation of post and telecommunications services, and the establishment of a regulatory commission. In addition, significant increase in stakes occurred.

In late 1998 the TCC solicited bids for a third mobile operator. South Africa's Vodacom won the bid and went into operation in August 2000. The mobile market was transformed, and there was· a significant initial drop in prices. Vodacom's entry into the mobile market also spurred Mobitel to accelerate by two years its plan to replace its analog Extended Total Access Communication System (ETACS) network with a global mobile communications system, and to significantly increase national mobile coverage.

Growing Pains

As competition grew, so did stress in the industry. Reportedly, some mobile operators bypassed the TCC and approached politicians directly with complaints about regulatory issues. Such actions confounded efforts by the TCC to avoid political interference and act professionally and transparently. In contrast, from the industry's perspective, the TCC lacked technical knowledge, inconsistently applied regulations, changed rules, and unduly interfered in business decisions. Perhaps as a result of pressure, ongoing disputes with Mobitel, and threats of court action in 2001, the Ministry of Communications amended the Telecommunications Act to strengthen enforcement by empowering the TCC to reallocate frequencies and to impose massive fines on defaulters.

Changes in the Telecommunications Act were concurrent with the TTCL's partial privatization. In 2001, 35 percent of TTCL shares were sold to an MSI Cellular Investment/Detecon consortium for US$120 million.[14] The strategic investor paid one tranche of US$60 million and assumed management control. The government provided the first tranche to the TTCL for reinvestment in the company in part so that it could proceed with the roll-out of rural connections. The subsequent establishment of CelTel, however, made observers suspect that the funds had been diverted. The MSI/Detecon consortium placed a moratorium on releasing the second tranche of US$60 million because of squabbling over the extent of TTCL debt prior to the transaction and disagreement on the amount of interconnection monies that were due to Mobitel. Until recently, this transaction remained mired in controversy, and both parties placed full-page ads in local newspapers presenting their positions. Demands were made for the removal of the minister of communications and transport. In the end, the parties reached a settlement and MSI/Detecon paid only US$5 million in the second tranche.

In exchange for maintaining its exclusivity on basic wireline and international connectivity through February 2004, the TTCL undertook to increase fixed lines nationally from 180,000 to 810,000, reaching all 9,000 villages in the country by the end of the period. As noted above, the TTCL has not made any serious attempt to meet this roll-out commitment. In fact, by defaulting on those targets, the company is now subject to a US$6.7 million fine.

The last of the major issues involved drafting rules for interconnection. The drafting process was drawn out, further delaying possible reductions in prices for both voice and data. The TCC's "interconnection determination," finally issued in September 2002, was widely acclaimed. The determination was expected to resolve nagging issues of competition, fair tariffs, and interconnection rates and disputes. The new rules, it was hoped, would level the playing field and reduce prices. The TCC saw the determination as an opportunity to counteract the angry accusations to which it had been subject. Early in October, however, the TCC suddenly announced a delay in enforcing the interconnection determination until 10 January 2003, due to "technical reasons." This opaque decision provoked an outcry that was only quieted when, effective 1 August 2004, the TCC reduced the interconnection fee from US$0.17 to US$0.10. Despite complaints from Vodacom, most operators have accepted and are implementing this ruling.

The Tanzanian Regulatory Authority Act of 2003 merged the TCC and the Tanzanian Broadcasting Commission (TBC) to form the Tanzanian Communications Regulatory Authority (TCRA). The TCC and TBC acts are being repealed, and a study of options for a new licensing regime has commenced. Already, a better process exists for selecting board members. New subcommittees have been created, and a review panel and a ten-member consumer consultative council were inaugurated on 16 July 2004. These changes are designed to improve dialogue and protect consumers. It is significant that the council has taken up Vodacom's complaint about the interconnection charges. Furthermore, an independent inquiry has resulted in a public and transparent process that appears to address consumer issues for the first time.

The continued liberalization of the telecom sector will bring in new players, especially international gateway operators. The extension of the submarine cable to Tanzania is a key project that is expected to make the country an attractive locale for businesses such as call centers and business process outsourcing.

During liberalization, key actors typically create alliances and institutions to advance their interests and projects; they also raise new policy concerns and spur adjustments. We see this dynamic playing out in Tanzania in different ways. For instance, the 1998 changes that took place in the TCRA were not the last that would occur. When a new minister for communications and transport (the late Ernest Nyanda) was appointed at the end of 1999, he replaced the incumbent TCC commissioners, and the president appointed a new chair. At the end of 2000 a new minister (Mark Mwandosya) was appointed. He retained the TCC team and decided to address the problems facing the sector. In August 2002 the minister of communications and transport changed the composition of the TCC by replacing some commissioners.

The Communications Operators Association of Tanzania (COAT) came into being in January 1999. It comprised private sector telecom operators such as mobile phone companies and data access providers, and encouraged industry to collaborate in dealings with government and the TCC. COAT subsequently spawned the Mobile Operators Association of Tanzania (MOAT), but both bodies were moribund by 2002, apparently as a consequence of industry infighting. Whatever the reasons, industry appears to have lost an important opportunity to speak with one voice on critical issues affecting telecommunications.

On a more positive note, the participation of civil society in telecom matters received a major boost in 2000 when an electronic forum, eThinkTank, was formed. The forum continues to play an important role in lobbying government and fostering public participation in ICT, particularly telecommunications.

CNI 3: ISP Licensing

Despite having to report directly to the communications minister and being subject to ministerial authority and intervention, the TCC jealously guarded its statutory independence. In the end, however, a dispute between the commission and Mobitel/Millicom raised too many concerns. In May 1997, the TCC's managing director, on the very same day that he visited Mobitel's offices in Arusha to take action in an alleged abuse of the telecom regulations, was suspended and later relieved of his duties. In his own words, he was "too independent, strong and pigheaded."[15]

The firing led to a regulatory hiatus that lasted for over a year, during which Mobitel sued the acting regulator as a protest against its geographically limited license. Political interference was alleged when an illegal out-of-court settlement with the attorney general was reached in which Mobitel was granted a national license. This effectively legalized Mobitel's Mwanza and Arusha operations.

By the end of 1998 the Telecommunications Restructuring Program was essentially complete, and 95 percent of the national fixed-line grid was digitized. Regulations that required telecom operators to apply for licenses for specific zones had been dropped in favor of national licenses. Formal licensing procedures for ISPs were in place, allowing them to apply to become data access providers and obtain their own international gateways.[16] Telecom costs and prices were falling. The TCC had new commissioners and a new director-general.

The TCC decided at an early stage to allow retail suppliers of telecom services to operate without licenses, provided their wholesale suppliers held TCC licenses. The early Internet cafes and Internet service providers therefore did not require licenses. The distinction between wholesale Internet access providers (IAPs) and retail ISPs was not clear, because ISPs were able to secure their own international access. In 1998 the TCC began negotiating with existing ISPs. It wanted to formally license ISPs that wished to establish their own international access rather than use the TTCL's links. The rationale was that if consumers could choose retail or wholesale Internet providers with independent international links, this would force the incumbent TTCL to become competitive. Issues included initial fees, annual fees, royalties on turnover, and whether arrangements should be retrospective. Clearly these issues could have a major impact on the pace of Internet diffusion in the country.

The TCC claimed that it sought to open and expand the market for Internet access and services and set acceptable fees. Yet its opening position appeared like a design for generating fees to support its annual budget: a US$50,000 initial license fee, a US$20,000 annual renewal, and 5 percent of revenue from Internet customers to be applied retroactively. The existing ISPs did not want retrospective charges and preferred minimal rates, because they were receiving no additional benefits. Additionally, the ISPs did not collaborate well with each other and operated with inordinate mutual suspicion. The agreed fee schedule that finally emerged was a US$2,000 initial licensing fee, a US$10,000 annual charge, and no percentage of turnover.

Soon after publication of the new licensing arrangements in April 1999, the number of IAPs and ISPs started to grow and prices gradually declined. While the openness of the negotiation process was regarded as valuable, some observers believe that the uncertainty it generated slowed the growth of the ISP industry for more than a year.[17]

In 1998 the number of ISPs increased from four to six, and Internet cafes proliferated. By 2000 there were six data service providers supporting sixteen ISPs that were sending and receiving data via satellite. By 2002 there were fourteen data access providers, twenty-two ISPs, and several hundred Internet cafes. Dial-up Internet accounts had grown from a few hundred to more than 20,000, and total Internet users were estimated to have grown from 3,000 to 300,000; Internet host names were nearly doubling each year.[18]

The opening of the telecom industry in Tanzania provided great encouragement for both international and domestic commercial interests to stake claims in a potentially lucrative arena. Inevitably this competition led to disputes and conflicts. The Tanzanian Telecommunications Commission had to build up human capacity and expertise in an increasingly complex field. In addition, the Telecommunications Act was subject to interpretation.

Resolving disputes sometimes required high-level political intervention. In the case of the 35 percent local shareholding requirement, the president stepped in to uphold the TCC's ruling. At other times, the TCC intervened on its own authority. An oil company, for example, was discovered using its "private point-to-point" communications license to communicate with its international business contacts via South Africa. The TCC disconnected the company's very small aperture terminal (VSAT). In another case, Mobitel illegally engaged in roll-out and provision of service in Mwanza and Arusha without a TCC license. The regulator traveled to Arusha, gave formal notice, and padlocked Mobitel's doors.

The period 1994–1998 was one of dramatic change in telecommunications in Tanzania. Important steps toward competition in the telecom arena were taken; mobile telephony was opened to two competitors and data communications to three. The first ISPs were launched and Internet cafes appeared. These were vital steps in the diffusion of the Internet in Tanzania. But the period was not without significant teething problems. The independence of the TCC was challenged on several occasions, and political interference eventually led to the regulator's dismissal. January 1997 to mid-1998 was a period of regulatory confusion, since there were no TCC commissioners and hence, legally, no constituted TCC. The foundation, vision, and regulatory culture established by the original commissioners and secretariat staff under the chairship of Awadh Mawenya were "shaken to the roots."[19] It is claimed that the situation was made worse because no experienced commissioners were reappointed in 1998. At the same time, the restructuring of the secretariat that followed removed some of the most experienced staff; those who remained felt intimidated and threatened.

To understand Internet diffusion in Tanzania, it is necessary to look beyond the Internet itself and examine some wider factors. For instance, the various disputes relating to fixed and mobile phones undoubtedly affected the Internet. Also, the TTCL was slow to meet its legal obligations, and the consequent limited roll-out of fixed lines seriously delayed access to the Internet in rural areas. Nevertheless, several measures indicate that Internet usage took off during the period. The rapid increase in ISPs—from six in 1998 to sixteen in 2000—has already been noted. Published statistics document a leap in dial-up customers from 4,500 in 2000 to 20,000 in 2001. Internet users increased from 115,000 to 300,000 over the same period. Network Wizard statistics indicate that in 2000, Tanzania-based Internet domain names (i.e., .tz hosts) rapidly multiplied. Exponential growth of hosts occurred from the beginning of 2000 to mid-2002, from a base of 218 to 1,684.[20]

While cybercafe statistics have not been recorded, informal observers report a rapid growth in their numbers over the same period. It is certain that competition has rapidly driven down the charge for access to a very low rate of US$0.50 per hour, a level analysts regard as unsustainable and likely to lead to a shake-out in that industry. There are conflicting estimates of Tanzania's international bandwidth, but it seems that outward bandwidth leaped from about 4 mbps in 2001 to 12–15 mbps in 2002. The bandwidth of the domestic backbone, if the capacity of all the backbone links in the country is accounted for, is over 40 mbps. These rates were achieved thanks to Simunet's roll-out of 2-mbps links to all twenty-two regional centers in the country over the 2001–2002 period.[21]

Spurred by the popularity of cybercafes, an Internet culture has rapidly developed in Tanzania. Some observers credit widespread Internet usage to the easy availability of VOIP in the cybercafes, despite the exclusivity of basic telephony and international voice traffic granted to the TTCL. In early 2001, for example, the TCC formed a high-level task force to examine options for VOIP. At issue is whether the VOIP regulations make sense in light of the convergence of voice and data communications and the inability to enforce the law. The VOIP task force, however, has not reported back. This is another issue that directly influences the future of the Internet in the country. By allowing the Telecommunications Act to be flouted, distortions in the marketplace, and disregard for the law, the TCC sent the wrong message to ISPs and potential investors in the sector.

The Telecommunications Act of 1997 accorded the TTCL exclusivity on so-called basic telephony services and international traffic. This exclusivity was confirmed for a four-year period following the partial privatization of the TTCL in February 2000. However, cybercafes and other clients of ISPs are sometimes blatantly providing VOIP services well below fixed-line or mobile rates. They often use the TTCL's national and international circuits and thereby illegally deprive the TTCL of revenue. The TTCL has objected to VOIP and insisted that the practice be stopped. In response, the TCC says that it regularly surveys cybercafes and threatens action against delinquent operators. So far, the only action taken by the TCC has been to remove violator's equipment. The eThinkTank forum has facilitated widespread public debate of this issue, and there is strong civil society support for consumer access to VOIP. Regardless of the law, end-users (including members of the Tanzanian diaspora) continue to make use of VOIP.

In the meantime, Simunet's recent roll-out of Internet connectivity to all regions will simply extend VOIP opportunities more widely throughout the country. The spread of corporate virtual private networks (VPNs) will make policy enforcement even more difficult. Several questions remain: Is the VOIP task force indulging in "benign neglect" by waiting for the TTCL contract to run out, thereby avoiding legal action against VOIP (which would be counter to international trends)? Eventually, should VOIP be allowed under some or all circumstances? Must the regulator turn a blind eye until the TTCL's period of exclusivity lapses?

Conclusion

Beginning in 2000, Tanzania witnessed more and more individuals, groups, and institutions becoming involved in Internet use, ownership, control, or blockage. Once engaged, actors mobilized like-minded interests to pursue common goals and strategies through overt and covert lobbying and negotiation. As other reforms in the TTCL and society were adopted, all telecom markets (other than land-line voice communications) were opened to vigorous competition, albeit under the eye of the regulator. Today, Tanzania is clearly enjoying a vibrant and competitive telecom marketplace.

The telecom industry has advanced rapidly despite many accusations and counteraccusations (especially in the mobile arena), court actions and threats of court action, criticisms of the competence and evenhandedness of the regulator, and delays in provision of infrastructure. Additionally, by many measures Internet activity has grown dramatically. It is easy to lose sight of the fact, however, that most of the action has occurred in Dar es Salaam and, more recently, in the major regional centers. If the notion of Internet diffusion is taken to include geographic "dispersion," then Tanzania has much to do. While Internet cafes are appearing in smaller towns, there is almost no evidence of Internet usage in schools or medical facilities. Although affordability is one factor, availability of infrastructure is another. So Tanzania has a long way to go before the Internet is widely accessible and of benefit to the population as a whole.

8

The Role of International Cooperation

Lishan Adem

THE STORY OF INTERNET diffusion in Africa is one of contradictions, a diversity of approaches, evolving critical negotiation issues (CNIs), and a fascinating variety of responses by states and international actors. In this process, what were the most critical negotiation issues? What patterns were emerging over the last decade and what outcomes ensued? What were the key political and institutional frameworks that influenced favorable and unfavorable policy outcomes for Internet diffusion in Africa?

This chapter aims to address these questions by reviewing the role of international development agencies. Bilateral and multilateral donor institutions have played a significant role in Africa by supporting Internet diffusion and other technological and infrastructure development. As we shall see, international donors were among the key actors that shaped Internet diffusion in Africa over the past decade.

Virtually every donor can claim some stake in Internet diffusion in Africa. Donors were the source of the computer and software infrastructure that made the growth of the Internet in Africa possible. Donors provided financial aid and equipment, built human resource capacity in support of Internet development, and included information communication technology (ICT) assistance in development projects like road construction, water resources management, and health services.[1] Donors lobbied for changes in government policies, including lower tariffs on personal computers and connectivity.[2] Among the donor institutions involved in Internet issues were national, bilateral, and international entities such as development banks, multinational private sector corporations, research and think tanks, and academic bodies.

Beyond African governments and Western agencies, Africa-based institutions played significant roles in coordinating interregional and intraregional negotiations on ICT infrastructure and applications. Such institutions included the UN Economic Commission for Africa (UNECA), regional economic communities like the Economic Community of West African States (ECOWAS), the Southern African Development Community (SADC), and the Common Market for Eastern and Southern Africa (COMESA), and associated regional regulatory organizations such as Telecommunication Regulators Association for Southern Africa (TRASA). African regional political organizations like the African Union and the African Telecommunications Union have also contributed to the debate on Internet issues.

Diffusion in the African Context

Before the advent of the Internet, African countries focused on telecommunications infrastructure development as a way to bridge the gap between those who had access to telephones and other ICTs, and those who did not. Experience in developed countries demonstrated that public sector monopolies could not attract the sizable investments needed to implement new infrastructure. Forward-looking states therefore began to change their focus from building infrastructure to promoting sector reform. A host of factors were spurring telecommunications sector reform around the world by 1990: the desire to improve telecommunication services, rapid changes in technology and technological convergence, reduction of public sector budgets, the establishment of telecommunications criteria for entry into the World Trade Organization, and pressure from international financial institutions (IFIs).[3]

Yet in many places, reforms were resisted. Opponents of reform argued, sometimes fiercely, that liberalization harmed efforts to promote universal access to service and that restructuring would threaten national security and other communal goods. In response, proponents of change expressed concern about the failure of the status quo to achieve the sociopolitical objectives that policymakers claimed to support.[4] In retrospect, this conflict between proponents and opponents of sector reform became a defining theme of efforts to promote Internet development in Africa.

At the very time when governments were grappling with the implications of reforming the telecommunications sector, the Internet was beginning to exacerbate debates of sectorwide reform. For reform proponents, especially international actors, the old regime was viewed as a centralized monopoly and a drain on public resources;[5] ultimately it was regarded as an obstacle to Internet diffusion. Governments held the opposite view. For officials, state retreat from a strategically important telecom sector and the loss of sizable and stable revenue streams were unacceptable. At that time, African policymakers could not envision how liberalization might satisfy consumer requirements and at the same time meet public policy goals. Moreover, government officials feared that the Internet would undermine their capacity to control information flows and reforms; in other words, they feared that it would threaten their legitimacy. Suspicion that the Internet could be used for political subversion was high, particularly in countries grappling with guerrillas, rebels, opponents, and diaspora dissidents. As stated by one high official, "[the] Internet has stripped us of information and exposed us to our opponents; nothing is left to hide."[6]

Beginning in this period, international actors like the World Bank, the International Telecommunications Union (ITU), and the US Agency for International Development (USAID) tied some of their ICT aid to liberalization in telecommunication sectors. They reasoned that African countries would not attract foreign investment nor be internationally competitive without sector reforms. During most of the 1990s, the World Bank and International Monetary Fund (IMF), as part of their structural readjustment programs, pressed for the privatization of incumbent telecommunications operators and made additional financial support conditional on liberalization. USAID, taking a somewhat different tack, made cost-based tariffing a requirement before it would provide grants to establish network operation centers in a number of African countries. Understandably negotiations and debates between states and international actors remained intense for most of the 1990s.

Despite being a government cash cow, the telecommunications sector in many African countries was underperforming. Monopoly operators maintained outdated and poorly administered networks and implemented unsustainable financial models that cross-subsidized international and local calls or urban and rural services. Nor were state monopolies able to cope with growing demands for telecommunications. Throughout the continent, 3.4 million people who could easily afford telephones waited in vain for providers to deliver services. Ironically, despite rapid expansion of mobile phones, today in Africa about the same number of people are waiting for fixed telephones.

It is important to recognize, however, that the results of negotiations, disputes, and discussions varied from country to country. The culture, values, viewpoints, interests, and experiences of local institutions helped determine the success or failure of internationally supported negotiations for sector reform. International actors offered disparate levels of technical and managerial assistance to different institutions in various countries, depending on the recipients' willingness and ability to reform. Tensions always existed between the neoliberal values of the international financial institutions and the concerns of states, which often argued that the IFIs did not appreciate their underlying social, economic, and political dynamics. Additionally, local institutions had difficulty responding in a timely manner to rapidly changing global telecommunications trends. In the case of countries that had successfully negotiated with international actors and had implemented reform, government leadership was often a key factor in overcoming gridlock and diffusing tensions between the different parties.

Thus negotiation outcomes reflected the complex social, political, and economic dynamics of each specific country. Internet diffusion somewhat mirrored the extent to which a country privatized its telecommunications sectors and developed a computing infrastructure.

Early Development, 1980s–1992

In the 1980s the UN Scientific and Cultural Organization (UNESCO) and the International Development Research Center (IDRC) promoted a model known as the International Information System for the Development Sciences (DEV-SIS), which was built around centralized input, centralized processing, and a decentralized distribution system that mirrored the mainframe and minicomputers of the day. In collaboration with the UN Development Programme (UNDP), these institutions helped establish the Pan African Documentation and Information System (PADIS), which was designed as a central node for Africa; national and regional institutions would maintain their own databases and exchange information with the central PADIS system.[7] By the end of the 1980s, the ubiquity of microcomputers altered the concept of a centralized cooperative information system and led to the quest for a more distributed approach.

Still, as elsewhere in the world, by 1990 few electronic networks existed in Africa. Bilateral and multilateral institutions had supported technology transfer and the installation of mainframe and minicomputers to enhance the ability of public institutions to collect, store, process, and disseminate information. International actors also supported national plans for telecommunications infrastructure development. World Bank and UN agencies, including UNESCO, the UN Industrial Development Organization (UNIDO), and the UNDP, and bilateral donors such as USAID, were among the institutions that funded information technology (IT) projects in Africa. These projects accounted for over half of the equipment and technical assistance received by Africa in the mid-1980s.[8]

A well-organized effort by the international community to support ICT needs in Africa began with the introduction of low-cost networking technologies at the end of 1989. By 1991 the Coopération Française, through its research arm Office de la Recherche Scientifique et Technique Outre-Mer (ORSTOM), initiated a Réseau Intertropical d'Ordinateurs (RIO) project that created low-cost, pre-Internet links to Burkina Faso, Cameroon, Côte d'Ivoire, Madagascar, Mali, Niger, and Senegal. RIO nodes were originally established to provide an electronic communications network among ORSTOM researchers. In 1992 the network was opened to anyone engaged in academic research or development work. The network grew substantially and nodes were established in twelve French-speaking African countries. These nodes served about 500 users in sixty organizations. RIO was able to connect outlying countries like Madagascar and the Republic of Congo. It built one of the few resources for Internet-protocol and

Unix expertise in Africa, and later became instrumental in extending full Internet connectivity to the whole continent. ORSTOM was phased out in 1998 in the face of extensive competition from local Internet service providers (ISPs) and the availability of local and international resources for the operation of more highly integrated, university-based networks.

The International Development Research Center, a public corporation of the Canadian government, was another institution at the forefront of early ICT initiatives. After piloting five separate projects in 1992,[9] the IDRC funded an electronic networking capacity-building project with the goal of connecting twenty-four African countries. The IDRC and the Swedish Agency for Research Cooperation with Developing Countries (SAREC) also played a supporting role in building ICT capacity at universities and scientific institutions in Africa. Furthermore, the IDRC was a pioneer in other areas such as using ICT in natural resource management and in the provisioning of healthcare. Finally, the IDRC forged close links with nongovernmental organizations (NGOs) such as the Association for Progressive Communications networks.[10]

A turning point in Internet development came in 1992, when UNESCO's Intergovernmental Informatics Programme (IIP) launched the Regional Informatics Network for Africa (RINAF), which was instrumental in disseminating the concept of the Internet protocol by forging links with the California-based Internet Society,[11] which in turn later emerged as a key advocate of Internet diffusion in Africa. The project was a collaboration with the Network Startup Resource Center (NSRC),[12] based in Oregon. It was coordinated by Internet pioneers Randy Bush and Steve Huter, and the Internet Society. RINAF introduced the vanguard of African ISP managers to Internet-protocol concepts.

Around the same time, the UNDP initiated two ICT projects. The Sustainable Development Networking Programme (SDNP),[13] launched in 1992, promoted connectivity between users and suppliers of information related to the environment and sustainable development. One of its main goals was supporting implementation of the Rio Declaration on Environment and Development. Another project, the Small Islands Developing States Network (SIDSNet),[14] was created in 1994 to examine the feasibility of establishing an electronic network for assisting the social and economic development of small island nations such as Cape Verde, the Comoros, Mauritius, São Tomé and Príncipe, and the Seychelles. The work of these projects provided an impetus for the entry of small ISPs into the market.

Initial Connectivity, 1993–1996

In addition to the rise of Internet literacy due, in part, to the initiatives reviewed above, other driving forces in the early 1990s included privatization, deregulation, and competition. The IFIs were advocating for reform of the telecommunications sector as part of their support for general economic reform in Africa.

By the mid-1990s, negotiations by the ITU and the IFIs, a ground swell of grassroots initiatives, and increasing realization of the Internet's impact on social and economic development led to a shift from piecemeal utilization of information technology to an approach that placed the Internet at the top of regional and national agendas.

The primary goal of the World Bank in this period was attracting capital investment to improve Africa's dilapidated telecommunications infrastructure and to privatize the sector. The prevailing state-owned, publicly operated model did not manage resources efficiently or attract investment and expertise from the private sector. The campaign to attract private investment was successful, and between 1995 and 1997 ten private investments in incumbent monopolies occurred.

At the regional level, interest arose in building infrastructure by using new cable and satellite schemes that promised higher capacities and lower costs for international telephone calls, and better access to the Internet via high-quality transmission bandwidth. Although the sparse populations that existed in many parts of Africa made satellite systems attractive, many planners argued that fiber optics would bring higher capacity and lower costs for international transmissions. Increasing demands for cost-effective bandwidth made optical fiber cables the cheapest and most reliable alternatives, particularly in Africa's coastal regions.

Early Adopters, 1996–2000

The second half of the 1990s in Africa was marked by increasing international cooperation in ICT projects and significant growth of economic and political reform. Both of these trends led to greater Internet diffusion. Political reforms such as multiparty elections, new constitutions, and legalization of political activities took root in many countries. These changes opened opportunities for civil society intervention in ICT policymaking. All African countries achieved Internet connectivity during this period (see Table 8.1), the number of Internet users grew dramatically, and bandwidth increased.

Table 8.1   Internet Access Availability in Africa, 1992–2000

1992	South Africa (one country)
1994	Algeria, Egypt, South Africa, Tunisia, Zambia (five countries)
1996	Algeria, Angola, Central African Republic, Benin, Côte d'Ivoire, Djibouti, Egypt, Ghana, Kenya, Madagascar, Mauritius, Morocco, Mozambique, Namibia, Reunion, Senegal, Swaziland, Tanzania, Tunisia, Uganda, Zambia, Zimbabwe (twenty-two countries)
1998	All countries except, Eritrea, Libya, Somalia
2000	All countries

Source: Jensen, 2002.

By 1998, Internet growth had soared and the role of the private sector had gained widespread support. By 2000, close to 40 percent of African countries were planning to privatize their incumbent telecommunication operators. In May 1996, the African Information Society Initiative,[15] sponsored by the UN's Economic Commission for Africa (ECA), was launched in South Africa, together with the Information Society for Development Conference (ISAD). These new organizations strengthened and heightened the political urgency of securing a place for Africa in the global information economy. The ECA played a key role in advancing the reform of national information and communications strategies throughout the continent.

The World Bank, the ITU, USAID, and the IDRC were among the key players of Internet diffusion during the 1996–2000 period. USAID funded a regional telecommunication restructuring program in southern Africa and launched the Leland Initiative in 1996. Both initiatives focused on promoting an enabling policy environment, strengthening ICT infrastructure, and utilizing the Internet for development. The World Bank and the ITU, besides funding pilot ICT projects and promoting infrastructure development, continued to pressure states to allow competition in the telecommunication sector.

The World Bank initiated an InfoDev program in 1996 with funding from a consortium of donors. InfoDev, in turn, funded a number of projects, including the African Virtual University, a study titled "The Economics of the Internet," participation by African experts in various international meetings, policy studies, data collection efforts, and publications. It also subsidized various ICT application projects designed to create a body of knowledge on the implications of the Internet for social and economic development in Africa. The IDRC, for its part, launched the Acacia Initiative, which focused on rolling out access to communities.[16]

The process and availability of funding unleashed a spurt of creativity in the delivery of Internet and universal services. The establishment of telecenters and the extension of services to rural areas were among the key concepts promoted by the international cooperation agencies. Other multilateral and bilateral agencies began to insist on universal access to ICT as a performance package in their credits and grants. Although rural access was encouraged, it has for the most part not been achieved. Results have been minimal despite vast amounts of resources expended to increase ICT access in rural areas, to adapt telecommunications tools to the specific needs of destitute communities, to promote awareness, to create effective policies, and to build institutional and regulatory capacities.[17] The millennium ended with mixed results in the areas of telecommunications, and critical negotiation issues remained anchored to policy reform and access issues. The language of international actors changed from "ICT for development" to "knowledge for development" and "digital opportunities," but full and widespread liberalization was not achieved.

The Information Revolution, 2001–2004

By 2000, proponents of reform had, for the most part, won the battle. Almost all countries permitted private investment in cellular services, paging, and the Internet. As of 2003, 40 percent of African countries had allowed privatization of their fixed networks.[18] Internet access expanded from less than 500 people in 1993 to 5–8 million by 2003. As of 2001, the number of cellular subscribers overtook users of fixed lines.[19] The reform process demonstrated that small, private enterprises could provide the kind of reliable, quality services that the monopolies failed to offer. Moreover, negotiations between states and international actors helped place Internet diffusion on course by putting all African countries on the connectivity map and in position to address the "digital divide."

At this time African states could be divided into three different categories:

- Those countries that were reluctant to open their markets and to liberalize their telecommunications sector.
- Those countries that were unable to attract international actors due to either internal instability or limited investment opportunities.
- Those countries that showed interest in conforming to global economic norms and that had successfully liberalized their communications sector.

Although in some African countries restructuring and privatization took place quite successfully, the institutional capacities, and sometimes even the independence, of regulators lagged behind. The African Internet market began to slow down as the bulk of users who could afford access obtained connectivity.[20] Improving the capacities of regulatory and civil society organizations to take over the negotiations process from international cooperation actors became more important.

New tools and technologies such as voice over Internet protocol (VOIP) became points of contention between incumbent telecommunications operators (who lost revenues) and joyous customers (who found a new cost-effective tool for their communications). Meanwhile, progress on introducing competition into the telecom and Internet markets slowed due to lack of knowledge and the financial self-interest of governments. International actors began to concentrate on empowering regulators and civil society organizations so that they could better bargain with policymakers. The strategy was simple: empower civil society organizations like media and business associations and build the capacity of regulators in order to "wear away" the dominance of the monopoly providers.

The tangle of issues being debated grew steadily and included participation in global ICT governance, creating local and regional Internet exchange points, transitioning from circuit-switched to Internet-protocol-based networks, defining broad-based national ICT strategies, and regulating wireless networks. In addition, a renewed emphasis was placed on bridging the digital divide.

The year 2000 was a time of change in information communication technologies. The plummeting value of ICT stock, the realization of a growing gap between those with Internet access and those without, and experience in promoting competition and privatization in the telecommunications sector all culminated in an expansion of the focus to include internal knowledge management strategies and external assistance frameworks with regard to ICTs.

*   *   *

In summary, a more than decade-long debate on telecommunications has witnessed the ebb and flow of different critical negotiation issues and changes in the agendas of international actors. Figure 8.1 lists the major bilateral and multilateral institutions and the critical negotiation issues that each institution advanced over the years.

But how did these general trends unfold in specific national contexts? How were these different critical negotiation issues resolved? A discussion of two donor-supported ICT diffusion programs with both continental and national scope for action, SatelLife and the Leland Initiative, can help us better understand these dynamics.

SatelLife's Ethiopian Experience

In 1991, SatelLife,[21] an international NGO, began to use low earth orbit (LEO) satellites to electronically link physicians and hospitals throughout the world, especially African healthcare providers and their US and European colleagues. Motivating this initiative was concern about a lack of input from developing countries on global debates about peace and health.[22] SatelLife's strategy was to utilize packet radio technology linked to an LEO satellite to bypass the "bad and costly telephones" barrier that prevented medical professionals in the south from communicating with their counterparts in the north. Doctors in Africa who could not afford costly telephone-based services would benefit from cheaper and more reliable e-mail based on a store-and-forward satellite connection. SatelLife's experience illustrates how foreign NGOs can negotiate with local stakeholders and governments over ICT access.

LEO-based technology required that ground stations be built, and their installation was negotiated in a two-step process. Negotiations began with a face-to-face meeting between Charles Clement, SatelLife's executive director, and African ministers of health. In turn, these ministers negotiated with their government colleagues in charge of the communications sector on SatelLife's behalf. Results, not surprisingly, varied from country to country. The intervention in Uganda was relatively smooth, thanks to the personal involvement of

Figure 8.1 Major International Actors and Their Telecommunications Agendas, 1990–2003

International Actor	Pre-Internet			Internet								New Millennium			
	1990	1991	1992	1993	1994	1995	1996	1997	1998	1999	2000	2001	2002	2003
Coopération Française (RIO/ORSTOM)	Connectivity and access													
IDRC	Connectivity and access, universal access, ICT policy, research													
UNDP					Access, pricing, ICT policy									
World Bank				Infrastructure, privatization, competition, regulation										
USAID							Infrastructure, pricing, regulation							
ECA	Low-cost connectivity				National e-strategies									
DFID												VOIP/IXP/ICT policy and regulation		

Ruhakana Rugunda, the minister of health and a former University of California–Berkley student who is a particularly charismatic leader. Ruhakana later became a SatelLife board member and played a key role supporting Health-Net's expansion into other countries. Mozambique, Tanzania, and Zambia conducted intense negotiations involving telecommunications regulators, Ministry of Health representatives, and local telecom companies. SatelLife's use of "associational power" in negotiations was later employed by other international actors. In this strategy it was sometimes necessary for SatelLife to intervene, because health ministries did not have the necessary technical knowledge needed to negotiate with telecommunications companies.

While SatelLife did enjoy rapid success negotiating with some countries, notably Uganda, it ran into difficulties in Kenya, Zambia,[23] Zimbabwe, and Ethiopia. In Kenya, negotiations were conducted by a personal physician of the former president, and there were allegations of smuggled equipment. In Zimbabwe, negotiations to obtain a ground-station license took two and a half years. The government of Zimbabwe expressed concerns about the "free flow" of information to the general population. In Zambia, delays were encountered because it was illegal to own third-party modems, which were required by the SatelLife system; violators were fined a hefty fee by the government.[24] Internet users, however, found ways to "work" within the prohibition. Some Internet enthusiasts, for example, attached third-party modems to government-registered modems so that they could pass inspections.[25] This "hide and seek" technique was one of the most prevalent strategies employed by Internet users throughout Africa to circumvent laws and regulations that inhibited Internet access.

When SatelLife first set foot in Ethiopia, the country was known for drought, famine, and civil war. Ethiopia was just emerging from a socialist economic regime managed by a military junta that had collapsed in 1991. The transitional government that took over after the military government was federalized based on ethnic groupings and state ownership of the land. The worldwide Ethiopian diaspora discussed Ethiopia's new government and other issues on the Internet. Amid unsettled conditions, the entry of SatelLife into Ethiopia was greeted with suspicion. In addition to concerns that the Internet could be used to oppose government policy, the state-owned monopoly telecom company was fearful of losing its lucrative revenue.

At the time the new government was sworn in, a wave of connectivity was under way. Store-and-forward e-mail had been available to a limited community since 1991 via the Economic Commission for Africa's Pan African Development Information System. The new government rapidly expressed concern about this e-mail service, which was gaining popularity, and its ability to spread opposition information to locals. It happened that some of the e-mail traffic carried by the PADIS network included discussion by members of the Ethiopian diaspora. As noted, the incumbent operator was apprehensive about the loss of foreign currency earned from the NGOs and UN agencies that were using the PADIS system instead of the government-owned system.

The proposal to install a HealthNet ground station became another "bone in the throat" of an already wary incumbent operator. Despite the humanitarian nature of HealthNet, SatelLife's request for installation of a ground station was rejected. Taking note of the complexity of the situation, SatelLife met with Addis Ababa University's dean of medicine, who was also a medical librarian, and with Ethiopia's Ministry of Health. Next a task force designed to negotiate quietly for the installation of a ground station was proposed and soon established at the university's medical college. Task force members were drawn from the university's medical faculty, the Ministry of Health, and the ECA.

After several meetings the task force formally requested a SatelLife license from the incumbent telecommunications operator. The telecom authority delayed responding to the request, claiming it needed time to "study" the technical specifications. The process entailed well over a year of back-and-forth negotiations. Finally the license was issued, but a high traffic compensation fee was imposed. Although the task force had argued that use of SatelLife by medical doctors was not comparable to telephones use, and that tariffs should be calculated differently, the incumbent insisted that licensing and traffic compensation fees should be paid as charged; and so they were.

SatelLife was also required to pay customs taxes for donated equipment. Paying these taxes became more and more difficult due to lack of funds. Furthermore, SatelLife found it morally unacceptable to pay duties on equipment that it had donated for humanitarian purposes. SatelLife's solution was to import equipment through the ECA, which had an agreement with the government regarding such donations. Once the equipment arrived, issues such as who would manage the network and who was to pay the annual licensing fee arose.

Eventually, the situation changed with the introduction of the Internet in Ethiopia. Additionally, it was realized that the traffic from the HealthNet ground station was not as large as expected, and so did not threaten the government telecom's revenue.

Interestingly, similar debates and discussions over Internet access continued to occur in Ethiopia, but these subsequent negotiations lacked the kind of enthusiasm that those who promoted the HealthNet ground station brought to the table. The success of the earlier negotiations demonstrated the endurance of Internet advocates dedicated to a specific cause. This was a pathbreaking effort that provided the impetus for wider access to global knowledge.

The experience gained while negotiating the installation of the HealthNet ground stations was helpful to the vanguard ISPs, which soon came onto the scene. The HealthNet precedent also informed subsequent debates on Internet access between international cooperation organizations and governments. Essentially, the same type of issues resurfaced when, a decade later, interest arose in using low-cost Ku/Ka band very small aperture terminal (VSAT) to connect small businesses, homes, and institutions to the Internet.[26]

Widespread utilization of HealthNet ground stations was ended for a variety of reasons, ranging from the cost of equipment, the need for skilled technicians to calibrate the system, and the availability of alternative connectivity options such as dial-up Internet. SatelLife employed the Internet for direct intervention in the area of healthcare, and furnished healthcare providers with diverse tools and content that met local needs. One additional contribution SatelLife made was helping to increase the technical knowledge and negotiating skills of its allies in various health ministries.

In retrospect, SatelLife's venture to connect medical professionals in Africa was the first example of negotiations between international nonprofit actors and monopoly regimes in Africa.[27] Installation of HealthNet's ground stations involved securing frequency licenses from the monopoly telecoms, passing "sensitive" telecommunications equipment through customs, and defining compensation fees for loss of revenue by incumbent telecom operators. Since SatelLife was a humanitarian organization, the demands made by telecommunications operators for licensing and traffic fees were highly contentious.

Cost-Based Pricing in Africa and the Malian and Leland Experience

Across Africa the birth and growth of Internet service providers in the mid-1990s portended an increase in privatization and competition by the end of the decade. Compared to other telecom operators, ISPs were small and nimble, and seemed particularly well suited for the private sector in poor, frequently authoritarian nations. The increase from 84 ISPs in 1996 to 450 in 2000 was largely due to the newly privatized and competitive environment.[28] In areas where monopoly ISP services were maintained, such as Rwanda, the "market" stagnated. The ISP retail sector eventually joined value-added service markets such as cell phones and paging; consequently, private investment and competition began to guide Internet diffusion.

The main obstacle to ISP expansion and survival was the cost, supply, and quality of the basic (and frequently monopolized) telecommunication structure. Indeed, the cost of dial-up telephone charges constituted a major expense. A 1997 World Bank survey showed that telephone charges represented 58 percent of users' local Internet access costs, 86 percent of the cost when users accessed an ISP from outside a local calling area. In addition, ISPs were paying over 48 percent of their revenues for Internet backbone connectivity and international leased lines.[29] The ISPs wanted an immediate reduction in call charges, but telecommunications operators felt threatened by the prospect of lower Internet access charges. Thus the monopolies were disposed to reject requests to lower their fees.

The dominant tariff structure for Internet access in Africa was based on cross-subsidies. A cross-subsidy charges more for one service, such as Internet access, to pay for another service, such as local pay-phone calls. This tariff of Internet access was also of great concern to international development agencies, since it artificially heightened access costs. Indeed, the expense of a leased line in Africa was more than several times its actual cost. The revision of Internet access tariffs in Africa (to stimulate Internet growth) was a goal articulated by local ISPs as well as international actors. Telecom operators were also under pressure from the unilateral benchmark established by the US Federal Communications Commission. This benchmark identified rates that US carriers should pay to foreign carriers for terminating calls originating in the United States.

Despite pressures, monopoly operators rejected requests to reform their pricing structures. Internet calls experienced longer holding times than did voice calls, and this resulted in added strain on poorly maintained infrastructure. A reduction in charges for Internet usage would have meant less revenue to monopolies for a service that increasingly choked their lines. Some operators also contended that Internet usage had already harmed their lucrative long-distance market, and they were concerned that cheaper dial-up access would lead to extensive usage of Internet telephony and reduced revenue streams.

Tensions between African telecom operators and international actors arose over the former's user-based tariff preference and the latter's cost-based tariff preference. This disagreement became a critical point of negotiation that gained momentum during the second half of the 1990s. ISPs and international cooperation institutions were unwavering in their demand for price restructuring. They contended that market needs and the Internet's potential to advance social and economic development could not be realized without increased competition and a reduction of costs. The telecoms continued to favor a pricing structure set by the monopoly in accordance with national economic policy.

In June 1996, USAID launched the Leland Initiative in honor of the late US congressman Mickey Leland, who died in a 1989 plane crash while on a famine relief mission in Ethiopia. The strategy of the Leland Initiative was to encourage states to adopt Internet enabling policies in exchange for assistance in the form of equipment and training. The Leland Initiative fostered the following: cost-based tariff structures to stimulate private sector competition,[30] the introduction or enhancement of full national Internet connectivity through the provision of requisite technologies,[31] and the achievement of broad-based utilization of the Internet and other ICTs for sustainable development.[32]

The Leland Initiative made grants conditional on an agreement to adopt cost-based pricing, liberalization of the market to third-party ISPs, and implementation of policies that allow for the unrestricted flow of information.[33] In testimony before the US Congress in 2001, Lane Smith, coordinator of the Leland Initiative, said:

> At the launch [of the initiative] we established one important principle. . . . We were only willing to help those countries that wanted to adopt modern, Internet-"friendly" policies. We offered to help them reach out to the private sector to implement these policies, and we offered to provide them with the equipment necessary to establish their national Internet infrastructure, and the training on how to use it. We noted that we would not help those who insisted on doing business the old-fashioned, state monopoly way.[34]

The Leland Initiative began its negotiations with visits to African countries. The purpose of these trips was to explain the initiative's basic principles to key policymakers in the region. John Mack of the US Department of State was a senior negotiator. In the first round of negotiations, he visited Eritrea, Ethiopia, Kenya, Madagascar, Mozambique. Mack recalls that the Leland Initiative "did not want to get into broad sector liberalization issues such as privatization, interconnection or universal access; we wanted to begin with a few critical success factors namely private sector involvement and cost based tariffs."[35] Dialogues between Leland staff and governments involved talks on the advantages of and how to transition from monopoly pricing to cost-based, affordable tariffs. Also discussed were why and how to allow free and open access to information on the Internet and why and how to set aside long-standing monopoly practices in favor of private sector ISPs. These exchanges constituted a process of awareness and consensus building. The Internet was new and frequently misunderstood; sometimes this was purposeful, at others it was due to unfamiliarity.

Beyond face-to-face negotiations, USAID used other techniques to advance its initiative, such as training high-level policymakers in the potential impact of the Internet. USAID sponsored the participation of African experts in the US Telecommunications Training Institute, and these experts were later instrumental in facilitating negotiations at local levels. In some cases, the Leland Initiative employed associational power. In Kenya, for example, a memorandum of understanding was secured through an alliance with a university network known as KeNet. In Rwanda, the education sector played a key role by joining the Leland Initiative in 1999, despite an earlier setback in which Rwandatel cut off competition after Rwanda received Leland equipment in 1996.

Despite achieving notable success in most countries, the Leland Initiative faced major problems in some cases. In Ethiopia, for example, the state-owned telephone monopoly did not agree to the condition of cost-based tariffs. The state not only prevented the private sector from entering into the telecommunications market, but also rationed access to telecommunication services and maintained extremely high prices for local and international calls. When governments failed to appreciate the link between increased usage of the Internet and economic development, negotiations were protracted. Gambia, Mauritania, Namibia, Nigeria, and Swaziland did not concur with USAID's conditional assistance. In Guinea-Bissau, the process was extended because of a change in government. The Leland Initiative, however, pressed ahead in partner-countries that were willing to end monopolies and allow private sector participation. Benin, Guinea, Guinea-Bissau, Côte d'Ivoire, Eritrea, Ghana, Kenya, Lesotho, Madagascar, Malawi, Mali, Mozambique, Rwanda, Senegal, and Uganda all benefited from the project.

The Leland Initiative was important in that it moved negotiations on cost-based tariffs forward. The initiative was also instrumental in forging links with, and inspiring, other international cooperation agencies to adopt principles of competition, free flow of information, and cost-based tariffs.

Two years after the launch of the Leland Initiative, the UN Development Programme launched a parallel enterprise titled Internet Initiative for Africa (IIA), which utilized some of the same strategies employed by USAID. The IIA assisted countries that had not joined the Leland Initiative, namely Angola, Burkina Faso, Cape Verde, Chad, Ethiopia, Ghana, Namibia, and Swaziland. Although the IIA engaged African states in policy dialogues, it did not stipulate policy reform as a condition for assistance. Rather, the UNDP required mandatory cost-sharing whereby each country was obliged to contribute an equal amount. This conditionality delayed implementation of most projects, because governments failed to allocate the necessary resources on time. In addition, these conditions restrained private sector initiatives by subsidizing monopoly telecom operators. Although governments were slow to contribute their share, they became more engaged in negotiations and were committed to the project, which spent, on average, over US$1 million per country.

Mali was the first country to participate in the Leland Initiative. The government had implemented forward-looking policies designed to liberalize the economy, open the political system, and expand social services. The proreform stance of the government, especially of former president Alpha Oumar Konaré, helped advance Internet development in the country. President Konaré was a scholar. After leaving office, he became the first secretary-general of the African Union and a member of the Comité du Pilotage for the University of Mali's networking efforts, and had made significant contributions to ICT promotion in higher education and using the Internet for development. His leadership was a key factor in support of smooth negotiations with Leland Initiative staff.

Discussion between USAID and the government of Mali began in April 1996, and were coordinated by a local team charged with a special objective for information and communications. Initial discussion between Leland staff and policymakers in Mali focused on establishing a national Internet gateway that would provide links to private ISPs.[36] The resulting memorandum of understanding, signed by the government of the United States (through USAID) and the government of Mali, stipulated the following:

- The incumbent Société de Télécommunications du Mali (SOTELMA; Telecommunications Company of Mali), in collaboration with USAID experts, would design, install, and test a high-speed Internet gateway.
- The government of Mali would adopt cost-based tariffs and first-year incentive discounts, thereby establishing Internet tariffs that were among the lowest in Africa.
- Mali would also establish a transparent process to bring the private sector into the Internet access business.

Before the Leland Initiative, only a handful of people had access to e-mail, mainly through RIO-ORSTOM; MaliNet's store-and-forward network based on Unix-to-Unix copy protocol, run by Eric Stevance; and a FidoNet system run by Madibo Tambura of the Balanzan Institute. Establishing the stipulated high-bandwidth point-to-point network allowed connectivity to the Internet and provided efficient Internet service. As such, the Leland Initiative supported ISPs and encouraged Internet diffusion.

The negotiated telecommunications rate structure that would promote increased usage was also key. Jonathan Metzger, who led much of the initiative's implementation throughout Africa, was tasked to assist with negotiations between the ISPs and SOTELMA to establish a cost-based and fair price that the ISPs could afford and that would provide a margin of profit for SOTELMA.

Having accomplished these goals, a fully functional international gateway was established. Given the availability of bandwidth to service providers, other issues cropped up that required renegotiation. A primary issue was the local loop, which became unreliable and prevented most ISPs from providing better service to users. Bringing the ISPs and SOTELMA together, the Leland Initiative negotiated improved and digitized local exchanges, installation of a redundant international link, implementation of a national call line, and management of the .ml domain and Internet-protocol addresses.

Overall, the Leland Initiative's efforts in Africa and Mali were largely successful. ISPs began serving hundreds of clients. Users in major cities other than Bamako were given access numbers and were charged at local call rates. The University of Mali's various schools and campuses were connected to the Internet. In 2000, SOTELMA not only revised tariffs, but was also able to improve the speed of its local network and host its international gateway to 2 megabits per second. Mali hosted two significant ICT conferences in Bamako, in 2000 and 2002. In short, Mali became one of the success stories and advocates of Internet development in Africa.

Conclusion

For more than a decade, Internet development was intensively debated by international agencies, government policymakers, and local actors (civil society, the private sector, academics, and other stakeholders), and between regional and subregional institutions and states. These discussions brought new agreements on issues, such as the "digital divide," that made international cooperation imperative. The advent of the awareness of a digital divide did not change the fundamental importance of negotiating access to networks, telecommunication liberalization, and cost-based pricing; rather, it brought new complexities to the table: wireless communications, intellectual property rights, universal access, content, VOIP, and more. The upsurge in the number of international institutions that expressed interest in using ICTs for development, and a shift from relatively distinct negotiation issues such as privatization and competition to more complex and interconnected challenges, demonstrated the urgency of ensuring broader access by policymakers to a wider set of stakeholders, nongovernmental actors, as well as government itself.

Early on, substantial Internet growth was achieved when negotiations on critical issues were straightforward. At later stages, when issues become more diffused and complex, Internet growth slowed. Early Internet diffusion in Africa brought about an impressive rise in the number of ISPs and users, but this dramatic rise leveled off once those who could afford access were connected. Figures 8.2A and 8.2B illustrate declining host and Internet dial-up subscription trends in Africa between 1996 and 2002. The figures document a high growth rate at the early stage and a flattening out during the consolidation phase. It remains to be seen if new technologies, economic growth, and wider participation will bring with them the higher diffusion rates of the past.

Figure 8.2A   Annual Percentage Growth of Internet Hosts in Africa, 1996–2002

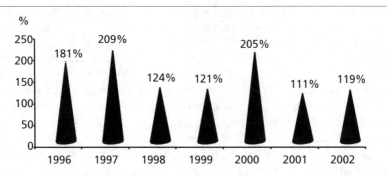

Figure 8.2B Annual Percentage Growth of Internet Subscribers in Africa, 1996–2002

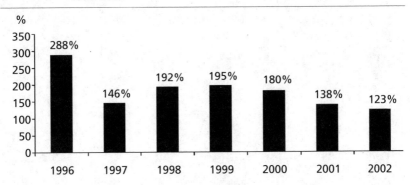

Source: Jensen, 2002.

9

Conclusion

Ernest J. Wilson III

COMPARING AND CONTRASTING THE critical elements of a fast-moving phenomenon like the information revolution is no easy task. In the preceding chapters we have attempted to do so by analyzing the critical issues of political give-and-take, what we call critical negotiation issues (CNIs), whose resolution is essential for successful information and communication technology (ICT) diffusion.

Having organized the chapters in this volume mainly on a country-by-country basis, we now concentrate on the CNIs themselves. This chapter describes their common political and institutional features and how they differ from one another across several distinctive issues. It also reviews their relative effects on ICT diffusion. In contrast to Chapter 1, which was more conceptual and academic, this final chapter reverses the balance, to analyze and underscore the most policy-relevant findings that emerged from our negotiating model and that are particularly relevant to practitioners.

The contributors to this volume have chosen to employ the CNI approach, over other available approaches, in order to pursue several distinct goals:

- To illuminate the essential contribution of politics to Internet diffusion, and to criticize the "technology first" approach.
- To provide common reference points of choice and action that can be consistently compared and contrasted within each country and across them.
- To give practitioners a consistent narrative and storyline with a beginning, middle, and end, to help them better understand the complicated processes of Internet diffusion.
- To identify lessons and best practices that could be learned and selectively applied in the African context.

- To demonstrate convincingly the effects that particular negotiation outcomes have on the pace and allocation patterns of Internet service diffusion.

The contributors have been able to advance all five of these expected benefits, some more completely than others. The most problematic goals have been the final two—best practices and impacts. In the rest of this chapter, I review these and other issues and begin by analyzing issues of CNI sequence, duration, and principal actors. Subsequently, I address matters of policy design and implementation, politics, and the especially problematic elements of best practices, lessons learned, and impacts.

A Brief Review of the CNIs

The contributors began their research with a repertoire of a dozen critical negotiation issues they judged initially to be most important in their case study countries. As depicted in Figure 1.1 (see p. 7), the CNIs involve four major categories: policy reform issues (privatization, liberalization, regulation), access issues (access to facilities, monopoly pricing, access legality), national information communication technology (ICT) policy issues (information society, universal access and services, policymaking capacity, implementation capacity), and technical issues (Internet exchange point [IXP], voice over Internet protocol [VOIP]).

Of these twelve, the contributors discovered through their two years of research that some CNIs were more important than others in the value-added "second market" of the Internet service providers (ISPs), which was our main focus. The first two CNIs (privatization and liberalization) were enormously important for the overall performance of the ISPs in their environment, yet the contributors concluded they were best analyzed as key upstream factors in the "first market" of the telecoms, not in the second market of the ISPs. The contributors had to refer to these two, but one step removed from the ISP market. The last two CNIs proved peripheral to most countries' overall CNI repertoire, because they were not as contentious as others, although they were judged rhetorically, in principle at least by the key players, to be "important" (Ghana was an exception where they were contentious).

Unquestionably, the most thorny and difficult issues proved to be the core four CNIs: access to facilities, anticompetitive behavior, monopoly pricing, and regulation. Table 1.1 (see p. 9) indicates how the several CNIs were ranked by the country contributors.

Conclusions About Policy Design and Implementation

A great deal of international scholarly and institutional attention has been devoted to whether, and how much, governments of less-developed countries (LDCs) articulate broad principles of liberal ICT diffusion, and whether they elaborate explicit policy frameworks and publicly commit themselves to common rhetorical positions about the value of ICT services and their potential contributions to national development. Analysts focus on statements by presidents and ministers, new legislation, and newly created or reformed institutions, and the whole juridical package designed, in principle, to promote beneficial outcomes like universal access and democratic growth. Examples of this approach are codified in national-level e-assessment documents of groups like McConnell International or the Center for International Development at Harvard (McConnell International, 2000).

No one would deny that the proper framing of broad principles and targeted ICT incentives is an essential element of successful ICT diffusion, whether in China or Botswana. Yet restricting the focus to rhetoric, intentions, and principles is insufficient. Perhaps the major contribution of these CNI studies is the determinative influence of other essential factors in successful Internet diffusion in Africa that tend to be overlooked: implementation, collective action, and political sustainability (Grindle and Thomas, 1991).

Studying how critical, contentious issues are resolved on the ground reveals that the relationship between rhetoric and reality can be distant or close. Policies can be pronounced and not implemented; and they can be implemented and not announced (through the slow accretion of small steps taken by various actors in response to facts on the ground). Being announced and implemented is only one option among several, and as indicated below, it is perhaps not the most prevalent. Whether an ICT policy is implemented in Africa is largely an empirical issue.

Internet diffusion policy is not just what governments do, but also results from many decisions made and actions taken by other stakeholders, including *private* ISP owners, individual members of the community of *university* experts, and the engagements of nongovernmental organization (NGO) leaders, often in reaction to government strictures. At some point in all countries where the Internet expands successfully and quickly, there emerges a small group of ICT collaborators drawn from different sectors of society who come together to advance their vision of the networked society.

Since action demands that stakeholders' interests must be aligned, moving from sharing a vision to actually implementing policies is difficult. "Implementing" requires that leaders must commit themselves, shifting from rhetoric to action and mobilizing scarce material and other political resources, resources that could be applied to other development challenges. These scarce resources will then be used to facilitate and reward the groups and individuals that promote liberal Internet diffusion, and punish those who oppose it. Different CNIs vary in their "implementation intensiveness" and susceptibility to political interference. Implementation has several distinct, if related, elements: sequence, intensity, duration, and stakeholders interests. Other issues concerning collective action and sustainability come into play as well, and are addressed later in the chapter.

Sequence

In politics and policy, the order and pace in which issues appear on the radar screen of decisionmakers has important consequences for outcomes. The adage that "timing is everything" certainly proved true in these African cases. Policymakers in Africa, as in other regions, discovered that issues of Internet diffusion came in waves, with some more likely to appear early in the process and others invariably later. Two interesting sequence patterns emerged in the cases, one tied directly to the CNIs as initially defined, the other somewhat more general.

In every case-study country, for example, the challenges of voice over Internet protocol and interconnecting national points of presence (POPs) into a national backbone appeared late in the process. By contrast, "access" terms arose early as one of the most contentious issues of all. Other issues like licensing and pricing were more spread out over the life of the diffusion process, likely to arise at different times in different nations. Succinctly put, the sequence of greatest consequence for ISPs runs from "access to facilities" through pricing, anticompetitive behavior, and regulation, and then to IXPs and VOIP.

For most countries, the sequence of issues strictly within the Internet service provision market was preceded by distinct but related policy sequences that arose in the broader telecommunications market. Commercialization and liberalization, for example, arose earlier in telecom reform, and their resolution shaped the national policy environment for the subsequent growth of ISPs. Where competition was permitted in the upstream telecoms market, Internet diffusion seemed to be facilitated.

The reasons for these differences in policy issue sequence are rather straightforward for the earliest and latest arrivals. Successfully interconnecting points of presence around the country to save money could only arise as a practical problem when there were in fact POPs already established and serving customers. Indeed, there is probably a minimal level of customers below which the financial and technical challenges of interconnection are much less pressing than others. The same holds true for VOIP. The technology to send voice over Internet protocol had to be invented and locally available. There had to be a threshold level of basic connectivity and customers, which is not insignificant. VOIP, therefore, was never the first negotiating issue confronting decisionmakers.

By contrast, an Internet service provider simply could not open for business without reliable, regular, and reasonably priced basic access to telephone lines. And because the owner of the lines—the incumbent telephone company—was unfamiliar with the Internet, and because the staff typically felt threatened by an innovation whose impact on their long-standing business model, on national security, on universal access, and on their own professional and personal prerogatives was possibly damaging, then in most countries it always began by hampering ISP access to its lines. Not surprisingly then, access became an early critical negotiation issue in Africa, as it did in Europe and North America.

In between the latecomers of IXPs and VOIP, and the early arrivals like access, we find issues of pricing, licensing, universal access, and institutional capacity drawing the interests of the different stakeholders in the developing ISP markets. These issues have greater leeway, and other nontechnical issues played a wider role.

Other temporal continuities emerged that were not as fully developed in the individual cases. Taken together, the African countries studied here experienced at least four phases of Internet expansion: precommercial, commercial, competitive, and consolidation. The first phase begins with the initial commissioning of the first Internet link in a country, always done in Africa as elsewhere by researchers and computer "geeks" usually housed at universities (compare Wilson, 2004, for similar processes in Asia and Latin America). A second commercial phase occurs a few years later with the entry of the first nonresearch, commercial ISP. Rapidly on the heels of the commercial stage comes the third competitive phase, when the first market maker is challenged by other entrants and the field becomes more competitive, prices fall, and service improves. After 2001 and 2002, the market begins to experience the fourth phase: more consolidation even as competition remains. Each of these phases has a different mix of CNIs, and a typical kind of politics, expanding out in concentric circles from mostly cooperative relations among a small group of Internet enthusiasts and champions who operate below the government's radar screen, to the commercial and competitive period when the challenges posed by the grassroots-oriented champions come to be recognized by the incumbents, who strike back in ways described below. In the fourth phase, the CNIs become slightly more technical again and less contentious, and the acrimony of the debates decreases somewhat. This is a kind of political turning point in the diffusion process.

An interesting common political point across all countries is when the Internet access issue appears on the "radar screen" of the telecom managers and senior ministry officials. The contributors to this volume have repeatedly drawn attention to this "Aha!" moment of recognition by the information conservatives, when they suddenly recognize the threat (and less frequently, the potential opportunities) they face from the information revolutionaries.

Intensity

The intensity of the CNIs appears to grow from the interaction of a number of separate factors: the number of stakeholders involved, their knowledge about how the technology works, their initial attitudes toward other actors, and their expectations about the outcomes of the interaction.

In a nutshell, the number of core stakeholders (ministry and telephone company) starts out small, and because their knowledge of the commercial and political implications of the Internet is very limited, they err on the side of caution and conservatism and view the new entrants as potentially threatening to their "turf" and intensely resist innovation. They expect that the results of interactions at best will be uncertain, and at worst will always be zero-sum—if the new ISPs and their backers win, then their own conservative coalition will lose. The ISP coalition takes note, also expects a win-lose situation, and negotiation intensity spikes. As the negotiations proceed over access, pricing, and other critical policies, the players in this new game invent the rules as they go along, and through an iterative process of hostility, conflict, and cooperation, come to learn more about the key elements than they knew originally—all parties learn more about the technology, the market, the other players, and themselves. One lesson they learn is that their core assumption about the future as a zero-sum, win-lose situation is wrong; it is in fact more like a positive-sum, win-win game. The evidence from most telecom reform campaigns is that, contrary to initial expectations, the telecoms can actually increase their revenues and other performance indicators when they reform their pricing, services, and other aspects of doing business, including providing leasing and other access to ISP resellers.

Heuristically, we can imagine a three-step process in this "market making." The first step is marked by few actors, low knowledge, low levels of trust, high uncertainty, perceptions of high risk, and expectations of zero-sum outcomes. After multiple negotiations comes a threshold point marked by new knowledge, new awareness, and new actors (including multilateral actors), all of which combine to occasion strategic recalculations by all parties. ISP owners, for example, gain self-confidence and create business self-help organizations. Finally, in the third step, the emerging market achieves quantitative and qualitative changes in all key components—the numbers, experience, knowledge, and expectations lead to greater awareness of the potential win-win nature of the arrangements, producing lower levels of conflict than occurred in the first cycle. Intensity of interaction starts low, climbs in a middle phase, then declines somewhat.[1] Still, market evolution certainly does not eliminate all conflicts—access and other regulatory issues remain contentious points for all the parties.

Duration

As there were some issues that arose early and others that emerged late, some CNIs were more likely to persist through time once they did emerge, and to resist easy or quick resolution. By contrast, others were more susceptible to expeditious resolution through negotiations. The former notably included regulation, access to facilities, and pricing, three tough, persistent issues that were themselves tightly bound together through the exercise of power by key ministries, large companies, and several other well-entrenched agencies, as well as the growing influence of rising smaller challengers. Issues like universal access, universal service, and the digital divide are especially long-lasting, given the extreme poverty and underdevelopment of the region. And because threshold levels of what is judged to be "universal" change along with technological innovation and increases in living standards, these issues remain critical even in developed countries. These CNIs were not susceptible to easy fixes, because in fact they were mainly reflections of the constantly shifting market conditions of demand and supply and the equally variable influences of consumers, producers, and other organized interests within and beyond government who spoke and acted on their behalf. This reflects technical changes that do not lend themselves to onetime resolution; it also reflects growing sophistication among the stakeholders about how to define and pursue their own interests and to calculate interests of others as well as greater facility in negotiating.

A few of the later CNIs, like IXPs and VOIP, are likely to be more neatly resolved than some of the earlier, continually contentious issues. Some negotiation issues were more akin to on-or-off switches—a company was privatized, or changed into a nonstate company, or it was not. Governments permitted more than one ISP to make the market more competitive, or they did not.

Other ICT-related issues have not yet been placed on the negotiating tables of most African countries, including electronic commerce or electronic government. This is hardly surprising given the low levels of penetration and commercial development. Yet we know that such new issues, along with continuing CNIs, will bedevil the negotiations for years to come among the different actors and stakeholders.

Stakeholders

For most of the CNIs, the range of actors was fairly consistent and surprisingly narrow. The telecommunications ministry, the incumbent telephone company, the regulator, the new ISPs, and some of the largest multilateral and bilateral aid organizations were the main interests engaged in virtually each of the CNIs. Indeed, one of the most interesting findings is the narrow range of players involved in the CNIs. The continuity of the key players before and after the telecom reforms was high—the ministry, the telecom, and the foreign donors. To this core group were added a few new players—ISPs, the regulator, and a few large consumers like universities.

The traditional closed policy system in place since the 1960s, if not before, was a duopoly of one state monopoly supplier company and one supervising ministry. In some countries, the ministry *was* the operator. In the middle to late 1990s, this duopoly began to expand slightly to encompass a few newcomers, but only sporadically and with limited effect. Nonstate, nongovernmental organization (NGO) stakeholders were allowed in to represent consumer or other interests only slowly. The closest to a real institutional and political innovation beyond government was the slow, tentative growth of the ISP associations.

Reviewing sequence, duration, and stakeholders we are reminded that policymakers and strategists among firms, government agencies, nonprofits, and education and research bodies will not resolve all the critical negotiation issues on their agenda easily or, in some cases, ever. Decisionmakers must be knowledgeable about continuing challenges and new ICT challenges not yet ripe for negotiation that remain just beyond the horizon. Being ready for the future requires knowing how critical issues were negotiated and resolved (or not) in the past. Aside from recognizing these new stakeholders and the shifts in relative power among them as individuals, an essential element of a "Negotiating the Net" (NTN) research strategy is to consider whether and how individual actors sought out and mobilized coalitions and tried to build constituencies for collective action.

Collective Action Around Internet Diffusion

Collective action refers to the challenges that arise when individuals seek to band together to pursue some (potentially) common purposes and must overcome barriers that block joint action. Because collective action issues are deeply embedded in the CNIs, conceiving of CNIs as collective action problems is illuminating (Olsen, 1965).

The Core Suppliers Coalition

One core group of stakeholders has been engaged in substantial collective action over many years, and has designed ways to institutionalize their cooperation to achieve their common ends—these are the communications ministry and the state-owned (usually) monopoly suppliers (i.e., the telecom). These two huge stakeholders usually do not have major collective action problems, because organizing two stakeholders with largely common interests is not very difficult, since they have been able to create repertoires of cooperation honed over many years. This is visible in all six cases studied in this volume.

The Excluded Who Do Not Engage in Collective Action

A second grouping demonstrates the difficulties of cooperation and collective action. Indeed, they are classical exemplars: these are the actual and potential *users* of the value-added services, and they are universally *excluded* from regular, serious negotiations with the core actors. No institutions exist in Africa to formally aggregate consumer interests. In no instance did the contributors report on an Internet *user* association, nor even a telecom *user* association that could bring consumers' perspectives and preferences to the councils of policymaking or policy implementation. There is an international telecom user association, the International Telecommunications Users Group (INTUG), and there are national equivalents in other developing countries (Brazil, for example). In all countries, especially in the developing world, consumers of a product or service suffer the classic barriers of being widely distributed with relatively low interest in the unfamiliar service and having low income. The potential benefits of action are widely scattered for these stakeholders but are concentrated for the core actors (the ministry and the telecom). Thus the ministry traditionally sides with the supplier.

The New Actors

Between the conventional political weakness of the final consumers and the political strengths and privileges of the traditional dyad are located the other important actors in the CNI drama. Such actors include the ISPs and their incipient associations. Typically, individual business owners and entrepreneurs do not coalesce into a formal business association unless and until they are sharply threatened by other stakeholders—usually by unexpected, intrusive, and worrisome government interventions that threaten sales and earnings. This is especially true in LDCs; there is a rich and sophisticated literature on business interest associations in developing regions that finds similar dynamics more generally. In Ghana and South Africa, for instance, the businessmen (always small businessmen) came together to try to aggregate their individual interests into a collective effort to protect the emergent sector. There were internal barriers among the ISP owners, and not all ISPs had the exact same interests, as in Ghana, where one ISP controlled half of the market. But in most cases, eventually some collective action was achieved that altered the pace and scope of Internet diffusion. While gaining mostly modest victories in the short term, the ISP associations will probably become more important over time.

In African countries there is not the same concentration of large industrial users of telecom services as in developed countries or even in other underdeveloped regions that might otherwise organize themselves to bargain for lower rates or improved service. The numbers of large firms (multinational corporations, for example) are few, and, relative to other costs of operating in a poor country, their Internet charges are low (Daly and Miller, 1998). Sizable firms typically internalize those ICT operations or make special arrangements to secure superior services through, for example, outsourcing.

One important exception to weak collective action by African consumers involved the steps taken by institutional leaders in some top African universities. In Kenya, Rwanda, and to some extent Tanzania, as top university administrators began to realize the importance of Internet connectivity for their faculty's research, for teaching their students, and for remaining engaged with knowledge creation and use globally, they began to lobby their governments individually and then collectively for improved access and lower prices. The country chapters point to these key examples of ICT-related collective action.

Sustainability

Another major analytic challenge for practitioners and scholars is whether the technical, institutional, and other innovations introduced in these African countries thus far are sustainable beyond the short to medium term. By "sustainable," I mean politically and institutionally sustainable, not just technically sustainable. The African landscape is littered with brilliant startups and well-intentioned first phases that failed, never making the transition to the second phase and long-term sustainability. Successful ongoing ICT initiatives require that effective collective action be launched and a stable political coalition be put in place to provide a continuous, predictable, and strategic flow of resources into the sector over the long haul—not for days and months, but for decades. It is still too early to determine whether the multiple Internet experiments in Ghana, Kenya, and Tanzania will be sustainable at the levels required to help African nations make the transition to a knowledge society genuinely rooted in the life of the people. The case studies provide ambiguous evidence.

Intimately tied to the capacity of African ICT stakeholders to aggregate their individual interests to group interests, and to achieve sustainability, will be the capacity of new and reformed institutions to facilitate progressive political interest aggregation. Central to that process will be the regulators. These new institutions must play an essential role in protecting consumers, promoting market competition, allocating licenses, and attaining other goals not achieved (or even pursued) by other bodies. The regulators thus regulate the access that different categories of stakeholders will have to rule-making and adjudication, shaping who gets to participate in negotiations and hence who is most likely or least likely to engage in efforts of collective action. To this extent, they are central to collective action in the ICT sector of African nations.

In turn, long-term sustainability requires that individuals, groups, and institutions heretofore quite separated from one another on these issues find ways to begin a process of enhanced, repeatable, and predictable communication built on growing trust and respect across four key sectors: public, private, NGO, and research and education. In the most successful communities and regions, like Bangalore (India), São Paulo (Brazil), Beijing (China), and Silicon Valley itself, ICT success is correlated with robust, reliable, and growing cooperation and partnerships across the four sectors (Wilson, 2003). This is a new form of social cooperation we call a "quad."

Let me further underscore the broader stakeholder issue by restating it in terms of the principal goals of the NTN/CNI project—to explain Internet diffusion in terms of its *process* elements, and in terms of visible performance *outcomes* measured through quantitative indicators like the number of dial-up subscriptions and the volume of broadband capacities in each nation.

Process Commonalities

There are certainly process commonalities across the cases studied in this volume. The contributors found that the *stakeholders* are fairly consistent across the cases—the supplicants are first the small private sector ISPs, outsiders who confront an entrenched, recalcitrant telecom incumbent and its allies in the supervisory ministry. Typically, some nongovernmental actor approaches the government to request more, and better, access to Internet services. The actor may, and usually does, approach again and again, until after repeated rejections the government consents to expand bandwidth by offering more capacity. The new actor may seek more capacity on its own, usually by getting access to a very small aperture terminal (VSAT) (as in Ghana). Alternatively, the incumbent may expand its own bandwidth and then agree to sell the new capacity to wholesale customers, who then resell it retail. This new dispensation by government almost always occurs only when the individuals or groups requesting expanded access construct a political coalition of players who also want more capacity, and the pressures of the proexpansion coalition trump those of the antiexpansion group inside the government, whose members fear losing their own political and economic influence, their access to scarce resources like foreign exchange, and even their jobs if competition leads to shrinking the public sector and public employment.

Leadership in the ICT Sector

For analysts to capture Internet diffusion accurately and to explain it rigorously, they need to pay more attention to the kinds of micro-macro linkages described in this volume. This means analyzing individual women and men and their individual contributions to Internet diffusion. In much of the ICT literature, the contribution of individual "information revolutionaries" has been given short shrift, set aside in favor of highly aggregated institutional or macroeconomic factors. I expand on this notion of micro-macro linkages that affect the emergence of social architectures, which in turn undergird the technological architectures of the Internet and other ICTs in other works (Wilson, 2003). In all African countries reviewed in this volume, some identifiable individuals emerged that recognized opportunities to spread these new resources and seized them well before other individuals even understood they existed. From Rwanda to Ghana to South Africa, their challenge was to transform their individual vision and will into real-world Internet diffusion.

In this regard, Africa confronts some special, indeed unique challenges in creating positive dynamics among early individual innovators, stakeholder groups, collective action, and sustainability. There are several reasons for this, some of which have been addressed in previous chapters. In communities like those cited above—Bangalore, São Paulo, Beijing—some early champions from the stakeholder groups who advocate strongly for a bottom-up, widely distributed, and inexpensive Internet are able to create robust links among themselves that enable them to mobilize the material and nonmaterial resources necessary to create and sustain diffusion. In Brazil, these cross-sector links were especially robust among enthusiastic university ICT researchers, committed professionals in government ministries, and some civil society organizations (Wilson, 2004). The information champions forge links of trust that lead to more than an academic network—they forge a kind of political alliance or coalition in favor of Internet diffusion and its antecedent telecom reforms. The case studies document varying degrees of cross-sector cooperation in the countries under review. In Africa, these essential linkages are less robust, partly because there are fewer experts in each of the four constituent nodes, because material resources are in short supply, and because the existing bridging institutions and norms are themselves weak.

Outcome Commonalities (Quantitative)

Exploring the linkages between CNIs and precise quantitative national diffusion patterns proved to be more problematic than tracing the negotiation processes. We pursued this question originally because we felt it to be important for theoretical and practical reasons. First, it would be one test of the extent to which politics and public policy make a difference in the diffusion of a technology. Experts in this field too often concentrate on the technical or financial aspects of promoting technological diffusion, because they lack the necessary insights into bargaining and politics that we offer in this volume. Second, exploring links between outcomes and political negotiations could identify and explicate "best practices," leading to improved policymaking as the various parties better understand the benefits of undertaking certain kinds of negotiation. Third, linking outcomes and negotiation does encourage greater conceptual and theoretical precision when scholars undertake comparisons across nations. Hence our search for causal relationships between political action and negotiation on the one hand, and identifiable aggregate outcomes on the other.

Yet as contributor Charley Lewis reminds us in Box 9.1, there are tremendous difficulties in successfully identifying such regularities. Selecting, obtaining, and using the right indicators, as well as problems of lag times and simultaneous causation, greatly muddy the analytic waters. Still, we can point to some relationships between CNIs and diffusion patterns that are highly suggestive.

Box 9.1
STATISTICS AND LIES, CAUSES AND EFFECTS
Charley Lewis

One of the intentions of the research undertaken in the country case studies collected in this volume was to explore what connection, if any, existed between the critical negotiation issues chronicled in each country case and their impact on the diffusion of the Internet. Our provisional hypothesis was that junctures in the negotiation process, where deadlock occurred, would impede that diffusion, and that a successful resolution would provide a measurable impetus toward further diffusion.

There is certainly anecdotal support suggesting such a conclusion. Interviewees repeatedly describe critical negotiation issues in terms that appear to bear out the hypothesis stated above. Several South African interviewees, for example, suggest that the establishment of the country's first fully fledged Internet exchange point, which was a direct consequence of the confrontation between the private sector ISPs and the incumbent telecommunications monopoly, had a direct and potentially measurable impact on intracountry Internet traffic.

continues

Box 9.1   continued

There are also certainly instances where the data appear to reveal some or other impact potentially traceable to a negotiated outcome—such as a dramatic increase in international bandwidth, a sharp spurt in numbers of Internet users, or a sudden change in the number of ISPs in the market. Certainly, in the case of South Africa, there was a sharp jump in the number of Internet users, particularly corporate and dial-up users, subsequent to the establishment of the first private sector ISPs, followed by a noticeable downturn in growth once the major dispute between Telkom South Africa and the Internet Service Providers Association flared up. Similarly, perhaps paradoxically, a sharp decline in the number of ISPs between 1998 and 2000 can arguably be ascribed to a belated wave of mergers and acquisitions once the dispute went into abeyance and the market stabilized again.

However, a consistent and directly traceable linkage between the kinks in graphed data and the vicissitudes of negotiations and their outcomes remains elusive. There seem to be a number of reasons for this. Fundamentally, the question of what is an appropriate marker for ICT diffusion needs to be addressed. Some of the more easily obtainable and accurate indicators, such as number of ISPs, or international bandwidth capacity, reflect more closely on the supply side of Internet diffusion. However, some of these are also prone to sudden jumps, such as the acquisition of an international circuit, which can dramatically lift the bandwidth of a country with relatively poor connectivity by an order of magnitude, but which may, initially at least, be underutilized. Numbers of Internet users may be a more accurate reflection of the demand side of diffusion, but even aside from the dubious accuracy of user statistics, the figures contain certain inherent distortions. For example, although no reliable estimates exist, it is widely recognized that the number of dial-up accounts corresponds to a considerably greater number of users—Telkom South Africa estimates an average of two users per dial-up account. But there is also a countertrend of duplication, whereby many users enjoy access via several channels that are measured separately, such as both a dial-up account at home and corporate access at work. The International Development Research Center of Canada has suggested outgoing bandwidth per capita as a more useful marker, but this still tends to reflect supply rather than usage. To gauge diffusion accurately, it would also seem important to include some more subjective indicators of the use and usefulness of the Internet for its users—the mosaic framework goes some way toward this, but arguably not enough.

continues

Box 9.1   continued

It therefore seems clear that further debate and additional work is required in order to secure a suitable measure for Internet diffusion. Perhaps a composite measure is required, trackable over time and incorporating a number of indicators, including possibly: number of ISPs, total outbound bandwidth per capita, number of users, number of points of presence, number of leased lines, number of domains registered, as well as some more subjective factors.

A second major difficulty of tracking the impact of negotiations on the diffusion of the Internet lies in the actual numbers themselves. This is acknowledged by both Arthur Goldstuck (the source of much of the best data) and Mike Jensen (probably Africa's leading authority). Many of their figures, particularly those with respect to users, are based on responses, which are not open to independent verification, from the various ISPs, which, for various reasons such as corporate prestige, have a vested interest in smoothing fluctuations and presenting a picture of steady growth. Further, such surveys typically enjoy a rate of return of around 60 percent, meaning that partial data have to be extrapolated to achieve numbers for the sector as a whole. In addition, estimates for numbers of corporate and academic users are just that: estimates, based on certain assumptions and extrapolations. Finally, the accuracy of the data tends to diminish the further back into the past one seeks to go. Similar problems underlie the International Telecommunications Union data, which are ultimately derived from the same sources.

Other factors beyond either the accuracy or the suitability of the various potential Internet diffusion indicators make tracing the impact of negotiations on diffusion a difficult exercise. For example, the relative "coarseness" of the data, which usually reflects the position in respect to each indicator only on an annual basis, diminishes its usefulness. Arguably, this makes it insufficiently accurate to mark the impact of the outcome of a particular set of negotiations, whose effect may well be measured in months rather than years.

In addition, there is the difficulty of demonstrating a causal relationship between a particular negotiating issue, whether it acts to restrain that diffusion or to impel it, and its impact on the diffusion indicators. Although one might intuitively expect stalled negotiations over the licensing of ISPs to make prospective users hold back on signing up for new dial-up accounts, it is hard to demonstrate that this is in fact so. Further, many of the potential indicators of Internet diffusion are subject to multicausality. Sluggish demand for new dial-up accounts may equally be restrained

continues

Box 9.1   continued

by poor or cyclical economic performance, or a price increase on local calls, or even a period of political tension.

Finally, there is likely to be a time lag between the resolution of a negotiation issue and its translation into any changes to the various diffusion indicators. The extent of the impact delay is largely indeterminate, likely to be the subject of debate, and probably varies from one negotiation issue to another.

All of this makes the demonstration of a simple linear relationship between negotiations and Internet diffusion fraught with difficulties. Nevertheless, the individual country case studies presented, described, and analyzed in this volume present a persuasive argument for the qualitative impact of negotiations, their blockages and resolutions, on the diffusion of the Internet. Further work, together with better data, is certainly required before this can be empirically demonstrated.

Selecting the Indicators

Before determining causal relations, we needed to agree on the most appropriate Internet diffusion indicators. As discussed in Chapter 1, we selected two main indicators, determined partly because they show complementary aspects of diffusion and partly because relevant data can be obtained more easily. The first indicator is ICT diffusion measured through the increase in dial-up subscribers (see Figure 9.1); the second is the rise in outgoing bandwidth availability (see Figure 1.2 on p. 11).

Of course, the two indicators are related—bandwidth facilitates and enables dial-up subscriptions—but they are certainly not identical in their purposes nor their growth patterns. Instead, there are noticeable and important differences, as the figures illustrate. The common question concerns *why* these trends exhibited the plateau-increase-plateau patterns when they did.

Some Broad Patterns in the Dependent Variables

Let us review several broad findings. First is the universally familiar story about the relationship between technology diffusion and its main determinant—the level of economic development—which generally holds true in the six cases at hand: the richer the country, the greater the Internet diffusion.

Figure 9.1   Dial-up Subscriptions by Country, 1998–2002

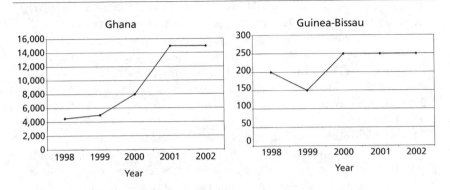

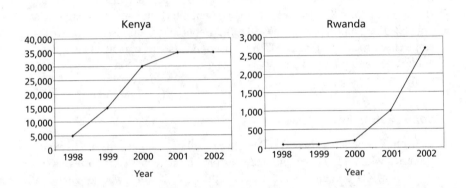

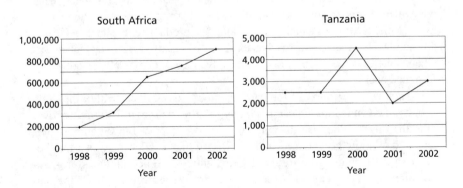

Source: Jensen, 2002.

Second, there is a common diffusion pattern during the period we review—the middle to late 1990s through the early 2000s. There are steady and relatively steep increases in both indicators, with several common break points when the slope of the line becomes more or less steep, typically around 2000 and 2001.

Most countries, for example, experienced sharp increases in roughly the same two years, 2000 and 2001. Bandwidth increases jumped sharply in Tanzania and South Africa in 2000; and in Guinea-Bissau, Kenya, and Rwanda in 2001. Ghana was an interesting outlier, because it experienced its bandwidth increase in 1999.

The contributors found it was not possible to state definitively the reasons for these common patterns. They probably reflect a combination of technological innovation and common learning patterns across countries as governments come to understand that accelerating the build-out of telecommunications infrastructure is an important development imperative. As Lishan Adem has shown in Chapter 8, these were the years when the attention of international organizations, and regional ones like the Economic Commission for Africa, emphasized the importance of IT for development. This coincided with stakeholders becoming more aggressive on the ground in each country, as we have seen in our cases.

Some Anomalies

Interesting anomalies also existed in the cases. For example, one might expect countries with higher per capita incomes (and more technical expertise) to resolve their ICT bottlenecks more swiftly than those with lower per capita incomes. If that hypothesis holds, we would find, in descending order, the most expeditious resolution of key Internet challenges (i.e., CNIs) in South Africa, Kenya, Ghana, Tanzania, Rwanda, and Guinea-Bissau. In general, that is what the evidence shows; however, as with some other outcomes, there are exceptions. While Kenya has a higher gross domestic product per capita than Ghana, and might be expected to resolve its CNIs more effectively, in fact it was Ghana that advanced further faster to resolve its key early CNIs of policy reform and access.

Another observation of the two outcomes can be cited: within the same country, the bandwidth indicator is likely to show sharper discontinuities over time than is the dial-up subscription indicator. Increases in outgoing bandwidth show more accentuated jumps. This probably reflects the fact that because of the technological design, bandwidth tends to be introduced in regular, often large increments. We saw this process especially in Ghana and Rwanda. By contrast, dial-up accounts are typically added much more incrementally, literally one by one.

Some Examples of Politics Affecting the Visible Patterns of Internet Diffusion

While the contributors could not perfectly account for each change in the diffusion patterns, there are political stories behind some of the fluctuation points. One is the sharp bandwidth jump in 2000 in Rwanda and Guinea-Bissau, both of which are small, poor countries that confronted security problems at the same time that the Internet was expanding. In both countries, the previous governmental ban on VSATs was overturned when educational institutions (Rwanda's national university and its Kigali Institute of Science, Technology, and Management) joined the proreform coalition lobbying the ministry and the president's office. When higher education leaders realized that their students needed Internet access, they swung into action and backed the reformers seeking access. In Rwanda, an external actor, the US Agency for International Development (USAID), also agreed to furnish resources in an effort to tip the policy balance—in this case, by agreeing to pay for broadband access costs for an entire year. USAID hoped to outflank the opponents of reform by demonstrating the benefits for the country. Once the beneficiaries recognized the value of the services, it was believed that all parties would be willing to pay for them. This political deal led to large broadband increases.

In Tanzania, we believe the visible jump in bandwidth (and relative increase in dial-ups) was brought about by the resolution of the muddled ICT policy environment that preceded the jump. The first regulator had earlier been fired from his position, which led to high uncertainty for the ensuing two years until the authority and direction of the agency were clarified.

Ambiguous Impacts: Internet, Democracy, and Economic Growth

If the relationships among the CNIs and quantitative indicators are ambiguous within the ICT sector, they are even more ambiguous beyond it. Here I review some additional ambiguous links between ICT diffusion on the one hand and other key conditions like democracy and growth on the other. Aside from a rather small group of experts and policymakers, most Africans, like most people in other regions, care less about the details of ICT and much more about the kinds of behaviors and outcomes that ICTs can advance in other sectors, whether health, employment, or better public services enabled through e-government.

In Africa, the multiple interactions among economic liberalization, political liberalization, and Internet diffusion proved complex and often contradictory. Economic liberalization seemed to have the most direct impacts on dif-

fusion. The causal arrow from such liberalizing telecom reforms as private investment, commercialization of state-owned telephone companies, and even
limited forms of competition and partial privatization accelerated the likelihood that ISPs would be able to offer cheaper, quicker, and more accessible
information resources. Economywide liberalization of competition and investment helped Internet growth on the supply and demand sides. Better upstream price, access, and performance conditions in the basic telecommunications infrastructure meant that the ISPs could offer better prices, access,
and performance to their own customers. Given the weak evidence, it is far
too early to conclude whether, in turn, Internet and other value-added services like cell phones have begun to influence economic performance in
Africa, though some evidence is available from selected sites suggesting initial positive benefits. But in Africa, claims of IT growth impacts must be
treated cautiously.

The relationship between political liberalization and Internet diffusion is
even more indirect and problematic. Charles Kedzie and others make a strong
case that Internet diffusion is closely associated with democracy, and large
cross-national surveys do find that the two are closely associated (see e.g.,
Kedzie, 1997). However, the work of Shanthi Kalathil and Taylor Boas
(2003), using more finely grained case studies of China, Cuba, the Middle
East, and other areas, finds no clear, evident, one-to-one ties between cyberspace and liberal politics. In this volume, only Mary Muiruri, in Chapter 4,
has found a close analytic association: a repressive Kenyan regime blocks
early access to mass communication, and then in the middle to late 1990s
grassroots populist movements use Internet and other media to organize
themselves and new constituencies against the regime. Activists then use the
Internet to help spread the message of mass resistance, and once the old
regime is voted out of office, the new more politically liberal regime then lib-
eralizes the Internet and other media. Muiruri's message: progressive political activists can use the Internet, cell phones, and other new technologies to
undermine and eliminate the old regime and bring in a new one that liberal-
izes the media. In Ghana and Tanzania, however, such liberalizing relationships were not so robust and direct (once in place, however, the technologies
do seem to enhance public discourse). In Rwanda, a security-minded regime
countenanced tight Internet controls that reflected tight political controls
more broadly. In South Africa, the opposite extreme—the end of vicious political repression and racial apartheid via rapid political liberalization—did
not count much on the Internet, nor did political freedom see a massive rise
in political uses of the Internet. Media reform rose quickly under the new
regime and then just as quickly hit a plateau, as the new African National
Congress government was perhaps reluctant to further privatize state assets
into foreign or nonblack hands.

Conclusions

Making and implementing policies in developing areas like Africa is challenging under the best circumstances, whether in healthcare, education, or trade. It is doubly difficult in fast-moving policy areas like telecommunications and information processing. Practitioners in Africa charged with making and implementing policy, whether in the public, private, or nonprofit sectors, should be able to draw on the latest analyses to help them make better decisions and help increase their likelihood of success. Yet precisely in the regions where informed, policy-relevant analysis is most needed, it is in the shortest supply. It was in this spirit that the Negotiating the Net project began.

To reflect accurately the empirical findings in our research, and to improve the chances that they will have a positive impact, we have stayed very close to the empirical evidence when drawing our conclusions. This is as important for good science and scholarship as it is for good practice. Faulty conclusions lead to misguided policies, and bad policies can produce harmful practice. Therefore we have been consistently conservative in our conclusions, pointing out, for example, the difficulty of tracing causality between CNIs and outcomes.

There are two kinds of interrelated conclusions that we draw from the case studies—those most relevant for *policy,* and those especially relevant for *politics.* Of course, the two intersect; politics is provoked and prompted by public policy, and policy is driven by politics, and together these two substantially define the pace and patterns of Internet diffusion. Still, it is helpful to distinguish among the lessons that can be learned from each distinct arena.

Political Findings

Because existing policy and institutional rules are supported by their own conservative coalition, and because policies and institutional rules largely drive diffusion, *successful Internet diffusion needs its own proreform countercoalition.* Typically, a successful countercoalition has a group of ISPs at its core.

To knit together such a countercoalition requires, at the outset, one or two individuals with exceptional vision and political skills, people like Bill Sangiwa in Tanzania, Nii Quaynor in Ghana, or Shem Ochuodho in Kenya. Such personalities possess rare skills, knowledge, and experiences, and provide unique leadership in the sector.

The importance of cooperation across the four key sectors—public, private, nonprofit, and research and education—cannot be overstated. Countries in which leaders are able quickly to mobilize expertise and legitimacy from these sectors cited above are best able to accelerate and sustain the pace and depth of ICT diffusion.

Finally, a curious and unexpected finding was the absence of ethnicity and tribalism as a salient factor in the politics of Internet diffusion in Africa. None of the contributors reported tribal favoritism in allocating scarce resources like licenses, for example. This runs counter to stereotypes about Africa. Some groups are better represented among Internet entrepreneurs, but that has not translated into ethnic politics.

Policy Findings: The Ambiguity of Best Practices

It is best to begin a search for best practices on a note of caution. Best practice recommendations are never unambiguous. Too often, "experts" use the term "best practices" but omit the essential modifier required—which is to state, "*under what circumstances* is something considered a 'best practice'?" (McNamara, 2003). African communities differ so much in size, wealth, economic organization, and technical capacity that "lessons" from one may not be applicable in another. A best practice in Rwanda may not be a best practice in South Africa. Indeed, a best practice in one village in Rwanda may not work in a neighboring village. For example, ISP activists in South Africa were able to create an association to advance their collective interests, while their counterparts in Rwanda failed to do so. In Ghana, an ISP association did not arise until later, and then mainly for market reasons.[2]

With this caveat in mind, there are several policy-based findings that seem to be generalizable across our cases:

- Just as there are best practices in ICT policy design, there are also best practices in policy implementation.
- Translating e-assessments and e-plans into e-action requires more attention to e-implementation.
- There is no single magic bullet, no single cause of effective diffusion, but a mix of technological, institutional, commercial, and political factors.
- To implement any policy framework requires close attention and management of stakeholder interests and dynamics.
- Implementation requires strong coalitions; policy statements and policy rhetoric do not.
- Designing and implementing effective future ICT policy in a country requires learning about that country's past ICT coalitions and constituencies.
- By far the single most important policy challenge is to design effective regulatory organizations.
- Best practices and lessons for learning should derive from careful and deliberate research that is comparative and policy-relevant.
- Teaching best practices and lessons through case studies and thematic analyses may contribute to improved performance in the ICT sectors of

Africa (this is more of a hypothesis than an empirical finding from the cases).

The final point suggests a positive feedback loop for Africa, a necessary nexus between knowledge and practice as careful research on good and bad practices, followed by genuine learning, and back again to inform good practice. In places like Bangalore, India, Silicon Valley, or São Paulo, such knowledge networks are closely knit, robust, and sustainable. Creating robust networks stands as a real challenge and an opportunity to all four key potential knowledge partners—public, private, nonprofit, and research and education. All four sectors must recognize that good knowledge is the basis for improved performance, and then they must take the steps necessary to obtain that knowledge. In this way, the slow buildup of trust, shared knowledge, and common expectations across these sectors can help resolve future critical negotiation issues on the path toward the African knowledge society.

Acronyms and Abbreviations

ACS	Accelerated Computer Service (Ghana)
ADP	Accelerated Development Programme 1994–2000 (Ghana)
ADSL	asymetrical digital subscriber line
AIDAT	African Internet Development Action Team
ANC	African National Congress
ARCC	African Regional Computing Center (Kenya)
BPO	business process outsourcing
CCK	Communications Commission of Kenya
CDITP	Center for the Development of Information and Telecommunications Policy (of the ANC)
CIC	Communication Infrastructure Company (Ghana)
CIDCM	Center for International Development and Conflict Management (University of Maryland)
CNI	critical negotiation issue
COAT	Communications Operators Association of Tanzania
CODESA	Convention for a Democratic South Africa
COMESA	Common Market for Eastern and Southern Africa
COSATU	Congress of South African Trade Unions
COSTECH	National Commission for Science and Technology (Tanzania)
CSIR	Council for Scientific and Industrial Research (South Africa)
CUASA	Communications Users Association of South Africa
CWU	Communications Workers Union (South Africa)
DEVSIS	International Information System for the Development Sciences
DFID	Department for International Development (United Kingdom)
DNS	domain name server
ECA	Economic Commission for Africa (United Nations)
ECDG	Export Credit Development Guarantee (United Kingdom)

ECOWAS	Economic Community of West African States
EDDI	Education for Democracy and Development Initiative
ELCI	Environment Liaison Center International
ESANet	Eastern and South African Network
ETACS	Extended Total Access Communication System
GDP	gross domestic product
GHAI	Greater Horn of Africa Initiative
GIFTel	Ghana Investment Fund for Telecoms
GISPA	Ghana Internet Service Providers Association
HIPC	Heavily Indebted Poor Countries (World Bank program)
IAP	Internet access provider
IBA	Independent Broadcasting Agency (South Africa)
ICANN	International Corporation for the Assigned Names and Numbers
ICASA	Independent Communications Authority of South Africa
ICT	information communication technology
IDN	Intercom Data Network (Ghana)
IDRC	International Development Research Center
IFC	International Finance Corporation
IFI	international financial institution
IGH	Internet Ghana
IIA	Internet Initiative for Africa (of the UNDP)
IIP	Intergovernmental Informatics Programme (of UNESCO)
IMF	International Monetary Fund
InfoDEV	Information for Development
INTUG	International Telecommunications Users Group
ISAD	Information Society for Development Conference
ISP	Internet service provider
ISPA	Internet Service Providers Association (South Africa)
IT	information technology
ITSP	Internet telephony service provider
ITU	International Telecommunication Union
IXP	Internet exchange point
KANU	Kenyan African National Union
kbps	kilobits per second
KeNet	Kenyan Education Network
KIST	Kigali Institute of Science, Technology, and Management (Rwanda)
KPTC	Kenyan Post and Telecommunications Corporation
LAN	local area network
LDC	least-developed country
LEO	low earth orbit
mbps	megabits per second

MOAT	Mobile Operators Association of Tanzania
MUCHS	Muhimbili University College of the Health Sciences (Tanzania)
NARC	National Rainbow Coalition (Kenya)
NASA	National Space and Aeronautics Administration (United States)
NCA	National Communications Authority (Ghana)
NCS	National Computer Systems (Ghana)
NGO	nongovernmental organization
NSRC	Network Startup Resource Center
NTF	National Telecommunications Forum (South Africa)
NTN	Negotiating the Net
NUR	National University of Rwanda
ODA	Overseas Development Agency
ORSTOM	Office de la Recherche Scientifique et Technique Outre-Mer (of Coopération Française)
PADIS	Pan African Development Information System
PDA	personal digital assistant
PIX	Proxima Internet Exchange
POP	points of presence
POTWA	Post Office and Telecommunications Workers Association (South Africa)
PSTS	Public Switched Telecommunications Service (South Africa)
PTI	Portugal Telecom International
PTT	post, telephone, and telegraph
RDP	Reconstruction and Development Program (of the ANC)
RINAF	Regional Informatics Network for Africa (of UNESCO)
RIO	Réseau Intertropical d'Ordinateurs
RITA	Rwandan Information Technology Authority
RPF	Rwandan Patriotic Front
RURA	Rwandan Utility Regulatory Authority
Rwednet	Rwandan Education Network
SADC	Southern African Development Community
SAIX	South African Internet Exchange
SAREC	Swedish Agency for Research Cooperation with Developing Countries
SATRA	South African Telecommunications Regulatory Authority
SAVA	South African Value-Added Networks Association
SBC	Southern Bell Corporation
SDNP	Sustainable Development Networking Programme (of the UNDP)
SIAG	SAIX ISP Action Group (South Africa)
SIDA	Swedish International Development Agency
SIDSNet	Small Islands Developing States Network (of the UNDP)

SITA	State Information Technology Agency (South Africa)
SiTec	Sila Technologies (Guinea-Bissau)
SMS	short messaging system
SNO	second national operator
SOTELMA	Société de Télécommunications du Mali (Telecommunications Company of Mali)
TAMWA	Tanzanian Media Women's Association
TBC	Tanzanian Broadcasting Commission
TCC	Tanzanian Communications Commission
TCRA	Tanzanian Communications Regulatory Authority
TESPOK	Telecommunication Service Providers Association of Kenya
TICSA	The Internetworking Company of South Africa
TIS	The Internet Solution
TPTC	Tanzanian Post and Telecommunications Company
TRASA	Telecommunication Regulators Association for Southern Africa
TRP	Telecommunications Restructuring Program (Tanzania)
TTCL	Tanzania Telecommunications Company Ltd.
UEMOA	West African Monetary and Economic Union
UNDP	United Nations Development Programme
UNECA	United Nations Economic Commission for Africa
UNESCO	United Nations Scientific and Cultural Organization
UNIDO	United Nations Industrial Development Organization
UNOPS	UN Office of Project Services
USAID	US Agency for International Development
UUCP	Unix-to-Unix copy protocol
VAN	value-added network
VITA	Volunteers for International Technical Assistance
VOIP	voice over Internet protocol
Voltacom	Volta Communications (Ghana)
VPN	virtual private network
VRA	Volta River Authority (Ghana)
VSAT	very small aperture terminal
Westel	Western Telesystems (Ghana)
WiFi	wireless fidelity

Notes

Chapter 1: Introduction

1. http://www.businessinafrica.net/features/telecoms/326937.htm.
2. Personal communication, April 2004.

Chapter 2: Ghana

1. William Foster, Seymour Goodman, Eric M. K. Osiakwan, and Adam Bernstein, *The Internet in Ghana* (2004), http://www.public.asu.edu/~wfoste1/ghanagdiff7.doc.
2. Interview with John Mahama, October 2003.
3. Interview with Kwami Ahiabenu II, August 2004.
4. Ernest J. Wilson III, *The Internet Revolution and Developing Countries* (Cambridge: MIT Press, 2004).
5. Interview with Mawuli Tse, April 2004.
6. Africa Online paid for the half circuit to Ghana Telecom. The other half circuit was purchased from Teleglobe directly.
7. Interview with Mawuli Tse, April 2004.
8. Interview with John Mahama, March 2004.
9. Interview with Edward Salia, June 2004.
10. ITU, *African Telecommunication Indicators 2004.*
11. Interview with John Mahama, March 2004.
12. Joseph Coomson, "32 ISPs Caught in NCA Dragnet," *Ghanaian Chronicle,* 1 October 2003.
13. E. Osiakwan and R. Southwood, *Ghanaian Regulator Looks Set to Issue Framework for New VoIP Landscape* (2003), http://www.balancingact-africa.com/news/back/balancing-act_148.html.
14. Interview with Leslie Tamakloe, April 2004.
15. Interview with Albert Kan-Dapạah, April 2004.

Chapter 3: Guinea-Bissau

1. Site visit and interview with Guine Telecom technicians, March 2003.
2. The independent ISP believes that this number is grossly inflated, and that even today there are not that many regular users in the country.
3. Paul Hamilton, Mike Jensen, and Russell Southwood, "Guinea-Bissau," African Internet Country Market Profiles, publication pending.
4. Interview with Isidoro Rodrigues, March 2003.
5. "Acordo Entre a CPRM e os Correios e Telecomunicações da Guiné-Bissau," Instituto de Comunicações da Guiné-Bissau, 2 October 1987.
6. "Desenvolvimento das Telecomunicações da Guiné-Bissau," Instituto de Comunicações da Guiné-Bissau, 2003.
7. "Acta da Reunião da Comissão Nacional de Coordenação Económica e Controlo, Alargada a Commissão para Análise da Proposta de Concessão e Seus Anexos, Apresentada pela Companhía Portuguesa Radio Marconi," Instituto de Comunicações da Guiné-Bissau, 27 January 1989.
8. This lack of appropriate documentation is at least documented in internal notes by Marconi and Portugal Telecom on file at the Instituto de Comunicações da Guiné-Bissau.
9. "Relatório e Contas 1993," Instituto de Comunicações da Guiné-Bissau, 1993. Author translation.
10. Isidoro Rodrigues during negotiations, August 1995.
11. "Caderno Reivindicativo dos Trabalhadores da Empresa Guiné Telecom," Instituto de Comunicações da Guiné-Bissau, 1995.
12. "Primeiro Encontro de Chefias e Cuadros da Guiné Telecom," Instituto de Comunicações da Guiné-Bissau, 25 November 1995.
13. Isidoro Rodrigues during negotiations, August 1995.
14. Briosa e Gala was assistant secretary of state for international cooperation at the time that Marconi, seeing privatization on the horizon in Portugal, sought exclusive telecommunications concessions in the former colonies.
15. "Deslocação à Guiné-Bissau," memorandum from José Manuel Briosa e Gala to Portugal Telecom, Instituto de Comunicações da Guiné-Bissau, 15–19 September 1996.
16. Address by Ansumane Mané, minister of transport and telecommunications, October 1996.
17. "Letter from José Saraiva Mendes, President of Portugal Telecom International, to Ansumane Mané, Minister of Transport and Telecommunications of Guinea-Bissau," Instituto de Comunicações da Guiné-Bissau, 16 December 1996.
18. Suplemento ao Boletim Oficial no. 34, 20 August 1999.
19. "Acta da Reunião de 20.04.98 no Ministério do Equipamento Social, Transportes e Comunicações Entre uma Delegação Guineense e uma Delegação Portuguesa," Instituto de Comunicações da Guiné-Bissau, 20 April 1998.
20. These two people are not identified. As the issue is very sensitive, particularly since Vieira is back in power, confidentiality is being maintained.
21. Carlos Schwarz Silva, minister of social works, government of national unity, 1 September 1999.
22. Declaração Política Sectorial, Decreto 9/99, Boletim Oficial, 20 August 1999.
23. Ibid.
24. Decreto 3/99, Boletim Oficial, 20 August 1999.
25. Lei Base das Telecomunicações, Article 25.
26. Artigo 3, Decreto 3/99, Boletim Oficial, 20 August 1999.

27. "Assembleia Geral Ordinária da Guiné-Telecom," Instituto de Comunicações da Guiné-Bissau, 1 September 1999.

28. Interview with João Frederico de Barros, adjunct administrator of Guine Telecom, March 2003.

29. "Letter from Portugal Telecom International to Carlitos Barai, Minister of Social Works of the Government of Guinea-Bissau," Instituto de Comunicações da Guiné-Bissau, 3 December 2001.

30. Contrato de Concessão do Serviço Publico de Telecomunicações da Guiné-Bissau (February 1989), Article 8: "Obligations of the Concessionaire" (author translation).

31. Most of the arguments were easily proven spurious with the documentation made newly available to the government.

32. Lei Base de Telecomunicações, Article 29.

33. Ibid.

34. Decreto 7/99, 20 August 1999.

35. Both Nhasse and Pereira favored the company for its accomplishments and professionalism. Both were dismissed by decree in the discretionary style of President Yalla. There were three prime ministers during Yalla's three years in office, and four ministers of transport and communications. Simões Pereira was replaced by Minister Cabí after only two months in the position. He returned to his position at the World Bank project, and as member of the technical/negotiation commission.

36. Interview with Abdulai Sila, June 2004.

37. Interview with Malam Fati, March 2003.

38. Interview with Aliu Quinharé, March 2003.

39. Interview with Richard Cox, December 2003.

40. Interview with Keith Bernard, December 2003.

Chapter 4: Kenya

1. "Kenyans Flock to Cyber-Cafes to Make International Calls," *Daily Nation,* 6 February 2001, http://www.nationmedia.com/dailynation.

2. http://www.brainyatlas.com/print/ke.html.

3. Michael Tyler, Janice Hughes, and Helena Renfrew Tyler, "Telecommunications in Kenya: Facing the Challenges of an Open Economy," http://www.vii.org/papers/tyler.htm.

4. In 1992, KANU was estimated to have spent US$377 million. This resulted in an inflation of the money supply by 76 percent. "Preview of Kenya's December 27 National Elections," *CSIS Africa Notes* no. 12 (December 2002).

5. Interviews with the three pioneer ISPs.

6. Interview with Shem Ochuodho, July 1996.

7. Interview with Yazim Nanji, July 1996.

8. http://www.nationaudio.com/news/eastafrican/03122000/features/supplement4.htm.

9. Interview with Amolo Ng'weno, Bakuli, and Kamande Muiruri, July 1996.

10. Kamande has no relation to me.

11. Interview with Africa Online, July 1996.

12. Interview with Kamande Muiruri, July 2003.

13. Interview with Africa Online, July 1996.

14. Interview with Kamande Muiruri, July 2003.

15. In 1996 the US government designed the Leland Initiative to help over twenty African countries, including Kenya, establish or improve Internet access by addressing policy barriers, establishing and improving ISP industries, and increasing the Internet user base. The program was designed in honor of the late congressman Mickey Leland, who died in a plane crash in Ethiopia while delivering food aid. Participation in the program required each host government in the target countries to sign a memorandum of understanding with the US government as a contract both sides were obligated to fulfill.

16. USAID's regional director, Keith Brown, appointed Mary Muiruri as the lead Kenyan negotiator for Leland. Brown departed Kenya before negotiations were concluded and progress was at a standstill. Fortunately, Brown's successor, Buff Mackenzie, came from USAID in Madagascar, where he had achieved great success with the Leland Initiative. Until Mackenzie arrived, negotiations were at a logjam after the Leland Initiative in Washington, D.C., categorically rejected the government of Kenya's counterproposal. Mackenzie successfully negotiated with Leland Initiative staff in Washington to accept the establishment of an education network for institutions of higher learning, in part because it would give USAID influence on some Internet-related policies in Kenya.

17. Interview with a former KPTC regulatory affairs staff, May 2004.

18. In 1999, only Nairobi University and the US International University could afford to pay US$4,500 for a 64-kbps Internet leased line from the KPTC. Word had been passed to the education sector that the US government was negotiating a memorandum of understanding with the government of Kenya (to enhance Internet access in the education sector at affordable rates).

19. All vice chancellors in Kenya are influential presidential appointees.

20. To this date, Jones and John Mack are remembered by key government of Kenya negotiators for their tact and diplomacy in negotiating with senior government officials. Thairu has remained a key negotiator on critical issues such as utilization of research frequencies for the education network with the regulator. He also played the critical role of coordinating the university donors' participation in the proposed education network.

21. Pledge made by Vivian Lowery, head of USAID in Africa at the inauguration of the Leland Initiative in Kenya on 24 January 2000.

22. Initial country budget for the EDDI countries.

23. Kenya was not on the list of targeted countries, but Muiruri and Kituto made compelling arguments to Carolyn Coleman and Sarah Moten of EDDI to provide funding for KeNet that was purely for education purposes. A budget was provided to fund KeNet, a female scholarship program, and a parliamentary network. All these projects were made possible by Coleman and Moten, who have continued to be great supporters of Kenya's education sector.

24. KeNet and Telkom Kenya memorandum of agreement.

25. "Kenyans Flock to Cyber-Cafes to Make International Calls."

26. Discussions with Muthoni Wanyeki of FemNet, May 2003.

27. Interview with Kamande Muiruri, May 2003.

28. http://www.businessinafrica.net/features/telecoms/326937.htm.

29. http://www.tespok.co.ke/members.html.

30. http://www.tespok.co.ke.

31. Global Internet Policy Initiative, "Internet Exchange Points—Their Importance to Development of the Internet and Strategies for Their Deployment: The African Example" (3 May 2004), http://www.internetpolicy.net/practices/ixp.pdf.

32. http://www.itweb.co.za/sections/internet/2000/0012140735.asp?o=s&ci restriction=tespok.

33. http://www.mail-archive.com/gkd@phoenix.edc.org/msg00386.html for an open letter from the TESPOK chair.

34. "Kenya's Cck Closes Internet Exchange After Only Two Weeks," http://www .balancingact-africa.com/news/back/balancing-act39a.html.

35. http://www.mail-archive.com/gkd@phoenix.edc.org/msg00386.html.

36. http://www.itweb.co.za/sections/internet/2000/0012140735.asp?o=s&ci restriction=tespok.

37. http://www.mail-archive.com/gkd@phoenix.edc.org/msg00386.html.

38. http://www.cck.go.ke/speech/speech15.htm.

Chapter 5: Rwanda

1. RITA is an executive body established to coordinate implementation of ICT policy on behalf of the government.

2. Old caseload refugees are those Rwandans who fled the country following clashes between Hutus and Tutsis during the revolution of 1959, and during various periods of violence in the 1960s and 1970s. Most remained outside the country, many in neighboring Uganda, Congo, and Burundi, until the RPF defeated the Armed Forces of Rwanda (government forces) and ended the genocide in 1994.

3. In 1994, Paul Kagame was the leader of the RPF, which had launched a war against the Habyarimana government beginning in 1990, and which defeated Habyarimana's forces to end the genocide in July.

4. Interview with Sam Nkusi, March 2004.

5. Ibid.

Chapter 6: South Africa

1. Quoted by Ant Brooks, private communication, 6 November 2002.

2. The conflict was foreshadowed by Arthur Goldstuck, writing about the pilot testing that preceded the launch of SAIX, initially billed as a service offered by Telkom South Africa to ISPs, in an article headlined, "Net Wars As Telkom Opens Shop," *PC Review,* October 1995.

3. ANC election slogan in 1999 and 2004.

4. Arthur Goldstuck, *Internet Access in South Africa 2002: An Annual Study of the ISP Market in South Africa* (Johannesburg: World Wide Worx, 2002).

5. ICASA was created in 2000, bringing together the South African Telecommunications Regulatory Authority (SATRA), which had been established in 1997, and the Independent Broadcasting Agency (IBA), which had been created in the run-up to the first democratic election in 1994.

6. Initial projections by audit firm Coopers & Lybrand suggested a market of 160,000–220,000 within eight years.

7. The Telkom South Africa Limited Group's 2003 annual report listed 4,844,000 telephone main lines as being in operation on 31 March 2003, an ongoing decline off a 1999 high of 5,492,838 lines. The annual reports of the three mobile operators claimed a combined total of 15,700,000 subscribers at the same point in time. Via its

website, Vodacom estimated the cellular market at 18.2 million users as of May 2004, of which just over 14.5 million were "active." http://www.cellular.co.za/stats/statistics _south_africa.htm.

8. Goldstuck, *Internet Access in South Africa 2004*.

9. The search directory http://www.ananzi.co.za had thirty-three entries for cybercafes as of May 2004, almost certainly an underestimate. As of June 2003, telecenter expert Peter Benjamin listed 71 universal service agency telecenters, some 200 multipurpose community centers of various types, as well as over 3,000 schools affiliated with SchoolNet South Africa.

10. According to James Hodge and Jonathan Miller's 1995 unpublished working paper "Information Technology in South Africa: The State-of-the-Art and Implications for National IT Policy," South Africa was then ranked fourteenth. It has since slipped, according to recent Harvard University benchmarks (their Networked Readiness Index, http://www.cid.harvard.edu/cr/pdf/gitrr2002_ch02.pdf), to a lowly fortieth place, sandwiched between Brazil and Mexico, although still ahead of its nearest African rivals, Mauritius and Egypt.

11. South Africa's early high levels of Internet connectivity may simply derive from the extreme levels of social inequality between an affluent, technologically advanced (white) elite with living standards on a par with those in Canada or California, and the country's underdeveloped, impoverished majority. Subsequent laggardly growth may in part be ascribed to some of the conflicts chronicled later in the chapter, but are also a consequence of policy failures.

12. Individuals who had played a prominent role in the development of the Internet in South Africa since 1990 were identified by a process of peer nomination. Of the forty-two individuals identified in this way, extensive, in-depth, semistructured interviews were secured with twelve individuals nominated by more than one source: Lucio de Re, Internet technical consultant, pioneer, and founder of Proxima Internet Exchange; Michael Silber, Internet and e-commerce lawyer now with South African Posts and Telecommunications and member of the new .za domain name authority; Anthony Brooks, Internet expert, head of the regulatory committee of the Internet Service Providers Association and administrator of the Johannesburg Internet Exchange; Anthony Gerada, chief executive officer of Digitec Computers and Internet pioneer; Mike Jensen, Internet consultant; Arthur Goldstuck, Internet researcher, journalist, and author; Mike van der Bergh, chair of the South African Value-Added Networks Association and of the Communications Users Association of South Africa, and managing director of FirstNet; Alan Barrett, managing director of Cequrux.com and founder of The Internetworking Company of South Africa; Mike Lawrie, current .za domain administrator and founder of UniNet, the university network; Victor Wilson, technology specialist of Telkom South Africa; Paul Nash, Internet consultant and founder of The Internetworking Company of South Africa; and Peter Davies, chief executive officer of AT&T in South Africa. Supplementary or corroborative information was subsequently acquired through e-mail correspondence with a number of those active in one or other aspect of the Internet's growth in South Africa.

13. The director-general in the Department of Communications, Andile Ngcaba, a central figure in most of the official policy processes, agreed to be interviewed, but canceled several appointments.

14. The one interviewee working for Telkom who agreed to be identified requested that he be interviewed purely in his personal capacity, outside working hours, and requested that certain of his comments remain "off the record."

15. It may also be remarked that the interviewees are overwhelmingly white, male, and English-speaking. This is not entirely unexpected in a country where, despite

majority rule and a policy of "black economic empowerment," the economy remains largely in white, male, and, to a lesser degree, English-speaking hands. The sample arguably thus accurately reflects the origins of the Internet in South Africa: its roots were under an apartheid government, at English-speaking universities in contact with their overseas counterparts, and at the hands of the graduates of those universities (although a few white Afrikaans-speakers, such as Ben Fouché of the Council for Scientific and Industrial Research, do feature). But even today there are only a handful of black-owned ISPs, and the demographics of the sector have barely begun to shift.

16. Interview with Mike Lawrie, 12 August 2002.

17. Interview with Peter Davies, 17 September 2002. He did believe, however, that an unstable, uncertain market and policy environment was a more serious impediment. These views are not entirely borne out in the South African case. Antelope Consulting, *Internet Costs Study: The Costs of Internet Access in Developing Countries* (DFID, 2000), http://www.clairemilne.btinternet.co.uk/telecommunications_development/dfid _internet_cost_report.htm, finds the Internet in South Africa more expensive than the norm in member countries of the Organization for Economic Cooperation and Development, but considerably cheaper than in countries like Cambodia and Uganda.

18. Interview with Mike Lawrie, 12 August 2002.

19. E-mail to IOZ mailing list, 20 March 2003.

20. See Mike Lawrie, *The History of the Internet in South Africa: How It All Began,* http://apies.frd.ac.za/uninet/history, for a participant account of the early days.

21. Interview with Lucio de Re, 19 June 2002.

22. Interview with Mike Lawrie, 12 August 2002.

23. Interview with Anthony Gerada, 24 June 2002.

24. Ibid. *PCReview,* April 1994, corroborates this, but gives the date a year later than Gerada's recollection. *PCReview*'s date is the one adopted here.

25. Interview with Lucio de Re, 19 June 2002.

26. Ibid.; *PCReview,* April 1994.

27. Interviews with Alan Barrett, 5 July 2002; Paul Nash, 22 August 2002; and Lucio de Re, 19 June 2002. For some reason, Lucio de Re, who had been part of the original group, was left out, a decision whose bitterness still rankles today.

28. Interview with Lucio de Re, 19 June 2002.

29. Ibid.

30. Interview with Mike Lawrie, 12 August 2002.

31. Former Telkom senior executive Alan Levin describes Telkom as a "large ship [which finds it] difficult to respond to change." Correspondence with Alan Levin, 25 May 2004.

32. Interview with Paul Nash, 22 August 2002. Nash does not indicate if the metaphor was adopted as a sales tactic to echo the CSIR's own positioning of itself within the innovation value chain (see the CSIR website, http://www.csir.co.za, for several references), or whether this is the interpolation of hindsight. It seems implausible that they were its originators.

33. OmniLink demanded a shareholding for itself and the CSIR far in excess of the 40 percent offered according to both Lucio de Re (interview, 19 June 2002) and Paul Nash (interview, 22 August 2002).

34. Interview with Paul Nash, 22 August 2002.

35. Interview with Lucio de Re, 19 June 2002.

36. Ibid.

37. Interview with Paul Nash, 22 August 2002.

38. Goldstuck, *Internet Access in South Africa 2002.*

39. E-mail from Paul Nash. See also Jacot Guillarmod, "Information on Southern African Networking," 13 January 1994, http://www.nsrc.org/africa/regional-reports/af-conninfo/faqsthafricannetworking.txt.

40. Interview with Paul Nash, 22 August 2002.

41. Guillarmod, "Information on Southern African Networking."

42. Interview with Paul Nash, 22 August 2002.

43. Dial-up ISP launched by Telkom in 1996.

44. Correspondence with Alan Levin, 25 May 2004.

45. Interview with Mike van der Bergh, 27 June 2002.

46. E-mail from Soren Aalto, Internet Services & Development, University of Zululand, 15 October 2002. Mike Lawrie, in an interview on 12 August 2002, expressed identical sentiments: "Later Telkom people were more worried about keeping their jobs in the new South Africa than about 3rd party traffic."

47. Interview with Mike Lawrie, 12 August 2002. TIS had been founded by computer scientists Ronnie Apteker, Tom McWalter, Joe Silva, and Phil Green (who later left). They were later joined by "business graduates" David Frankel and Alon Apteker. See Arthur Goldstuck, *The Goldstuck Report: Internet Access in South Africa, 2004* (Johannesburg: World Wide Worx, 2004).

48. E-mail from Paul Nash, 26 June 2002, and interview with Paul Nash, 22 August 2002.

49. Interview with Lucio de Re, 19 June 2002. The comment is echoed by Goldstuck: "While TICSA clearly gave birth to the ISP industry, it becomes clear from interviews with numerous industry players that it was the arrival of TIS that commercialised the Internet access business. Until that point, TICSA was broadly-speaking a non-profit organisation with the odd commercial interest." Goldstuck, *The Goldstuck Report.*

50. E-mail from Paul Nash, 26 June 2002, and interviews with Anthony Gerada, 24 June 2002, and Lucio de Re, 19 June 2002.

51. They might more correctly be termed Internet access providers (IAPs), since their control of international leased lines puts them in a position to sell Internet access to other ISPs (sometimes termed second-tier ISPs) like Digitec Online, PIX, and a range of others.

52. Alan Levin noted that these were dial-up trials to ensure Telkom's "technical capability," and pointed out that some "commercial selling of SAIX connectivity" preceded the official launch (correspondence, 25 May 2004).

53. See Goldstuck, "Net Wars As Telkom Opens Shop."

54. Interview with Victor Wilson, 19 August 2002. See also Marina Bidoli, "Telkom Fights Back," *Financial Mail,* 25 November 1994, which quotes senior Telkom executive Rhynie Greef, while acknowledging that "nobody owns the Internet," as saying that Telkom would permit it to be used only for "information retrieval" and "personal electronic messages," and that Telkom considered electronic data interchange, e-commerce, and "third party voice and data traffic" illegal.

55. Interview with Anthony Gerada, 24 June 2002.

56. Interview with Mike Lawrie, 12 August 2002.

57. Correspondence with Alan Levin, 25 May 2004.

58. Goldstuck, "Net Wars As Telkom Opens Shop."

59. Quoted in ibid.

60. According to an anonymous source within Telkom, the pricing calculation may have failed to take account of the cost of half of Telkom's international leased-line circuit (interview, late 2002, name and date withheld at the request of the interviewee). However, in an e-mail to me dated 6 November 2002, ISPA's Anthony Brooks sug-

gested that the subsequent process around the Competition Board showed that "Telkom wasn't able to calculate accurately the cost of providing Internet access."

61. Victor Wilson wondered why the commercial ISPs were "so opposed" to SAIX, which he saw as merely having "positioned itself as a hub for other ISPs . . . intended as a service to them" (interview, 19 August 2002). The argument is somewhat disingenuous, since SAIX's pricing, however arrived at, undercut ISP profit margins, which had already been trimmed considerably by the bitter infighting described earlier.

62. E-mail from Anthony Brooks, 6 November 2002.

63. Interview with Anthony Gerada, 24 June 2002.

64. E-mail from Anthony Brooks, 6 November 2002, who commented on "how little that list has changed in seven years!"

65. Interview with Anthony Brooks, 21 June 2002. The invitation to the first AIDAT meeting had played the CEOs against each other, suggesting that all other CEOs had already accepted!

66. E-mail correspondence from Anthony Brooks, 6 November 2002. The initial meeting was held at TIS on 9 June 1996, two days before the launch of SAIX, and involved what Brooks described as a "gang of five": Dave Frankel of TIS, Jon Oliver of Global Internet Access, Mark Todes of Internet Africa, Steve Corkin of Sprint, and Anthony Brooks. In the words of Anthony Brooks: "Several other significant ISPs in the market . . . were phoned shortly after the meeting to brief them on the plans and [to invite] them to participate. Amongst those who got calls were Anthony Gerada (PiX) and Angelo Roussos (Club Internet)."

67. Interview with Arthur Goldstuck, 6 June 2002. Anthony Brooks, in an interview on 21 June 2002, gave a slightly different date (7 June) but also put this the day after the launch of SAIX. *Computing SA,* however, in an article titled, "Telkom vs the ISPA: The Continuing Saga" (8 December 1997, http://www.computingsa.co.za/ 1997/12/08/feature/feat10.htm), also gave the date as 10 June 1996, but stated that SAIX was officially launched only the *following* day. The same sequence of events was borne out by Anthony Brooks and Lawrence Edwards in *The South African Internet: First World vs. Third World* (http://www.isoc.org.gh/ans97/brooks.htm). Perhaps this merely demonstrates how fickle even recent memory can be.

68. The Competition Board was a body initially established in terms of 1979 legislation to "provide for the maintenance and promotion of competition in the economy, for the prevention or control of restrictive practices, acquisitions and monopoly situations, and for matters connected therewith" (see http://www.compcom.co.za/thelaw/ act96of1979.doc), before it was replaced in 1998 by the Competition Commission and the Competition Tribunal (see http://www.polity.org.za/html/govdocs/legislation/1998/ act89.pdf).

69. See "Telkom vs the ISPA."

70. Interview with Michael Silber, 20 June 2002.

71. E-mail from Anthony Brooks, 6 November 2002, who traces the establishment of South Africa's first Internet exchange directly to this meeting.

72. Value-added network services (VANs) operators had existed for some time, providing, among other things, network management, protocol conversion, electronic data interchange, and management services, but were required to acquire telecommunications facilities from Telkom.

73. Interview with Mike van der Bergh, 27 June 2002.

74. See "Telkom vs the ISPA."

75. The launch of intekom.co.za may also in part have been a counterstrategy against ISPA's complaint. However, the timing of the leaked memos (a few days after the launch of SAIX) suggests that the launch of a dial-up ISP was integral to Telkom's

strategy all along. Alan Levin rather archly suggested, in Telkom's defense, that Telkom "did not say that they wouldn't enter the market—they said that SAIX would not sell dial-ups." However, despite "extreme efforts to establish Intekom as a separate entity with totally separate governing structure, in order to compete with the ISPs on an equal and even basis [with] all accounting . . . done at an arm's length" (correspondence from Alan Levin, 25 May 2004), Telkom, SAIX, and Intekom were widely perceived as a single telecommunications entity, as their subsequent integration under the banner of Telkom Internet perhaps bears out. The private sector ISPs certainly perceived a de facto vertical integration that was an anticompetitive threat.

76. "Virtual" ISPs are entirely reliant upon a major ISP (SAIX, in this case) for the Internet access and associated services that they rebrand and resell to their clients.

77. Correspondence with Alan Levin, 25 May 2004, who further suggested that it was due to Telkom that the "concept of the Virtual ISP was born."

78. See "Telkom vs the ISPA."

79. See "South African Internet Time Line," Cyberlaw, n.d., http://www.legalnet .co.za/cyberlaw/timeline.htm; and "Telkom vs the ISPA."

80. See "Internet Blue Paper," August 1997, http://internet.org.za (copy in my possession); and "Telkom vs the ISPA."

81. "Outrage at Telkom Bid to Take Over the Internet," *Business Times,* 27 April 1997, http://www.btimes.co.za/97/0427/news/news3.htm.

82. "Telkom vs the ISPA."

83. SATRA was established on 10 February 1997 according to "South African Internet Time Line."

84. Short interview with former SATRA councilor Alison Gillwald, May 2003.

85. Interview with Anthony Brooks, 21 June 2002.

86. Telkom's argument was that the provision of Internet services, which are not among the license categories specified in the 1996 Telecommunications Act (these included public switched, mobile cellular, national long-distance, and local access telecommunications services, public pay-telephone and value-added network services, as well as private telecommunication networks), was in fact part of the public switched telecommunications service, in respect of which there was "a fixed period during which no person other than Telkom shall be licensed." http://www.polity.org.za/html/govdocs/legislation/1996/act96-103.html.

87. "Freedom of Expression Institute Roundup," August 1997, http://fxi.org.za/update/augup/saaug97.htm.

88. "Telkom vs the ISPA."

89. Interview with Michael Silber, 20 June 2002.

90. *CyberServ Newsbrief,* 19 August 1999, http://www.cyberserv.co.za/cyber/whatnew.htm.

91. Interview with Mike van der Bergh, 27 June 2002.

92. Ibid.

93. See Phillip de Wet, "ISPs, VANs Take Telkom to Competition Commission," *ITWeb,* 8 May 2002, http://www.itweb.co.za/sections/telecoms/2002/0205081129.asp.

94. Successor, under new legislation, together with the Competition Tribunal, to the Competition Board.

95. ICASA was created in 2000 as the new sector regulator, bringing together SATRA and the IBA.

96. Reported by Pinweb Consulting, April 2002, http://www.pinweb.co.za/news _apr.htm.

97. News release from the Competition Commission, mirrored on the website of VAN operator MetroWeb, http://www.metroweb.co.za/news/antitrust.php.

98. Rodney Weidemann, *ITWeb,* 25 February 2004, http://www.itweb.co.za/sections/telecoms/2004/0402251257.asp.

99. Anton Klopper, Telkom's head of litigation, quoted in Marina Bidoli, "Telkom vs Vans: Challenge to Fine," *Financial Mail,* 14 May 2004.

100. E-mail from Paul Nash, 26 June 2002.

101. Interview, late 2002, name and date withheld at the request of the interviewee.

102. Correspondence with Alan Levin, 25 May 2004.

103. The *ISPA Submission to the Competition Board (1996)* (copy in my possession) alleges pricing levels up to 40 percent lower than the rates charged by existing ISPs.

104. Goldstuck, *Internet Access in South Africa 2002.*

105. Interview with Anthony Brooks, 21 June 2002.

106. Ibid.

107. Interview with Paul Nash, 22 August 2002.

108. Although the 1996 Telecommunications Act was amended in 2001 (see http://www.internet.org.za/telecoms_act.html) to provide for a second PSTS license, as well as licenses to provide PSTS services in underserviced areas, no such licenses had been issued. The sector regulator, ICASA, has twice rejected both bids for the second PSTS network operator license (see, for example, Rodney Weidemann, "A SNO Train That's Not Running," *ITWeb,* 3 September 2003, http://www.itweb.co.za/sections/columnists/doubletake/weidemann030903.asp), and the underserviced area licensing process drags on (see, for example, Rodney Weidemann, "Rural Licenses Closer to Being Awarded," *ITWeb,* 1 October 2003, http://www.itweb.co.za/sections/telecoms/2003/0310011152.asp?a=com&o=f). "Carrier-of-carriers" and "multimedia" licenses were awarded to the state-owned broadcasting signal distributor, Sentech, in May 2002, but neither allows Sentech to provide access to ISPs, IAPs, or VANs operators.

109. This situation is set to change dramatically with the February 2005 inception of a substantial liberalization of this market, announced by Communications Minister Ivy Matsepe-Casaburri as a series of ministerial determinations on 3 September 2004.

110. Interview with Peter Davies, 17 September 2002.

111. Lawrie, *The History of the Internet in South Africa.*

112. Ibid.

113. Interview with Anthony Gerada. The article was reported by him to have appeared in *Computing SA,* but I have been unable to trace the original.

114. Quoted in *PCReview,* October 1995.

115. Interview with Victor Wilson, 19 August 2002, who described this as the "conception that what the Postmaster General does, no-one else may do."

116. Interview with Mike Lawrie, 12 August 2002.

117. The phrase "total onslaught" was coined in the era of then–South African president P. W. Botha to refer to the perceived global campaign against apartheid.

118. Interview with Mike Lawrie, 12 August 2002.

119. Ibid.

120. SBC Communications, one of the "Baby Bells" created through the antitrust breakup of AT&T, was the major investor in the partial privatization of Telkom. In terms of a strategic services agreement never made public, a number of senior management position were filled by SBC Communications executives.

121. Interview with Mike van der Bergh, 27 June 2002.

122. Interview with Peter Davies, 17 September 2002.

123. Ibid.

124. Phillip de Wet, "AT&T Ready to File Telkom Court Order," *ITWeb,* 10 July 2002, http://www.itweb.co.za/sections/telecoms/2002/0207101204.asp?o=te.

125. There are some doubts about this date. Official AT&T documents refer to 8 February, which was a Thursday. Peter Davies, interviewed on 17 September 2002, was emphatic about it being a Friday, but placed it in late 2001. SAIX, for its part, denied that there was ever a peering arrangement in the first place.

126. de Wet, "AT&T Ready to File Telkom Court Order."

127. Ibid.; ICASA ruling, http://www.icasa.org.za; interview with Peter Davies, 17 September 2002.

128. Interview with Peter Davies, 17 September 2002.

129. In another ruling, for example, also in June 2002, ICASA upheld the right of leading ISP, Internet Solution, to provide a protocol switching service, branded as IP-Net, which Telkom had argued contravened its legally entrenched monopoly by permitting the carriage of voice traffic.

130. See de Wet, "ISPs, VANs Take Telkom to Competition Commission."

131. Interview with Mike Lawrie, 12 August 2002.

132. Interview with Peter Davies, 17 September 2002.

133. South Africa's telecommunications reform process has been documented relatively well and publicly, most notably in R. Horwitz, *Communication and Democratic Reform in South Africa* (Cambridge: Cambridge University Press, 2001); D. Cogburn, "Globalization and State Autonomy in the Information Age: Telecommunications Sector Restructuring in South Africa," *Journal of International Affairs* 51, no. 2 (Spring 1998); and A. Gillwald, "Experimenting with Institutional Arrangements for Communications Policy and Regulation: The Case of Telecommunications and Broadcasting in South Africa," *The Southern African Journal of Information and Communication* 2, no. 1 (2002), http://link.wits.ac.za/journal/j0201-ag.htm. The analysis here draws extensively on these commentators, but focuses on those aspects of relevance to the diffusion of the Internet, and makes no claim to be comprehensive.

134. "South African Internet Time Line," http://www.legalnet.co.za/cyberlaw/timeline.htm.

135. A financial services company, originally founded in 1918 as a vehicle for the economic empowerment of Afrikaans-speaking white South Africans.

136. See Horwitz, *Communication and Democratic Reform in South Africa.*

137. Interview with Mike van der Bergh, 27 June 2002. The NTF was an initiative of the ANC-aligned Center for the Development of Information and Telecommunications Policy and brought together the key stakeholders including government, business, organized labor, and Telkom. See Fikile Khumalo, "National Telecommunications Forum (South Africa)," in Tina James, ed., *An Information Policy handbook for Southern Africa,* 2001, http://www.apc.org/books/ictpolsa/app/app-8.htm.

138. CODESA was established in December 1991 as a multiparty forum to negotiate South Africa's transition to democracy.

139. Interview with Mike van den Bergh, 27 June 2002.

140. See especially "Chapter 2.8" at http://www.polity.org.za/html/govdocs/rdp/rdp2.html#2.8.

141. South African parliamentary practice officially follows the UK model, in terms of which a green paper is used to spell out broad policy options, followed by a white paper to set out government policy, and finally legislation is enacted. In recent years, shorter and less formal processes have been used, over the objections of some in the sector, to implement changes in policy.

142. Willie Currie had been appointed by the first ANC minister in the sector, Pallo Jordan, to run the national telecommunications policy process described here.

143. See the extensive analysis in Horwitz, *Communication and Democratic Reform in South Africa.* I myself have heard, on more than one occasion, the latter justi-

fication made to members of the National IT Forum by then–postmaster-general Andile Ngcaba.

144. See ICASA (2006) Telecommunications Act (103/1996), "Public Switched Telecommunication Service Licence in Terms of Section 36 of the Act," Notice no. 197, *Government Gazette* 488, no. 28483, Independent Communications Authority of South Africa, Johannesburg, 8 February 2006.

145. For a useful analysis of Telkom's pricing levels and structure, see W. H. Melody, *Assessing Telkom's 2003 Price Increase Proposal* (LINK Center, 2002), http://link.wits.ac.za/research/wm20021130.htm.

146. Interview with Peter Davies, 17 September 2002.

147. Interview with Mike Lawrie, 12 August 2002.

148. See, for example, the analysis in A. Gillwald and S. Kane, "South African Telecommunications Sector Performance Review" (LINK Center, 2003), http://link.wits.ac.za/papers/tspr2003.pdf.

149. The analysis presented here has benefited from additional comments and suggested improvements to wording made by Michael Silber.

150. http://search2.ananzi.co.za/about_us.

151. *PCReview,* December 1996.

152. Ibid., March 1997.

153. Ibid., February 1997. Only one of two finance houses had a Web form. The car dealer only responded to the Web query after he'd bought the car.

154. http://docweb.pwv.gov.za/ecomm-debate/myweb/index.htm.

155. http://docweb.pwv.gov.za/ecomm-debate/myweb/docs/discuss00.html.

156. The themes were a security and privacy group; Internet governance and domain naming; customs and taxation; education, awareness, and enablement; intellectual property; technical standards; infrastructure; access and convergence; contracting and trade laws; and electronic payment systems. http://docweb.pwv.gov.za/ecomm-debate/myweb/groups/index.htm.

157. http://docweb.pwv.gov.za/ecomm-debate/myweb/greenpaper/index.htm.

158. COSATU made formal responses to both the green paper (http://www.cosatu.org.za/docs/2001/ecommgp.htm) and the final bill (http://www.cosatu.org.za/docs/2002/elecomic.htm), expressing particular concerns about the process.

159. Interview with Michael Silber, 20 June 2002.

160. CUASA is an umbrella "body representing the interests and needs of users of communications."

161. See Phillip de Wet, "NameSpace Moves Towards Controlling ZA Names," *ITWeb,* 3 September 2001, http://www.itweb.co.za/sections/internet/2001/0109031154.asp.

162. For NameSpace's version of events, see http://www.namespace.org.za.

163. Interview with Mike Lawrie, 12 August 2002.

164. See Phillip de Wet, "Support Grows for Offshore .za," *ITWeb,* 14 June 2002, http://www.itweb.co.za/sections/internet/2002/0206141210.asp?o=fpt.

165. http://www.sealandgov.com.

166. http://www.havenco.com.

167. http://www.itweb.co.za/sections/internet/2003/0309151136.asp.

168. Interview with Lucio de Re, 19 June 2002.

169. Interview with Michael Silber, 20 June 2002.

170. The story of the dial-up subscribers to Lucio de Re's Proxima Internet Exchange, coming at the end of the period, is perhaps symptomatic. Faced with an astronomical telephone bill, and unable to manage the collection of subscriptions effectively, de Re transferred his subscriber base to Anthony Gerada in exchange for settling

the telephone bill. Interviews with Lucio de Re, 19 June 2002, and Anthony Gerada, 24 June 2002.

171. For example, Telkom recently unilaterally (and possibly illegally) cut outgoing telecommunications services from one of its potential PSTS rivals. See "Telkom's Salvos Announce Telephone War," *Business Day,* 8 December 2003, http://www .bday.co.za/bday/content/direct/1,3523,1228307-6078-0,00.html.

172. In 1990, Lucio de Re was doing contract work for Naspers, an Afrikaner publishing and newspaper conglomerate in Cape Town. Needing a telephone to call long-distance in order to send and receive the e-mail messages that had recently become for him such a "revelation," he found an unused external phone jack in the office he had been assigned. A chance incoming call allowed him to discover the telephone number for the line. After that, it was easy. A computer was soon connected, functioning as a store-and-forward e-mail hub based on Unix-to-Unix copy protocol. This arrangement went undetected for almost six months, carrying international traffic for Lucio, his group of friends, and much of South Africa, until a phone bill of over US$500 led to an internal investigation and this network's abrupt closure, amid protestations of innocence. Interview with Lucio de Re, 19 June 2002.

173. http://www.info.gov.za/gazette/bills/2003/25806.pdf.

174. Including Internet protocol, effectively legalizing VOIP for VANs.

175. Phillip de Wet, "Internet Providers Want Telkom to Play Fair," *ITWeb,* 19 March 2003, http://www.itweb.co.za/sections/telecoms/2003/0303191229.asp?s= internet&a=int&o=frgn.

Chapter 7: Tanzania

1. The *ujamaa* (familyhood) policy of the 1960s supported collectivized agriculture in a number of government-sponsored planned settlements. These settlements overrelied on government finance and gradually dwindled in number.

2. UNDP, *Human Development Report 2005: International Cooperation at a Crossroads—Aid, Trade, and Security in an Unequal World,* http://hdr.undp.org/statistics/ data/indicators.cfm?x=133&y=1&z=1.

3. Voice over Internet protocol became legal on 22 February 2005.

4. A major training house in Dar es Salaam fills two large rooms with trainees learning to type on manual typewriters.

5. This in a country of over 30 million people, but it is estimated that each Internet account has ten users.

6. Compared with cybercafes, telecenters typically offer a wider range of services, such as training facilities, other information resources, professional support services, and the like.

7. SIDA report on ICT in Tanzania, http://www.sida.se.

8. Fatma Alloo, "Women Encountering Technology," in *Rowing Upstream: Untold Stories—The Beginning of ICT in Africa,* http://www.piac.org/rowing_upstream/ chapter5/full_chapter_5.html.

9. SatelLife purchased 60 percent of the capacity on the UK University of Surrey-built low earth orbit (LEO) satellite to enable this service.

10. The department in turn had to get clearances from government security functions for specific allocations.

11. These reforms resulted in changing the policy that required a license to import or own a computer or television set, which had been in place since 1974.

12. Personal communication with Emmanuel Olekambainei, April 2002.

13. Three applicants were awarded data communications licenses—Datel (jointly owned by the TTCL and France Telecom), Wilken AFSAT, and the State Information Technology Agency (SITA) (airline industry)—and there was a promise of five-year exclusivity for data transmission. These licenses allowed international data communications, and, independent of the TTCL, the licensees established satellite links to the outside world. Although there was competition between the providers, charges for dial-up access remained about US$70 a month before tax, "exorbitant" in the view of some. This was partly due to each of the operators using expensive outside gateways (Dubai, Paris, and London) and their refusal to implement a joint "international Internet hub" in the country as recommended by some in the sector, including the TCC.

14. MSI Cellular has now been licensed by fourteen governments in Africa, representing more than one-third of the population of the African continent, to operate global mobile communications cellular networks. Investors include the CDC Group, the IFC, WorldTel, AIG Infrastructure Fund, Citigroup, GE Capital, Mitsui, Bessemer Venture Partners, and Palio. Detecon is a German-based consulting company operating on a worldwide basis in the fields of telecommunications and information management. Its shareholders are Deutsche Telkom AG, Deutsche Bank AG, Dresdner Bank AG, and Bau-und Handelsbank, which holds 14.6 percent. http://www.psrctz.com.

15. Personal communication with Emmanuel Olekambainei, April 2002.

16. ISPs are not allowed to operate their own international gateways. Unless they apply to become access providers (which to date none have), they must connect through the data operators' gateways.

17. Personal communication with Bill Sangiwa, April 2002.

18. With the notable exception of fixed-line telephony, this was the start of an essentially open and competitive telecom environment in Tanzania, and the result was significant growth in the sector. By September 2002, mobile subscribers had grown from 38,000 in 1998 to 360,000, more than double those with fixed lines.

19. Personal communication with Emmanuel Olekambainei, April 2002.

20. http://www.nw.com; author observations at several cybercafes.

21. The statistics in this paragraph are author estimates based on several interviews.

Chapter 8: The Role of International Cooperation

1. Nancy Hafkin and Kate Wild, "ICT in Africa: The Challenge to Donors in the Global Information Society," in *Rowing Upstream: Untold Stories—The Beginning of ICT in Africa,* http://www.piac.org/rowing_upstream/chapter5/full_chapter_5.html.

2. Personal communication with John Daly, March 2004.

3. Scott Wallsten, *An Empirical Analysis of Competition, Privatisation, and Regulation in Telecommunications Markets in Africa and Latin America,* World Bank Policy Research Paper no. 2136, http://econ.worldbank.org/docs/553.pdf.

4. On sociopolitical objectives, see, for example, ITU, *Trends in Telecommunications Reform 2002,* http://www.itu.int/publications/docs/trends2002.html.

5. Ernest Wilson, "Inventing the Global Information Future," http://www.cidcm.umd.edu/library/papers/ewilson/futures.pdf.

6. Personal communication with an African minister.

7. Hafkin and Wild, "ICT in Africa."

8. Mayuri Odedra Straub, "Is Information Technology Really Transferred to Africa?" http://www.straub-odedra.de/artikel/27%20-is%20information%20technology .pdf.

9. The five IDRC projects were NGONet, which linked nongovernmental organizations; ESANet, which connected universities in eastern Africa, including in Kenya, Uganda, Tanzania, and Zimbabwe; ARSONet which connected regional standards organizations; HealthNet, which connected medical practitioners; and PADISNet, which connected national and regional information centers that were part of the Pan African Development Information System at that time.

10. SangoNet, GreenNet, and the Institute for Global Communications were among the key networks of the Association for Progressive Communication, which promoted early connectivity in Africa.

11. Evaluation of RINAF project by Mike Jensen, http://unesdoc.unesco.org/ images/0011/001137/113766eo.pdf.

12. http://www.nsrc.org.

13. http://www.sdnp.org.

14. http://www.sidsnet.org.

15. http://www.uneca.org/aisi.

16. http://www.idrc.ca/acacia.

17. Kerry McNamara, "Information and Communication Technologies, Poverty, and Development: Learning from Experience," background paper for the InfoDev annual symposium, Geneva, 9–10 December 2003.

18. ITU, *Trends in Telecommunications Sector Reform 2002,* http://www.cidcm .umd.edu/library/papers/ewilson/futures.pdf.

19. Paul Hamilton, "Mobile: New Markets, Unseized Opportunities," in Paul Hamilton, ed., *The African Communications Infrastructure and Services Report 2002/2003* (AITEC Africa, 2002).

20. Mike Jensen, "The Internet Infrastructure," in Hamilton, *African Communications Infrastructure and Services Report 2002/2003.*

21. SatelLife was founded in 1988 by Bernard Lown, professor emeritus at Harvard University, as an effort to use satellite technology to address some of the world's health needs, particularly in developing countries.

22. Julia Royall, "SatelLife: Linking Information and People—The Last Ten Centimetres," *Development in Practice* 8, no. 1 (1998).

23. Mark Benett, "HealthNet in Zambia: The Technical Implementation of a Communications System for Health Workers," http://www.sas.upenn.edu/african_studies/ comp_articles/healthnet_zambia.html.

24. See Karry Galivan's account at http://www.hopkinsmedicine.org/ccp/conf/ panel2.html.

25. Kerry Galivan, "Field Study: Electronic Networking for Health in Zimbabwe," http://www.sas.upenn.edu/african_studies/comp_articles/health_net_zimb.html.

26. "At least three electronic mail nodes at the University of Zimbabwe are accessible to the public sector, research community and non-governmental organizations in Zimbabwe. . . . The first which uses a UUCP [Unix-to-Unix copy protocol] link to the Internet, for electronic mail only, to Rhodes University in Grahamstown, South Africa, has nearly 2000 registered users. The second is a node using Front Door software and the Fidonet Protocol, as part of the Eastern and Southern Africa Network (ESANET) project linking five universities in the sub-region, with about 30 users in Zimbabwe. The third, a Healthnet/SatelLife ground station, is experiencing difficulties in securing an operating license." John G. Shepard, University of Zimbabwe, 1993.

27. The Volunteers for International Technical Assistance (VITA) was using the same LEO satellite and was active in the licensing debate in some countries in Africa.

28. Mike Jensen, "Internet Update for ISOC Geneva's DEVSIG Meeting," http://www-sul.stanford.edu/depts/ssrg/africa/24connec.html.

29. InfoDev, "Economic Internet Toolkit for African Policy Makers," http://www.infodev.org/projects/internet/010toolkit/afpt1.pdf.

30. These goals were negotiated and implemented in partnership with the US State Department.

31. The US National Space and Aeronautics Administration (NASA) was a key partner here.

32. Here Leland worked extensively with intergovernmental and nongovernmental organizations.

33. The launching of the initiative took place at a meeting of African communications ministers organized by *Africa Communications Magazine* at George Mason University in Virginia. Indeed, the project was a blow to most of the twenty-five African ministers in attendance, because they were responsible for their respective state-owned telecommunications companies.

34. Lane Smith, "Bridging the Information Technology Divide in Africa," testimony to House Committee on International Relations, Subcommittee on Africa, May 2001, http://usinfo.state.gov/topical/global/ecom/01151703.htm.

35. Personal communications with John Mack.

36. Leland Initiative, "Memorandum of Understanding Between Government of Mali and USAID," unpublished.

Chapter 9: Conclusion

1. Kelly Wong of the University of Maryland pointed out these potential factors to me.

2. See the Global Internet Policy Initiative's excellent collection of best practices for Internet expansion, which concentrates on a few substantive policy recommendations for practitioners, http://www.gipiproject.org/practices.

References

Addy-Nayo, C. 2001. *3G Mobile Policy: The Case of Ghana.* Telecommunication Case Studies, ITU. http://www.itu.int/osg/spu/ni/3g/casestudies/ghana/ghanafinal.pdf.

Balancing Act. 2005. *Afridigital Country Reports.* http://www.afridigital.net/country _profile.php?id=41.

Bertolini, R., O. Sakyi Dawson, A. Anyimadu, and P. Asem. 2001. *Telecommunication Use in Ghana: Research from the Southern Volta Region.* http://www.itu.int/itu-d/ fg7/case_library/documents/ber001.html.

Bilodeau, Denis. 1999. USAID/Leland/Mali briefing. Washington, DC, June.

Boyer, Mark A., Brigid Starkey, and Jonathan Wilkenfeld. 2005. *Negotiating a Complex World: An Introduction to International Negotiation.* 2nd ed. Lanham: Rowman and Littlefield.

Bratton, Michael, and Nicholas van de Walle. 1997. *Democratic Experiments in Africa: Regime Transitions in Comparative Perspective.* Cambridge: Cambridge University Press.

Cukier, Kenneth. 1998. "Firm Voice Demanding Fair Deal for Africa." *Communication Week International,* May 18.

Daly, John. 1999. *A Comparison: Leland Versus Non-Leland Countries.* CIDCM Telematics for Development Working Paper Series. College Park, MD.

Daly, John, and Robert R. Miller. 1998. *Corporations' Use of the Internet in Developing Countries.* IFC Discussion Paper no. 35. Washington, DC: World Bank, July. http://ifcln1.ifc.org/ifcext/economics.nsf/attachmentsbytitle/dp35/$file/dp35.pdf.

de Wet, Phillip. 2003. "Internet Providers Want Telkom to Play Fair." *ITWeb,* 19 March 2003. http://www.itweb.co.za/sections/telecoms/2003/0303191229.asp?s=internet &a=int&o=frgn.

Drake, William J., and Ernest J. Wilson III, eds. 2005. *The Governance of Global Electronic Networks.* Cambridge: MIT Press.

Esselaar, P., H. Hesselmark, T. James, and J. Miller. 2001. *A Country ICT Survey for Rwanda: Final Report Status and Development Priorities for Rwanda's ICT Sector.* SIDA. http://www.eldis.org/static/doc11602.htm.

Esselaar, P., O. Hesselmark, T. James, and J. Miller. 2001. *A Country ICT Survey for Tanzania: An Overview of Current Use and Future Needs for ICTs in Tanzania.*

Tanzania Online. http://www.eldis.org/cf/search/disp/docdisplay.cfm?doc =doc10280&resource=f1.

Freepong, G. K., and W. H. Atubra. 2001. "Liberalisation of Telecoms: The Ghanaian Experience." *Telecommunications Policy* 25.

Gadio, Cheikh Tidiane. 1995. "Institutional Reforms of Telecommunications in Senegal, Mali, and Ghana: The Interplay of Structural Adjustment and International Policy Diffusion." Diss., Ohio State University.

Gillwald, Alison. 2001. "Case Study: Broadband the Case of South Africa." LINK Center, Graduate School of Public and Development Management, University of Witwatersrand. http://www.itu.int/osg/spu/ni/broadband/workshop/southafricafinal.pdf.

Gillwald, Alison, S. Esselaar, P. Burton, and A. Stavrou. 2005. *Towards an E-Index for South Africa: Measuring Household and Individual Access and Usage of ICT Survey of South African Telephone and Internet Usage Patterns.* Research ICT Africa. http://www.eldis.org/cf/search/disp/docdisplay.cfm?doc=doc19544&resource=f1.

Government of Rwanda. 2000. *An Integrated Socio-Economic and ICT Policy and Strategies for Accelerated Development.* http://www.uneca.org/aisi/nici/country _profiles/rwanda/rwanpap3.htm.

Grindle, Merilee S., and John W. Thomas. 1991. *Public Choices and Policy Change: The Political Economy of Reform in Developing Countries.* Baltimore: Johns Hopkins University Press.

Gutierrez, L. H., and S. Berg. 2000. "Telecommunications Liberalization and Regulatory Governance Lessons from Latin America." *Telecommunications Policy* 24.

Hernandez, J. 1998. "Creation of New Regulatory Regimes in the African Region." *Africa Communication* 9, no. 2 (July–August).

International Institute for Communications and Development. 2004. "ICT Sector Performance in Africa: A Review of Seven African Countries." March. http://www .ftpiicd.org/files/articles/01329%20ict%20book%20-%2001-32.pdf.

ITU. 1996. *The Development of Telecommunications in Africa and the General Agreement on Trade in Services.*

———. 2002–2003. *Basic Indicators.* http://www.itu.int/itu-d/afr/statistics/basic _indicators.htm.

———. 2003. *Africa Information Technology.* http://www.itu.int/itu-d/afr/statistics/ information_technology.htm.

———. 2003. *African Telecommunication Indicators 2003.* http://www.itu.int/itu-d/ afr/statistics/general.htm.

———. 2004. *African Telecommunication Indicators 2004.*

———. 2004. *Country Profile.* http://www.itu.int/itu-d/treg/profiles/guide.asp?lang=en.

———. 2004. *Regulators Profile.* http://www.itu.int/itu-d/treg/profiles/guide.asp ?lang=en.

———. 2004. *Universal Service Profile.* http://www.itu.int/itu-d/treg/profiles/guide .asp?lang=en.

Jensen, Michael. 2000. "Making the Connection: Africa and the Internet." *Current History* 99 (May). http://www.currenthistory.com.

———. 2002. *Information & Communication Technologies (ICTs): Telecommunications, Internet, and Computer Infrastructure in Africa.* http://www3.sn.apc.org.

Kalathil, Shanthi, and Taylor Boas. 2003. *Open Networks, Closed Regimes: The Impact of the Internet on Authoritarian Rule.* Washington, DC: Carnegie Endowment Fund.

Kedzie, Charles. 1997. "The Third Wave." In Brian Kahin and Charles Nesson, eds., *Borders in Cyberspace.* Cambridge: MIT Press.

Levy, Brian, and Pablo T. Spiller. 1997. *Regulations, Institutions, and Commitment: Comparative Studies of Telecommunications.* Cambridge: Cambridge University Press.

Longwe, Brian. 2003. "Current and Future Status of National & Regional Internet Exchange Points in Africa." Presentation to the second Latin American Regional Network Access Points Meeting, Buenos Aires, 21 August 2003.

Maxfield, Sylvia, and Ben Ross Schneider, eds. 1997. *Business and the State in Developing Countries.* Ithaca: Cornell University Press.

McConnell International. 2000. *Risk E-Business: Seizing the Opportunity of Global E-Readiness.* Washington, DC.

McNamara, Kerry. 2003. "Global Information and Communication." Geneva: World Bank, Department of Technologies. http://www.infodev.org/symp2003/publications/learning.pdf.

Metzger, Jonathan. 1998. *Leland Madagascar Report.* CIDCM Telematics for Development Working Paper Series. College Park, MD.

Mureithi, M. 2002. *Kenya: The Role of Civil Society in the Development of ICTs in Kenya.* Africa ICT Policy Monitor. http://www.eldis.org/cf/search/disp/docdisplay.cfm?doc=doc12346&resource=f1.

Mutagahywa, B., and J. Kajiba. 2000. *Serious Bottle-Necks Prevent the Development of E-Commerce in Tanzania.* Connectivity and E-Commerce Series. Economic and Social Research Foundation. http://www.eldis.org/cf/search/disp/docdisplay.cfm?doc=doc9183&resource=f1.

National Research Council. 1996. *Bridge Builders. African Experiences with Information and Communication Technology.* Washington, DC: National Academy Press.

———, Office of International Affairs. 1998. *Internet Counts: Measuring the Impacts of the Internet.* Washington, DC: National Academy Press.

National Telecommunications and Information Administration. 1999. *Falling Through the Net.* Washington, DC: US Department of Commerce, Economics, and Statistics Administration.

Negroponte, Nicholas 1996. *Being Digital.* New York: Vintage.

Olsen, Mancur. 1965. *The Logic of Collective Action: Public Goods and the Theory of Groups.* Cambridge: Harvard University Press.

One World Broadcasting Trust Conference. 1994. Transcript, London, 27–28 October. http://www.oneworld.org/owbt/conf94/africaon.html.

Ott, Dana, and Lane Smith, 2001. "Tipping the Scales? The Influence of the Internet on State-Society Relations in Africa." *Mots Pluriels* no. 18 (August).

Oyelaran-Oyeyinka, B., and K. Lal. 2002. *The Internet Diffusion in Sub-Saharan Africa: A Cross Country Analysis.* Maastricht, Netherlands: UN University/Institute for New Technologies INTECH. http://www.intech.unu.edu/publications/discussion-papers/2003-5.pdf.

Petrazzini, Ben, and A. Guerrero. 2000. "Promoting Internet Development: The Case of Argentina." *Telecommunications Policy* 2, no. 24.

Project for Information Access and Connectivity. 2002. "Rowing Upstream: Snapshots of Pioneers of the Information Age in Africa." Johannesburg: Sharp Sharp Media.

Pryor, J., and J. G. Ampiah. 2002. *ICTs in Rural Ghana: Bringing Schools and Communities Together?* Center for International Education, University of Sussex. Development Reporting Service.

———. 2003. *ICTs as a Positive Force for Education in Ghana.* DFID. http://www.eldis.org/cf/search/disp/docdisplay.cfm?doc=doc14164&resource=f1.

Pyramid Research. 1999. *Telecom & Wireless African/Middle East,* March 19.

"Review of African Political Economy." 2004. *Special Issue on IT in Africa* 31, no. 99 (March).

Rodrigez, Francisco, and Ernest J. Wilson III. 1999. *Are Poor Countries Losing the Information Revolution?* CIDCM Telematics for Development Working Paper Series. College Park, MD.

UN, Department of Public Information. 2000. *Africa Recovery,* April.

UN, Economic Commission for Africa. 1998. Seminar, "Information and Communication Technology Policy for the Government of Rwanda." Kigali, 30 November–3 December. http://www.un.org/depts/eca/news/vicepres.htm.

Wilson, Ernest J., III. 1996. "The Information Revolution Comes to Africa." *CSIS Africa Notes* no. 185 (June).

———. 1998. "The Asian Economic Crisis and the Information Revolutions." *Inter Media* 26, no. 3 (June).

———. 1998. *Globalization, Information Technology, and Conflict in the Second and Third Worlds.* New York: Rockefeller Brothers Fund.

———. 2003. "Scholarship and Practice in the Transitions to a Knowledge Society." *Items & Issues* (Social Science Research Council) 4, nos. 2–3 (Spring–Summer). http://www.ssrc.org/publications/items.

———. 2004. *The Information Revolution and Developing Countries.* Cambridge: MIT Press.

Wilson, Ernest J., III, and Kelvin Wong. 2000. Conference proceedings, "New IT and Inequality: Resetting the Research and Policy Agendas." University of Maryland, College Park, 16 March. http://www.cidcm.umd.edu/ict/papers/itconf1999.pdf.

———. 2003. "African Information Revolution: A Balance Sheet." *Telecommunications Policy* 27, nos. 1–2 (February–March): 155–177. http://www.sciencedirect.com.

World Bank. 1998. *Economic Toolkit for African Policy Makers.* Washington, DC.

The Contributors

Lishan Adem is an independent consultant and researcher specializing in ICTs in the development of Africa; associate professor at the Center of Knowledge Dynamics and Decision Making, Department of Information Science, University of Stellenbosch, South Africa; and adjunct professor at the Unity University College, Ethiopia. For fourteen years he worked at the UN Economic Commission for Africa in Addis Ababa as programmer, trainer, network manager, and regional adviser. He was one of the pioneers that introduced low-cost connectivity in Africa in the early 1990s. From 1993 to 1997 he was project officer for Capacity Building for Electronic Communications in Africa, which helped establish the first electronic communications nodes in twenty-four African countries. From 1998 to 2002 he was regional adviser on information technology and connectivity, in which capacity he provided advice on ICT applications in health, education, agriculture, and business and commerce, and on the development of national ICT policies and strategies. He holds a PhD in information science from the University of Sheffield, United Kingdom.

William Foster is a research scientist with the Institute for Next Generation Internet. He has twenty years of experience in the information technology field. Much of his research is focused on the interaction of technology, government, and culture. He received his doctorate from the University of Arizona, with a dissertation on diffusion of the Internet in China. He is a member of the MOSAIC Group, which has studied Internet diffusion in forty countries. In addition to his work in China, Foster has completed case studies of Internet diffusion in Ghana, Mexico, and India. Between 1995 and 2001, he was international policy editor for the Commercial Internet Exchange, the world's first Internet service provider association.

Brian Michael King is Internet adviser for USAID's Africa Bureau. He was formerly Guinea-Bissau country coordinator of USAID's Leland Initiative, in which capacity he negotiated enabling policy, planned installation of an Internet node, and trained a hundreds-strong user base. He is cofounder of the record label Cobiana Records, which represents Bissau's most cherished musical heroes. King has worked in Guinea-Bissau over the years as a tour manager, an agriculture extensionist, and a telecom policy consultant. Most recently he was ICT manager for InterAction, a coalition of 160 US nongovernmental organizations, in which capacity he wrote a column on ICT for development and supported members' ICT projects. He has also worked as an independent consultant and writer specializing in communications technology and development.

Charley Lewis is lecturer and researcher at the LINK Center of the School of Public and Development Management, University of the Witwatersrand, where he focuses on ICT and telecommunication policy and regulation. Lewis also coordinates the master's degree and certificate programs in ICT policy and regulation at LINK. He has undertaken a range of ICT projects, including the production of a series of videos on ICT development projects and the writing of an interactive training CD-ROM on online research and advocacy. His research areas include Internet policy, call centers, consumer protection, e-learning and cyberactivism in the labor movement, and universal service. He has published a number of articles in refereed journals, and has written several forthcoming book chapters. Before joining LINK, he was head of information technology at the Congress of South African Trade Unions, where he was responsible for ICT policy interaction, was webmaster of its highly acclaimed website, and managed the IT support function, as well as representing organized labor in a range of ICT processes and activities. Lewis holds a master of commerce degree in management of information systems from the University of the Witwatersrand.

Jonathan Miller holds a PhD in information systems from the University of Cape Town, and is a fellow of the Computer Society of South Africa. Based in South Africa, he has worked in management of the manufacturing and oil industries, carried out business-school teaching and research, and in recent years consulted via his company, Trigrammic, which focuses on ICT policy and practice, especially in the developing world. Miller's assignments have included ICT policy formulation in South Africa, Namibia, and the eastern Caribbean states; e-readiness assessments in several African countries; assessment of ICT investment opportunities in east Africa; devising ICT funding programs for the European Commission; and in South Africa, technology road-mapping, ICT diffusion studies, a major census of ICT firms, and formulating ICT policies for small and medium-sized enterprises and policies for open source. Miller has published over twenty refereed articles, many professional articles, and conference papers on topics such as measurement of ICT effectiveness. He was formerly president of the Computer Society of South Africa and currently chairs the board of the International Computer Driving License Foundation.

Mary Muiruri owns and manages Afrika ICT Strategies Inc., Maryland, which has a subsidiary in Nairobi, Kenya, and specializes in empowering African countries to utilize ICT for sustainable economies by applying telecom policies that promote competition. She has consulted extensively with African countries on the use of e-government as a tool for increasing economic growth and promoting democracy, transparency, and procurement integrity. Muiruri worked for USAID's Nairobi regional office for seventeen years and managed several ICT projects to enhance Internet use in seven African countries. She was the lead negotiator for the Leland Initiative and the formation of the Kenya Education Network (KeNet). Muiruri holds a PhD in international business administration from Newport University, California. Her dissertation focused on increasing job opportunities in Kenya through Internet cafes, with special emphasis on marginalized communities.

Albert Nsengiyumva is director of the Computing Center at the National University of Rwanda (NUR). He is a graduate of the Higher Institute of Applied Electronic and Automation of Liege, Belgium, with an advanced diploma in ICT from the University of Liege, Belgium. Nsengiyumva worked for a number of European institutions before returning to Rwanda, where he has been involved in the development of the Internet and ICT, from installation of the first VSATs in 1999 at the NUR and the Kigali Institute of Science and Technology, to involvement in the Cisco Networking Academic Program, the World Bank Development Gateway, and the computer science and ICT degree programs at the NUR.

Eric M. K. Osiakwan is executive secretary of both the African Internet Service Providers Association and the Ghana Internet Service Providers Association. He is also visiting fellow and scholar at Stanford University and Reuters Foundation Digital Vision Program, and is affiliated with the Berkman Center for Internet and Society at Harvard Law School. Osiakwan has published widely on ICTs in local and regional journals and newspapers, both on- and offline. He produced and presented "ICT World" on Ghana's premier FM talk radio station, Choice, from 2001 to 2003. He has been involved in a number of ICT-related projects and initiatives in the United States, Europe, and Africa. He is currently a consultant to the World Bank's Information for Development Program on Open Access for Africa, to BusyInternet, and to the UNDP in Ghana. He coauthored *The Internet in Ghana* with the Mosaic Group.

Anne Pitsch Santiago is faculty research associate at the Center for International Development and Conflict Management, University of Maryland, and adjunct professor at the University of Portland. She has specialized in conflict and development studies focused on Africa, and has worked in Rwanda. She has worked in Ghana as a researcher, and in Mauritania as a Peace Corps volunteer.

Ernest J. Wilson III has worked extensively on information and development in Africa and elsewhere. He is author of *The Information Revolution and Developing Countries,* coeditor of *Governance of Global Electronic Networks* and *National Information Infrastructures,* and editor in chief of the MIT Press journal *Information Technologies and International Development.* Wilson has been senior adviser on information technology to the Economic Commission for Africa, the World Bank, USAID, the Food and Agriculture Organization, the IDRC, the National Research Council, Cisco Corporation, and the governments of South Africa and China; and has advised on international communications policy at the Clinton White House and as deputy director of the Global Information Infrastructure Commission. He holds degrees from Harvard and Berkeley, and has taught at the University of Pennsylvania. He currently teaches at the University of Maryland, where he is government professor and senior research scholar at the Center for International Development and Conflict Management, which he headed from 1995 to 2002.

Kelvin R. Wong is senior associate at the Center for International Development and Conflict Management, University of Maryland, and coordinator of the center's Telematics for Development Project, which focuses on research, policy reform, and project implementation in the field of information and communication technology and international development. Wong has consulted or collaborated on issues of ICT, conflict, and education and development with the UNDP, the World Bank, the IDRC, USAID, the Ford Foundation, the UN High Commissioner for Refugees, the Commission on Human Security, and the UN's Economic Commission for Africa. He is coauthor of *Africa's Information Revolution,* and author of a number of evaluations, analyses, and project design documents. Wong received his PhD in political science from the University of British Columbia.

Index

227

About the Book

WHY DO NATIONAL PATTERNS of Internet expansion differ so greatly throughout Africa? To what extent does politics trump technology? Who are the "information champions" in the various African states? Addressing these and related questions, *Negotiating the Net in Africa* explores the politics, economics, and technology of Internet diffusion across the continent.

The "Negotiating the Net" framework is applied consistently to chapters on Ghana, Guinea-Bissau, Kenya, Rwanda, South Africa, and Tanzania, allowing a rich, comparative analysis based on in-country research and extensive interviews with key stakeholders. Three broader chapters reflect a crosscutting perspective. The result is a comprehensive discussion that, while dealing specifically with Africa, is also highly relevant to other regions in the developing world.

Ernest J. Wilson III is professor of government at the University of Maryland and senior research fellow at the university's Center for International Development and Conflict Management (CIDCM). His numerous publications include, most recently, *The Information Revolution and Developing Countries,* and he is founding editor in chief of the journal *Information Technologies and International Development.* **Kelvin R. Wong** is assistant research scientist at the University of Maryland and senior associate at the CIDCM. He coordinates the Telematics for Development Project, which focuses on research, policy reform, and project implementation in the field of information and communications technology.

iPolitics: Global Challenges in the Information Age

Renée Marlin-Bennett, series editor

Governing the Internet:
The Emergence of an International Regime,
Marcus Franda

Launching into Cyberspace:
Internet Development and Politics in Five World Regions,
Marcus Franda

Knowledge Power: Intellectual Property, Information, and Privacy,
Renée Marlin-Bennett

Negotiating Privacy:
The European Union, the United States,
and Personal Data Protection,
Dorothee Heisenberg

Intellectual Property Rights: A Critical History,
Christopher May and Susan K. Sell

Negotiating the Net in Africa:
The Politics of Internet Diffusion,
edited by Ernest J. Wilson III and Kelvin R. Wong

Overselling the Web? Development and the Internet,
Charles Kenny